Laughter's Always the Best Medicine

T0273613

Chicken Soup for the Soul: Laughter's Always the Best Medicine
101 Feel-Good Stories
Amy Newmark

Published by Chicken Soup for the Soul, LLC www.chickensoup.com
Copyright ©2025 by Chicken Soup for the Soul, LLC. All Rights Reserved.

The publisher gratefully acknowledges the many individuals who granted Chicken Soup for the Soul permission to reprint the cited material.

Front cover photo of left side and right side alpaca courtesy of iStockphoto.com (©Bobbushphoto), photo of middle alpaca courtesy of iStockphoto.com (©Marta Urbanska) Back cover and interior image generated using Adobe Firefly from the prompt "laughing emoji on white background"

Photo of Amy Newmark courtesy of Susan Morrow at SwickPix

Cover and Interior by Daniel Zaccari

Publisher's Cataloging-in-Publication Data

Names: Newmark, Amy, editor.
Title: Chicken soup for the soul : laughter's always the best medicine , 101 feel-good stories / Amy Newmark.
Description: Cos Cob, CT: Chicken Soup for the Soul, LLC, 2025.
Identifiers: LCCN: 2024949194 | ISBN: 978-1-61159-113-2 (paperback) | 978-1-61159-348-8 (ebook)
Subjects: LCSH American wit and humor. | Anecdotes. | Humor. | Literary collections. | BISAC HUMOR / General | HUMOR / Form / Essays | HUMOR / Form / Anecdotes & Quotations
Classification: LCC PN6157 .C45 2025 | DDC 817.6--dc23

Library of Congress Control Number: 2024949194

PRINTED IN THE UNITED STATES OF AMERICA
on acid∞free paper

30 29 28 27 26 25   01 02 03 04 05 06 07 08 09 10 11

Laughter's Always the Best Medicine

101 Feel-Good Stories

Amy Newmark

Chicken Soup for the Soul, LLC
Cos Cob, CT

Changing lives one story at a time ®
www.chickensoup.com

Table of Contents

❶
~Domestic Disasters~

❷
~I Can't Believe I Did That~

❸

~It's All Relative~

❹

~Technology Is Not Your Friend~

❺

~Happiness Ever Laughter~

❻
~Mistaken Identity~

❼
~Laughing at Ourselves~

❽

~That Was Embarrassing~

❾

~I Kid You Not~

❿

~Not What I Meant~

⑪
~Sometimes, You Just Have to Laugh~

Chapter
1

Domestic Disasters

Now That's a Nice-a Meatball

But some secrets are too delicious not to share.
~Suzanne Collins, Mockingjay

could smell the heavenly aroma of the garlic and other Italian spices even before I opened the front door. Mama was cooking because Uncle Vince was coming to dinner. As the only non-Italian in the family, Mama wanted to impress Uncle Vince, who was the "Italian of Italians" in the D'Antoni clan. She had been simmering homemade spaghetti sauce all day.

About an hour before Uncle Vince arrived, Mama grabbed the bag of meatballs that she had cooked and frozen two days before. She had made them extra big just like my Italian grandma did. She carefully ladled the meatballs into the bubbling pot of sauce.

The salad was made and covered with a damp towel to keep it crisp, the table was set, the garlic bread was ready to pop into the oven, and the water for the spaghetti was almost at a boil.

Uncle Vince arrived about twenty minutes early. No problem. We did the Italian kissing-on-the-cheek thing. Then, he and Daddy sat in the living room to "shoot the breeze" while Mama and I dished up the food.

"Come on in, guys. Food's about to be served," Mama said, smiling confidently.

I passed Uncle Vince the bowl piled high with spaghetti, and he scooped up a big portion. Then, Daddy handed him the platter of meatballs that had heated to perfection in the big pot of sauce. When

Uncle Vince saw the size of them, his eyes widened, and he licked his lips. He helped himself to three meatballs while Mama held her breath.

Chewing on a piece of crusty garlic bread, he twirled spaghetti around his fork and put it in his mouth. He gave a nod of approval.

"Great sauce, Nellie," he said. Mama burst into a big smile.

Then, he speared one of his meatballs and took a huge bite. He paused and blinked.

"Interesting texture and spices in this meatball, hon," he said. "Different, but it's good."

Mama relaxed. In fact, the meatballs were so good that, after eating three, Uncle Vince had two more. Mama beamed with joy. She knew she had passed the test.

The next morning, while I made coffee, Mama opened the freezer door to remove a roast for dinner. She gasped, threw her hand over her mouth, and stood pointing at something.

"Mama, what's wrong?" I touched her shoulder.

She kept pointing. When she could finally speak, she said, "Oh, Barb, that's the bag of meatballs."

I laughed at her. "We ate them last night for dinner!"

She shook her head in disbelief and said, "No. A couple of days ago, I made a dozen bran muffins because I know how much you like them. I even put in raisins and extra cinnamon." She shut the freezer door and leaned her head against it.

"I can't believe it. I must have grabbed the wrong bag and put the bran muffins in the spaghetti sauce!"

"What are you going to do? Are you going to tell Daddy and Uncle Vince?"

"Nothing. I'm going to do absolutely nothing," she said. She looked up and grinned. "And don't you tell either! But I'll say this, everyone's going to have healthier systems today... and Uncle Vince will be the healthiest of all!"

— Barbara D'Antoni Diggs —

The Day We Cremated a Pig

Obviously, if I was serious about having a relationship
with someone long-term, the last people I would
introduce him to would be my family.
~Chelsea Handler

When I was growing up in a small town in Washington, our summer family gatherings would often include classics like potato salad, hot dogs, and hamburgers. But one Fourth of July, my family decided to roast a whole pig in a pit. This entailed a lot of planning, including finding a farmer who would sell us a ready-to-cook pig, digging a pit, gathering firewood, and estimating the time to fully cook a hundred pounds of meat. The aunts and uncles didn't have a recipe or instructions, but they'd seen a pig roasted at touristy luaus in Hawaii. How hard could it be?

My uncle John was the designated fire tender. The morning of the Fourth, he dug the pit in the yard and lined it with big rocks to hold the heat. Next, he built a large fire, stoked it, and then let it burn down to coals. My aunts seasoned the pig and wrapped it in what seemed like a mile of aluminum foil. It ended up looking like a shiny mummy.

It took three uncles and a little red wagon to move the pig out to the fire and place it on top of the hot coals between the pre-heated rocks. Then, because we were fresh out of banana leaves, the whole thing was covered with a sheet of steel and then loose dirt.

During the hours when the pig roasted, the adults chatted, told jokes, drank beer and wine, worked on the rest of the dinner, and discussed how good the pork would be, including how they would distribute and use all of the leftovers. We couldn't possibly eat the whole thing in one sitting. We cousins listened to the stories and jokes, tried to play badminton in the yard, and successfully avoided falling into the hot fire pit while diving for the birdie. It was a good afternoon!

Uncle John and my mom kept checking the pig and peeking under the steel sheet. It didn't seem hot enough, so Uncle John built another fire on top, just to be sure. No one wants to eat undercooked pork. More wine was poured, and the jokes, stories, and food prep continued.

Finally, around 4:00, the chips and snacks had been devoured, and we were all getting hungry. My mom went out one last time to check the pig in the pit. She pushed the upper coals and ashes off the top with a shovel and moved the steel sheet aside with her oven mitts. The pig was gone! There was just a lump about the size of a groundhog covered with aluminum foil.

My family had inadvertently incinerated the pig!

Mom carried the remaining charcoaled hunk of meat into the house to show the rest of the family. At the sound of the loud laughter we cousins stopped our game and ran in to see what all the racket was about. Just then, my cousin Stacy arrived from her shift at the sandwich shop with a six-foot submarine sandwich. We wouldn't starve to death after all!

We enjoyed our all-American dinner of cold sandwiches and sides with a minuscule morsel of roasted pork each. Aunt Carol thought that it would be a lot easier the next year to simply toss a bunch of dollar bills directly into the fire and watch them go up in smoke. Or, better yet, use the money to buy another giant sub sandwich.

— Michelle Eames —

The Broccoli Parade

When your mother asks, "Do you want a piece of advice?" it is a mere formality. It doesn't matter if you answer yes or no. You're going to get it anyway.
~Erma Bombeck

My mom was always the organized one. With four kids, she had to be. When we all grew up, got married, and took turns hosting gatherings, she had a natural tendency to jump in to direct traffic.

One fall, my husband and son and I were visiting from out of state and had rented a house for a few weeks. I was excited to host Thanksgiving dinner. After being away for many years, I could treat my family and show off my entertainment skills. I went to the local hobby store and bought fall decorations, collected the most appealing tableware, and started planning. It was to be a potluck, with our contribution being the turkey, stuffing, mashed potatoes and gravy, and cocktails.

My mom wasn't happy with the way I was preparing for the party. While I provided the main dishes, I instructed the guests to "bring whatever." It would be fun! Full of surprises!

She insisted that I needed to assign dishes to each branch of the family. She wouldn't let it go. "You need to designate a starch, a vegetable, an appetizer, a salad, rolls, or dessert," she said. "Call everyone back! That's the only way it works!" I retorted that it was no big deal. Why go there? I didn't want to be the family food boss. She threw up her hands, declaring that I would regret this laissez-faire approach to Thanksgiving.

The day came. Our part of the meal was ready, filling the house with mouth-watering aromas. I scattered flowers and decorations around. We were appropriately dressed up.

My sister and her husband were the first of our twelve guests to arrive. I hugged her and offered her a glass of wine. She handed me a broccoli casserole, which I set on the end of the table. It looked delicious, with a cheesy crust on top.

Next to arrive were my brother and his wife, who handed me another broccoli casserole, looking lovely as well, which I placed next to my sister's dish.

My nephew walked in with steamed broccoli and cheese.

My niece walked in with steamed broccoli and some kind of special seasoning.

Hmmm, there's a lot of broccoli so far, I thought. But the dishes made a nice presentation at the end of the table. A broccoli corner, of sorts. A broccoli cornucopia.

My mom walked in with a plate of uncooked broccoli with a side of ranch dressing. A tray of crudités, with just broccoli.

My friend walked in with something broccoli.

My other friend walked in with something broccoli.

Almost everyone had arrived. Everyone had brought broccoli.

This is hilarious! I thought. *How did this happen? Does everyone love broccoli that much? Well, it's okay. Broccoli is yummy. It'll be a healthy Thanksgiving. I have no appetizer, salad, rolls, dessert, or other vegetable, but it'll be fine. But no pie?*

My other niece walked in a bit late. She handed me a produce bag of raw broccoli, as if she'd just brought it from the grocery store. *What the heck?* I was a little annoyed that she expected me to figure out what to do with her contribution at the last minute. Should I just throw it on a plate? My alluring "broccoli corner" had taken over most of the table.

"What should I do with this?" I frowned at her. "We have a lot of broccoli already. So much, you won't believe it! It's such a coincidence!"

She didn't say a word, but I caught a smirk. Looking around, I realized all the guests' eyes were on me.

"Wait a minute!" I cried, looking at their faces. "What the...? What is going on here?"

The entire gang started laughing. Mom walked up and told me that this is why you assign food groups. The risk is too great that you may get nothing but broccoli, or worse. My mouth flew open in shock and confusion until I, too, laughed until I had tears running down my cheeks.

Mom had orchestrated the whole thing along with her accomplices—my family and friends.

Life is full of lessons. This is one I'll never forget. Sometimes, all it takes is too much broccoli.

—A.J. Hughes—

Too Much Trouble

I am too lazy to be lazy.
~Author Unknown

Despite the array of crockery and kitchen tools I have, I am lazy about using them. I do have fancy kitchen shears but the pair I have has a locking mechanism, so you have to press the handles closer together to "unlock" them in order to use them. Right next to those kitchen shears in our knife block is our set of Quikut paring knives that cost all of $5 for three back in the day. They're tiny, but they can slice through just about anything, which turns out to be an unfortunate attribute.

I was fixing dinner one night alone. I needed to open a plastic bag for the Hamburger Helper I had chosen to feast on. I reached for the kitchen shears but thought, *Nah, that's too much trouble!* Instead, I grabbed one of the paring knives sitting in a slot next to the shears.

Something inside me said, "Don't do it. This is a bad idea," but I threw caution to the wind. The bag was slashed open in a flash! But so was my right index finger. Blood spurted all over the place.

There I stood, going off like a sprinkler system, trying my best to remember what to do beyond applying direct pressure to my finger. Water. Cold? Hot? Something occurred to me about maybe elevating it above my heart. So, with direct pressure applied, I hurried to my bathroom at the back of the house to run cold water over it. It just seemed unsanitary to do it in the kitchen sink where I was fixing dinner.

I ran icy cold water over my finger until the bleeding stopped. I turned off the water and reached for a hand towel. There she sprang again. Nothing I did stopped the blood for more than a few seconds.

I started feeling dizzy. Should I call 911? No, first I'd call my husband at work. He'd know what to do; he's a nurse. I had to call three times before he answered. By then, I was back in the kitchen, holding my finger under the kitchen faucet, no longer caring about cross-contamination. I told him what I'd done. "What should I do?"

"Drive over to the hospital," he answered calmly. We lived five minutes from the nearest emergency room.

"No, you don't understand how much blood I've lost. I'm on the verge of passing out." I really was by then, whether from loss of blood, fear, or something else.

"If you call 911, they're going to send the ambulance. It's going to take time, and it's going to cost a lot of money."

"But I need them. I can't drive myself. You don't understand." I started crying, which did nothing to make the situation better for either of us.

"Go ahead and call 911. I'll come to the hospital as soon as I can get away from here."

"Thank you," I sobbed and hung up.

Then I dialed 911. "What is your emergency?"

"I was cutting open a bag of Hamburger Helper mix to fix dinner, and somehow my finger got in the way. I've been bleeding for twenty minutes, and I feel like I'm gonna pass out."

The 911 operator started asking me a lot of questions. I'd seen it all on TV a thousand times before. Yes, she needed information, but she was also trying to help me calm down and stay alert in case I really was going to pass out. Address? I told her where I lived. Was anyone with me? Alone, and my husband was far away. How did this happen again? I told her the whole sordid tale.

"Don't you have any kitchen shears?" she asked.

I vaguely remember telling her, "Yes, I have kitchen shears, but they're too much trouble."

I told her to please have the ambulance come to the back door because I was way too woozy to walk down the front steps. I heard the ambulance long before it arrived. The paramedics came to the front door. I was sitting in my pajamas with my arm raised over my head.

"How did you do this?" the first ambulance attendant asked. So, I gave a shorter version. "Don't you have any kitchen shears?"

"Too much trouble," I mumbled under my breath. Then, they stood me up, leading me toward the steps. "Guys, I'm way too dizzy to make it down these steps," I said as we walked out into the brisk night air.

"We've got you," the second guy said, each of them with one arm wrapped loosely around my shoulders. They had parked a good fifty feet away from the steps on a steep, downhill slope. When I reached the back of the ambulance, the driver had the stretcher out, ready for me to lie down so they could strap me in and put me inside. But as they were doing so, they dropped the stretcher, and the brake wasn't on. I started rolling down our driveway with no way of stopping myself. One of the guys managed to grab it at the last minute and haul me back in. At this point, I was thinking that driving myself probably would have been safer. They loaded me and closed the doors, and we were on our way, sirens and all.

Unloading me was far more successful than loading me had been. But now I was in the ER, the wonderful part of the medical universe where you must explain everything that you have already explained to a dozen people another dozen times.

"Don't you have kitchen shears?" the desk agent asked.

"They're too much trouble," I answered blankly.

By the time an ER doctor came in, my husband had arrived and was sitting with me. The doctor removed the gauze and tape that the ER nurse had applied to my finger. The bleeding seemed to have finally stopped. But about the time the air hit it, the blood shot straight out again. "Whoa! That's some cut! How did you do that?"

I sighed and gave him an even shorter version than I'd given anyone else up to that point. Frankly, I was tired of talking about it.

"Don't you have any kitchen shears?" the ER doctor asked as he examined the wound more closely.

"I do, but they're too much trouble," I answered, exasperated.

The wound went through my top two layers of skin. It was deep.

Even a novice like me knew that this was a stitch-worthy wound. He brought in some surgical glue. As he started to apply it to my skin, I asked why he had chosen the glue over stitches. He looked at me like I, of all people, should understand this situation.

"Because stitches are… well, they're just too much trouble."

— Chrissie Anderson Peters —

Alexa Saves the Day

If Alexa were a person, she'd be the funniest
stand-up comedian out there.
~Author Unknown

My begonia plants were well on their way to becoming pot-pourri. In fact, every plant in the newly landscaped yard was fading fast. I stepped from the lazy coolness of the house into the sweltering heat of a summer day in Texas with a record-breaking heat index of 112 degrees.

"Wow, I better make this fast," I said to myself. As the blistering sun beat down with a vengeance, I laboriously dragged the hose the length of the yard, generously watering as I went and thinking that a hat might have been in order. My dear daughter, Katherine, popped her head out the back door.

"What are you doing out here, Mom?"

I turned, using my shirt to mop the sweat out of my eyes so I could see her.

"I've got to water everything, or it will disintegrate."

"Well, be careful. I'm off to class."

Perspiring more by the minute, I continued my mission to save my yard, ignoring the spots dancing before my eyes. Finally, I soaked the last plant. With a sigh of relief, I reached the back door, greatly anticipating the rush of cool air on my beet-red face. Relief quickly turned to disbelief and shock; Katherine had flipped the deadbolt out of habit. The door was locked.

My mind quickly processed a slideshow of reality: padlock is on gate; key to padlock is in house; cell phone is in house; three hours until my husband, Jonathan, comes home. I'm going to cook! My backyard was an oven, and I was the picnic ham.

In my head, my right-brain, positive voice said, "Don't worry. Something will work out." But my left-brain, logical voice shouted, "What? It can't possibly work out!"

I told myself to calm down and think. There had to be a way. I entertained the idea of climbing to the top of the gate and waving, but the gate isn't visible from the street. Thoughts of my arthritic, "mature" body falling six feet to the sunbaked ground quickly nixed that idea.

I huffed back and forth from side to side of the yard shouting, "Heeeeeeeeelp meeeeeee!" at the top of my lungs. No response at all, only the hot, dead-quiet heat of a merciless Texas swelter, dictating that anyone possessing any sense of self-preservation remain indoors. There was no shade in the yard. The patio, so inviting in early morning, was now unbearable in the scorching sun.

I pondered my options. My three wiener dogs faithfully tried to help. They stayed right with me, tails wagging, dancing in and out of the doggie door from time to time as if to say, "Get out of the heat, Mom. It's easy."

I took a close look at the very small and low doggie door. Would I fit through? Ha ha, not a chance. How about reaching my arm through the opening and up to flip the bolt lever? I had seen my son do that, so I carefully lowered my round, stiff-jointed self to the concrete. My arm was too short to reach the lock. The porch broom was too long. The metal "Love my yard" sign was a joke in more ways than one. I pictured myself, hair askew and sweaty, rolling around on the hot porch and burst into hysterical laughter that morphed into sobs.

Suddenly, the sobbing ended in a hopeful gasp. Like a bolt from the hot blue sky, I had an idea, and the idea had a name: Alexa. She was there, just twenty feet away on the kitchen counter. If I could just get my head through the doggie door, maybe Alexa could save the day. I struggled to stretch out on my belly and then worked my head through the small opening.

I found myself eye-to-eye with my very confused puppies, tails tucked and whining as they tried to understand why Mom had no body. "Alexa!" I shouted. I was immediately rendered incapable of further speech by the dogs pouncing to vigorously lick my face in alarm. With no hands to ward off their ministrations, I sputtered something that caused Alexa to begin reading Wikipedia's definition of the word "ship." As Alexa droned on, I squeezed my head back outside, hauled the dogs out one by one, and then quickly pushed my head back through. I was ecstatic with hope. Alexa had heard me!

My interaction with Alexa up to this point had been limited to mundane questions such as "What's the time?" "What is the capital of Montana?" or "How old is Jane Fonda?" Could Alexa send a text or call someone for me? *Please, God, let the answer be yes.* I lifted up my chin as far as possible and shouted, "Alexa, call Jonathan!"

"Did you say 'Jonathan'?" she replied.

"Yes!" I shouted. When I heard the ring tone, I was filled with all the joy of a trapped miner beholding a glimmer of light. But there was no answer. At the beep, I yelled a voice message and then spent the next half-hour chafing my neck on the edge of the doggie door while yelling in a regulated monotone to the voicemail of one family member after another. All the while, the dogs were glued to my back, whining and licking my neck.

Finally, my six-months' pregnant daughter-in-law, Jami, answered on the first ring.

"Jami," I screamed, "don't hang up."

"Mom?"

"I'm locked out… in… the… backyard… yelling… through… the… doggie…door."

"What? Mom, are you okay?"

"I'm overheated, and I need help. Please come. The garage code is…"

I caught her shriek of "Oh, my God!" as the call dropped. I rested my cheek on the deliciously cool tile floor, hoping she was on her way.

Rushing to my aid, Jami was stopped doing 67 in a residential area. She hysterically told the officer, "Just give me a ticket and let me go. My mother-in-law may be dying in her backyard." The faithful blue issued no ticket but gave escort to my house to make sure that Jami arrived safely.

Soon, I heard the blessed sound of the garage door opening and then saw her tiny, swollen feet making their way to the back door. I pulled my head out and struggled to a sitting position. Jami opened the door and offered me a cup of ice-cold water.

"You are red as a tomato," she said.

I nodded gratefully, took a few sips, struggled to my feet, and shuffled further inside to collapse in a chair. At this point, Katherine stormed through the door and said in a demanding tone, "I got your message! How on earth did this happen?"

I pointed to the deadbolt and said, "When you flip that lever, the door locks, even if someone is outside."

Now there is a key hidden in the backyard, I have a smartwatch, our front and back doors can be unlocked by an app on our cell phones, and my "doggie door voicemails" will forever be a source of family entertainment. The dogs are still in recovery.

— Story Keatley —

6

Dad Paints the Porch

All you need to paint is a few tools, a little instruction,
and a vision in your mind.
~Bob Ross

First, here are a few things you need to know about my dad. He was a slightly impatient kind of a guy. If he wanted something done, he wanted it done NOW, if not sooner.

Second, you need to know that Dad was an early riser. Every single day. No exceptions. No excuses. Work or no work. Holidays or vacation days, there was my father, up and ready to go. We'd often start vacation trips at 3:00 or 4:00 a.m. "to beat the traffic."

Oh, and you should know that Mom was a night owl, up late watching a late movie or a wrestling match. It didn't matter to Mom. She enjoyed staying up late, late, late.

One more thing about my dad. He was color-blind. That usually doesn't matter. And he was a fairly conservative kind of person. For instance, he bought our new home out in the country and objected immediately to the stucco being a pale peach color. Way too "flashy" for Dad. He hired a painter to cover up all that peach with a nice, not-flashy gray. Dad was fond of gray anyway.

And so, we arrive at the Saturday morning when Dad popped out of bed as bright-eyed and bushy-tailed as ever, felt restless, and looked around for something that needed doing. Mom was sound asleep, as usual. My brother and I slept in a bit. There was nobody around to keep an eye on Dad and whatever he decided to do next.

So, Dad decided that the porch on our newly gray house needed a fresh coat of paint. He headed off to the hardware store to get paint and painting supplies. He did not tell any of us. Nor did he invite any of us along.

We've never been sure what happened at the hardware store. Did he ask for advice? Did he study color samples? Did another shopper help him choose? Or a store clerk? Or a circus clown?

Who knows?

But we're all pretty sure that Dad had no clue what color he was painting the wooden porch.

He worked hard at the task.

My brother and I woke up, wondered where Dad was, and went looking for him.

We found him. Out front in old work clothes, busily painting our front porch with a sort of fluorescent, intense, circus-tent-pink paint. It was a glow-in-the-dark pink. A be-seen-for-miles pink. A stop-your-car-to-stare pink. A honk-your-horn, point-and-laugh pink.

My brother and I made a quick dash for Mom.

"Come quick!" we told Mom. "Hurry!"

She could tell how urgent it was by the hysteria in our voices.

Stumbling around in her robe, floppy slippers and hair curlers, Mom rushed outside.

We three stood out front, staring.

Mom later swore if she hadn't been in hair curlers, she would have torn out her hair at the roots.

Dad was nothing if not efficient. He was putting the finishing touches on his paint job.

"All done," he declared, with a wide grin and a booming jolly voice.

"Oh, no," Mom moaned.

"What?" Dad asked. "What's wrong?"

"It's pink," Mom pointed out, as if we couldn't all see it just fine.

"Is it?" Dad asked, looking at it as if he'd never seen it before.

"Oh, wow, it sure is," my brother and I told him.

Staring at the porch as if he'd only just now noticed how pink it was, Dad frowned. "It is a bit bright, isn't it?" he asked.

Mom sadly shook her head. My brother and I grinned — it would sure draw interesting comments.

Just then, a car went by, the occupants honking, pointing and whistling at us and our pink porch.

Dad wore his bewildered look. "Should I redo it?" he asked.

"No, hon," Mom told him. "We'll leave it for now. But please don't ever, ever, ever choose a color for anything, at all, ever, ever again. Okay?"

Dad nodded. Two more cars drove by with honking, yelling and laughter. When they waved, Dad waved back.

From that moment on, everyone in our area included us in their directions. "Just hook a left when you've passed the pink porch."

— Karen M. Leet —

Dogs Are Lousy Drivers

*Without my dog, my wallet would be full and my
house would be clean, but my heart would be empty.*
~Author Unknown

ogs can be taught to do a lot of things. Sit. Roll over. Fetch. Play dead. Play poker. (I know because I've seen paintings of dogs doing this.) But, no matter how skilled they might be at many tasks, dogs are lousy drivers. Take Belle.

Belle was a Golden Retriever and the apple of my eye. She was also the extra digit in our grocery bill and the reason that we received a call from a neighbor at 3:00 a.m. But I digress.

We lived in the country where dogs were pretty much able to live a free-range lifestyle. In fact, we only had one neighbor on our dead-end street, about a hundred yards downhill from us. The downhill part will be very important in this story later.

Belle knew her share of tricks. She could catch a ball, slobber on it, and then bring it back to you. She also knew how to catch a Frisbee and how to slobber on it before returning it. Belle also learned how to scratch her own back, but not using the ground like a normal dog. No, she insisted on using the undercarriage of my small pickup truck.

I had no idea until I looked out the window one day and noticed that my truck was rocking. I don't mean rocking as in, "Man, that cool truck is really rocking," but rather as in, the whole truck was swaying. Although this was a new one on me, I knew there had to be some rational explanation for it — perhaps car thieves, young lovers, or poltergeists. I made my way slowly out the door and toward the swaying truck. About that time, Belle came from beneath it, gave her body a shake, and trotted off, the truck swaying no more.

From then on, I did my best to discourage this new trick and took extra care before driving off, fearful my dog might still be underneath, lost in back-scratching nirvana.

As much as I loved her, Belle was not a house dog. Lord knows we tried to domesticate her with plush doggie beds and squeaky toys. In cold weather, she would come in at night, but during the summer she refused, preferring to sleep on the front porch. We allowed this because she never caused any nighttime trouble — until that one night.

That night, it all came together like a big cosmic joke: the small pickup truck, the doggie backscratching, the steep hill, and the 3:00 a.m. phone call. Although you've likely already figured out the outcome of this story, you haven't lived until you've heard the details.

Belle and I had gone fishing that afternoon, and as usual she had frolicked in tall grass, mud puddles, and questionable pond water. This gave her an itch, as it always seemed to do. Once we got back home, she couldn't wait to get under the truck to do some serious back scratching. Meanwhile I took a shower, ate dinner with my family, and was in bed by 11:00 p.m.

The good news is that I had four great hours of sleep. The bad news is that the phone rang at 3:00 a.m.

"Hello?" I mumbled.

"Uh, yeah, this is your neighbor down the hill. You have that little red truck, right?"

"Unhuhahyeah," I said, yawning.

"Well, could you move it? I won't be able to get to work in the morning until you do."

Even as foggy as my brain was, I sensed something was amiss. "Um, I park at the top of the hill. You must be mistaken. I didn't block your driveway."

"Well, your dog did. She's standing here beside your truck, wagging her tail. You need to come down here."

I walked out of my house, clad only in pajamas and the work

boots I'd slipped on, and saw both the truck and dog were gone. Fearing the worst, I walked fifty yards down the hill to where the neighbor's entire family had gathered. There, squarely blocking their driveway, my truck had come to rest with its tailgate smashed against the neighbor's huge oak tree.

"I think you'll need a wrecker," the neighbor said as he panned his flashlight over the scene. Meanwhile, his wife stood in the carport soothing a crying infant as a boy of about eight, clad in a mismatched *Star Wars/SpongeBob* PJ ensemble, stroked the head of a happy Belle. The dog was always quick to recover from trauma, especially if kids and head petting were involved.

By now, I was awake enough to put the facts together. The truck was in neutral, meaning that somehow the transmission had been disengaged, allowing gravity to have its way with the vehicle. The meeting of car and tree woke the neighbors, who came out and saw a wrecked vehicle with a large Golden Retriever prancing around it.

"It was odd," the neighbor said. "We couldn't find a driver, just the dog, so I figured it must have rolled down here."

"Maybe the dog drove it, Daddy," the PJ-clad boy said.

As ridiculous as that idea was, it got me to thinking. Because of the steep hill, I always double-checked that the shifter was in park, especially because the emergency brake was faulty. So, how had it shifted into neutral? I looked at the dog, who was now scratching her back under the neighbor's truck, and the truth hit me. Even though she couldn't drive, she had shifted the transmission into neutral while wallowing down below.

I was sure that finding a wrecker at 3:00 a.m. would be both hard and expensive, so I was surprised to get an answer at the first one I called. Not only did they dispatch a unit quickly, but the price was more reasonable than I expected. Once the driver arrived, we chatted as he hooked up my truck.

"We get a lot of early morning calls like this. I bet you forgot to put it in park, huh?" the driver said.

"Oh, no, I always put it in park. The dog did this."

Although it was dark, I knew the tow-truck driver was rolling his eyes. I suspect that third-shift wrecker operators hear a lot of things like that at 4:00 a.m. It's the equivalent of the old "dog ate my homework" excuse that every teacher has heard.

"The dog drove it!" the boy shouted.

Thirty minutes later, my truck had been towed back to the top of the hill, the transmission locked in park, and the wheels chocked. I signed the form on the driver's clipboard as he petted Belle.

"Pretty dog," he commented. "Too bad she's such a lousy driver."

— Butch Holcombe —

My Kitchen Ceiling Will Never Be the Same

Much like life, baking makes a mess of things in the
process, but the end result is worth savoring.
~Author Unknown

A few years ago, my husband and I moved to Texas, a couple of hours' drive from my sister and her family. It had been a long time since we lived near one another, a good thirty years.

That first year, my sister announced that she was going to make me a special meal for my first birthday in Texas, in my new house, using my kitchen. Well, it wasn't new. In fact, it was over sixty years old, but it was new to me. My sister is a phenomenal cook, so turning my kitchen over to her was a no-brainer.

The day of my birthday, she brought all the fixins and proceeded to put together all the dishes for my special birthday dinner. Honestly, I don't remember any of the dinner except the dessert, but not for the reasons you would think. Knowing that my favorite dessert is coconut cake, she brought the cake already baked at her house and proceeded to start making a classic Seven-Minute Frosting, which is cooked for seven minutes on the stove in a double boiler. I asked her why she was making a Seven-Minute Frosting, as the only frosting I'd ever had on a coconut cake was buttercream, chock full of shredded coconut. She wrinkled up her nose and informed me that a cake like this deserved a much better frosting than buttercream. I told her that I really like buttercream frosting. She assured me that Seven-Minute Frosting was sooooo much better than buttercream and that I would like it even better.

Well, what was I gonna do? Turn down a gift horse, as our Nana used to say? Nope, I shut up and trusted that I'd love my birthday cake. I mean, she's an amazing cook, so what could go wrong?

She got out all her ingredients and proceeded to start making the Seven-Minute Frosting in the top of my double boiler. I don't remember all the ingredients she used. I'm pretty sure that, besides the egg whites, she stirred in sugar, a bit of salt, light corn syrup, vanilla extract and probably cream of tartar because that's pretty much a given in Seven-Minute Frosting recipes. Either she used a large whisk or maybe a spoon and began stirring and whisking away, her fingernails twinkling with some unusual, sparkly fingernail color that made it look like she was stirring pixie dust. In retrospect, the pixie dust might have been a good addition. Anyway, everything seemed to be going well — until it wasn't. She was at least ten minutes into stirring the frosting concoction, but nothing was happening. I kept walking over and peeking into the top of the double boiler.

"Isn't it supposed to be done in seven minutes?" I asked.

"Stop being so impatient," she admonished me. "Sometimes, it takes a little longer."

Well, what did I know? I'd never made Seven-Minute Frosting, but it seemed to me that if it was named Seven-Minute Frosting, shouldn't it take just seven minutes? I refrained from asking her because I could see she was getting annoyed. I wasn't sure if it was with me or the frosting.

Time marched on. It wasn't finished in fifteen minutes, or twenty or even thirty. It just wasn't coming together. I vaguely recall that I suggested that we bag the Seven-Minute Frosting and make a buttercream frosting instead. Oh, if looks could kill, I would have been seriously dead. I backed off and kept my distance.

When we'd passed the forty-five-minute mark, or maybe it was an hour, I don't know if she turned up the heat or what happened when, suddenly, the No-Longer-a-Seven-Minute-Frosting exploded. It shot up in the air like a fast-moving helium balloon. It didn't just explode upward; it exploded everywhere—all over the copper pots hanging on the overhead pot rack, the stove top, the counters, floor, us, and even a few feet behind us into the sink. I was just about to burst out laughing when I saw her face. She didn't think it was funny at all. In fact, she was about to cry.

I tried to reassure her that it was okay; it was just frosting. Wrong thing to say. It didn't help at all. She was devastated. Right about then, the menfolk came running into the kitchen, having heard the frosting explosion. They stood there frozen with their mouths wide open. I don't know if it was one of my nephews, my husband, or my brother-in-law who asked what had happened. All I remember is that they got "the look," too.

At that point, all we could do was start cleaning up. The sticky mess was stuck like glue to everything. Note: Cooked corn syrup is a really good substitute for Super Glue or that Gorilla stuff if ever you find yourself short of it. I don't remember much else of that eventful meal other than we did eat the cake, without frosting, and it was really good. I also remember, with great fondness, that when I opened my birthday present, which was in a very large box and quite heavy, I found a brand-new KitchenAid mixer. Oh, was I happy! So what if I was going to be living with dried frosting all over my kitchen until the end of my days? I had a new KitchenAid!

About a year later, my husband was looking up at the pot rack and pointed to something odd. He got out the stepstool and peered close to the glob for a better inspection. It was the now-petrified No-Longer-a-Seven-Minute-Frosting. Although it took a bit of elbow grease, he got it off. A year or two later, once again we noticed something strange on the pot rack. Upon closer inspection, we found another glob of the now-infamous frosting. I'm pretty sure there's probably more up there, but I figure that if I can't see it, then it can stay. It would likely take a jackhammer to remove it at this point.

Someday, whenever we move, which I hope is never, and we take down the pot rack, there will probably be gobs of old frosting stuck in places we didn't notice before. And there's probably some on the ceiling that is fused into the crevices. I imagine that, a thousand years from now, some archeologists will unearth my house and find some ancient bits of fossilized frosting and initiate a scientific inquiry to discover what it is.

—Jeffree Wyn Itrich—

I Can't Believe I Did That

Road to Realization

The embarrassment of a situation can, once you are
over it, be the funniest time in your life.
~Miranda Hart

"Hey, look at us! We're twins!" I shouted out of the car window as I drove to work one morning. It had been an exciting week for me and my family as we had just bought a brand-new PT Cruiser.

Other than the Volkswagen Bug, I could think of no other automobile that possessed such vintage coolness as Chrysler's PT Cruiser. My husband and I had been drawn to it from the get-go, ever since we had seen one on Sunrise Highway. It was black with bright, detailed Greased Lightning flames covering the hood.

We still kept our reliable, less-than-cool minivan as it was the more practical vehicle. It afforded us the space we needed now that we had a baby and all that goes with the territory: a car seat, a playpen for visits, a stroller for walks and shopping, formula, bottles, the essential diaper bag, etc.

But, on this particular sunny day, I felt free.

As I drove north along the Cross Island Parkway, I spotted the same exact car. Kindred spirits! Two silver PT Cruisers sparkling like diamonds in the sun.

I stepped on the gas pedal to align myself with the other PT that drove steadily along in the right lane. Surely the other driver was experiencing the same sense of freedom I was in his new PT. There he sat, a middle-aged stranger, with salt-and-pepper hair, as ordinary as can be, yet encased in a shimmering piece of art.

This was a man with good taste and now my brother in the PT club.

I pressed the window button down and inched up in order to be right next to him. Once there, I honked the horn and gave him a big thumbs-up as he looked over at me. He didn't seem to respond, however, so I shouted out the window, "You and me! You and me!" adding, "We've both got good taste!"

Being that it was a Monday morning, I accepted his rather unenthusiastic reaction.

I shouted a few more terms of endearment, gave him an A-okay hand sign, and then continued on my way to work, allowing him his privacy and respecting our PT kinship.

I felt sorry for him actually. Perhaps he wasn't experiencing the same sense of liberty — that feeling of true authenticity when you've bought a car based solely on aesthetics.

It wasn't until I reached the parking garage on Second Avenue in Manhattan and exited my car that I realized my husband was driving the PT Cruiser that day. I was in our old blue minivan.

— Mary C. M. Phillips —

Save That Duck!

My entire life can be summed up in one sentence:
Well, that didn't go as planned.
~Darynda Jones

want to say at the outset how embarrassing it is to write about this incident. However, in our defense, my husband John and I had lived in the city our whole lives and were completely clueless about life in the animal world.

John and I were in our twenties when we moved to an upscale condo development complete with canals and interlocking ponds surrounded by gardens with walking paths. One fine October morning, we were strolling along beside a duck pond when we heard frantic squawking.

A few feet farther down the path, we discovered a big duck with a green head jumping on the back of a much smaller brown duck. The attacker kept pecking the feathers out of the smaller duck's head and continually pushing it under the water. There were only a few feathers left on its head by the time we arrived on the scene.

Having been a lover of birds since I was little, I was very alarmed for the welfare of the little duck, who looked as if it might be drowning and seemed too weak to resist the onslaught.

I shouted to John, "Save that duck! Get that big duck off the little duck before it drowns! Go, go, go!"

My kindhearted, gallant husband didn't wait. He jumped into the shallow pond and, with water up past his knees, grabbed the bully and threw it off into the nearby water. This action didn't deter the big duck at all. It just swam back and clambered up on the little duck's back again, wagging his tail back and forth and forcefully pushing the little duck's head under the water with its beak.

John tried to dislodge the bigger duck once more, but it was a losing battle. We were both upset and wondering how to resolve this violence in nature when we heard footsteps come up behind us.

We both turned around and saw an older man standing on the path, a stranger to us. "You'll never get that mallard off that duck, son," he said. "They're mating!" Then, he strode away with a smirk.

John immediately removed his grip on the bully duck and slogged back to shore. Neither of us spoke as we headed for home, both of us blushing from embarrassment and accompanied by the sound of John's shoes squishing out brown mud with every step.

I still cringe with humiliation when I recall that incident even though many years have passed.

We were exceedingly glad that we never met that man again and feel lucky that we have not since encountered any amorous ducks.

— Christine Clarke-Johnsen —

The Parking Problem

The rate at which a person can mature is directly
proportional to the embarrassment he can tolerate.
~Douglas Engelbart

Confusion, followed closely by panic, gripped my heart after I
left the grocery store and arrived at the spot where I'd parked
my car. But where was it?

I wasn't one to forget where I parked, and even if I was,
there weren't that many cars in the parking lot. It would've been easy
to find mine.

Plus, there was a memorable car I'd passed on my way into the
store. Its back bumper was covered in stickers with funny sayings.
It was still there. I was in the right place, but my car was nowhere
to be found.

That's when panic set in. And despair, too. It was early afternoon
on a weekday. I knew theft could happen anytime, but it seemed like
such a random one in this case.

And my car? Really? Why choose it? There weren't many other
options in the parking lot, but there were certainly nicer and newer
ones than mine.

Before I called the police, I wanted support, so I called my husband
Wayne, who was working from home that day. Besides, I was going
to need a ride back to our house.

"Babe, can you come get me? Someone stole my car."

"What? Are you sure?"

"Not entirely, but I don't see it, so I'm guessing that's what happened."

That's when the tears started to fall.

"Did you lock it?" he asked.

"Of course!" I said. That was something I was always vigilant about.

"I just don't get it," I lamented. "Who would want my fifteen-year-old car? Its parts can't be worth much, right?"

"Who knows, babe? But it'll be okay. Hang tight. I'm on my way."

In the background, I heard the jangling of his keys as he grabbed them before he hung up.

While I was on the phone, a gentleman had parked near where I stood with my cart of groceries and no trunk to put them in. He'd hesitated after exiting his car.

"Are you okay, miss?" he asked. "I didn't mean to eavesdrop, but did I hear you say that your car just got stolen?"

I nodded solemnly.

"I don't get it," I said, repeating what I'd told my husband. "It's a fifteen-year-old Altima. Not exactly the kind of car that most thieves target."

"Can I help in any way?"

"No, thank you. My husband's on his way."

Just then, my phone rang.

"Speaking of," I said to the man as I picked up, only to hear my husband laughing.

"What's so funny?" I asked. I'd never seen him respond to a stressful situation by cracking up before, but I guess there was a first time for everything.

"I found your car!"

"What?" I asked incredulously. How could that be?

"It's right here where you left it. Look again. You drove my car today, remember?"

I turned and looked. Sure enough, his SUV was parked right where I'd left it.

So, apparently, just as I always knew, I don't have a problem remembering where I parked, just which car I'm driving.

— Courtney Lynn Mroch —

The Pastry Chase

*Because the greatest part of a road trip isn't arriving
at your destination. It's all the wild stuff
that happens along the way.*
~Emma Chase, Tamed

dear friend of mine and her husband moved to Sarasota, Florida from New York in the early 1980s, and I enjoyed visiting them on occasion. One year, I was making a trip there in March, and my visit coincided with Saint Joseph's feast day. To Italians, this is an important day, and they celebrate by enjoying a special pastry that is made only at that time of the year. Since the pastry is filled with a creamy center, it's not something that you can leave unrefrigerated for a long time, so I wasn't able to bring it down from New York.

I figured I would ask my friend to take me to an Italian bakery when I landed in Florida. Her husband was of Italian descent, and I knew he would appreciate having Saint Joseph's pastry.

When I arrived and my friend picked me up at the airport, I asked her where the nearest Italian bakery was. She laughed and said, "What Italian bakery? There aren't any here. The only bakeries we have are in the supermarkets."

I was shocked and figured there had to be one somewhere nearby. Perhaps she just didn't know. I said, "Well, we can look in the Yellow Pages when we get to the house and maybe find one that way."

Later, we combed through the Yellow Pages and, not finding an Italian bakery anywhere in the Sarasota area, we were once again shocked. Being from New York, I naively thought the whole world operated like we did, with a bakery or two in every town. I called a couple of Italian restaurants in the area and asked if they had any of the pastries, but no luck.

My friend had Yellow Pages from other areas of Florida because of her husband's job, so we started looking at the Orlando area, which was a two-hour car ride away. The only thing I was able to find was a wholesale Italian bakery near Orlando. They sold only to restaurants, not to the public.

I decided to call anyway, and someone put the owner on the phone. He didn't speak much English, so I used my limited knowledge of Italian to explain that I was visiting from New York and wanted to get some Saint Joseph's pastries for my friends who lived two hours away from his store. He was surprised but sympathetic and said, "I don't sell to the public, but if you call me tomorrow morning at about 7:00, I can tell you if I will have extra pastry for you."

When I called the next morning, we were in luck. I asked him to put aside a dozen for us.

We took a Styrofoam cooler with us to fill with ice so we could keep the pastries cool. We drove up to Orlando and stopped at a convenience store to get ice. Following directions, we pulled up to a pink cinder-block building with only a front window and glass door. It didn't even have a sign in the front, but since it was the correct address, we went in.

They brought out a tray of pastries and filled a box for us. There were people working in the back who were peering out the kitchen door just to see who would drive over two hours just to get a piece of pastry. We could tell by the looks on their faces that they thought we were crazy.

When we got back in the car and started driving, it was feeling really warm. Even though the compressor was running, it was blowing hot air, and our worst nightmare was about to come true: The air conditioner was broken! The only thing we could do was get home as fast as possible, so we kept driving and opened all the windows. I was praying we wouldn't be stopped by highway patrol and have to tell the officer we were speeding due to a pastry emergency!

It was so hot that the ice in the cooler was melting. Every fifteen minutes, I would lean over into the back seat, uncover the cooler, take out the pastry box, and pour the water from the cooler out the window. I had plastic wrap from the sandwiches we'd bought on our way home, and I spread it out under the box on the ice that remained in the cooler. I took some napkins left from lunch and used them to line the inside of the box, hoping it would absorb some of the moisture and keep the pastries from getting wet.

Over an hour into the trip, the heat was overwhelming. Even with everything I was doing, the box was a bit damp. I took a couple of pastries out of the box and told my friend we should at least eat those in case the rest were ruined.

When we finally got home, we ran into the house with a slightly soggy box of pastries. We quickly took them out of the box and got them into the refrigerator. Surprisingly, they still seemed okay! I was glad all my efforts had paid off.

A little while later, my friend's husband came home. We were excited to share the story of our adventure. He took one look at the St. Joseph's pastries and said, "Ugh! I hate those things!"

I said, "What? Are you kidding?"

He said, "No, my mother used to buy them, and I never liked them!"

My friend and I didn't know whether to laugh or cry. She called a few of the neighbors and invited them over for pastries and coffee.

She and I had wine.

— Jeanne Cassetta —

Life of the Party

*Sometimes crying or laughing are the only options
left, and laughing feels better right now.*
~Veronica Roth, Divergent

I moved to rural China to teach English to high school students. It was a huge transition for me, especially coming from a small town in Arizona, but I was more than excited to accept whatever challenge came my way. It was going to be a real adventure.

Since I continued working right up until my flight there, I didn't have time to prepare. I knew less than a dozen phrases in Chinese and had done very little research about the culture or my new village.

I was nervous, of course, but as soon as I settled into my school, I was amazed by how welcoming everyone was. An English teacher named Miss Sun was my liaison, and she gave me a quick tour of everything. Whenever we talked, she mostly asked me questions about America. But every time I got the chance, I asked her for advice about how to make friends.

She basically told me to just be myself. My village was a safe place, and people would be happy to meet me. All I had to do was go out there and explore.

That's exactly what I did. The village was pretty small by China standards, although there were still tons of people on the main streets when I was walking around.

Since there were less than ten of us foreigners living there, I very quickly started feeling like a celebrity. People would constantly come up to me and ask for photos. The shyer ones would secretly take my photo when I walked by. Several times, elderly women would come up to me, touch my arm hair (which most Chinese people don't have), and then either tell me something in Chinese or just give me a thumbs-up. It was a bit surreal.

The whole time, I felt supremely welcome wherever I went. As a foreigner in a small village, I never felt alone. Even though I hadn't made any close friends yet, I was constantly invited to sit with people at their tables or join in on street-side games of Ping-Pong. (I was terrible at it.)

After about a week of this, I quickly learned to just say yes to whatever was offered. I had come to this new place for the experience, so I might as well embrace it, I told myself.

One weekend, I was walking alone on the street behind my school and saw an outdoor party. People dressed in white were standing under a tent with tables lined with food. They were all talking to each other, and while no music was playing, I could tell it was a nice little party. I walked past, and one of the people there gave me a smile. I took that as an invitation to join them.

None of them knew any English, so the best I could do was say "hello" and "thank you." An older man gestured me toward the food table. Even though there was a line of people waiting, he had me cut in front of everyone. That kind of situation happened a lot in this extremely respectful culture, so I didn't argue.

As I was eating, though, I noticed that the people around me didn't seem too happy for me to be there. They were still friendly and welcoming, and one lady still came up and touched my arm hair, but there was a bit of coldness among them that I hadn't experienced during my other outings in the village.

I quickly finished my food, thanked everyone with my limited Chinese, and rushed home.

When I went back to school on Monday, Miss Sun asked me about my weekend. I told her about my village exploration. I talked about all the new food I got to try. And I mentioned that party. When I told her that everyone was wearing white, her eyes widened. I asked her what was wrong, and she said, "That was a funeral."

— Evan Purcell —

The Newbie

To make mistakes is human; to stumble
is commonplace; to be able to laugh
at yourself is maturity.
~William Arthur Ward

I was just a teenager, working at a small restaurant in Northport, Alabama. The restaurant was "country-style," serving what we in the South call "meat and three" lunches and dinners. For those of you unfamiliar with the term, it means one serving of a type of protein (meat) along with three side dishes.

I had only been working at the restaurant for a few weeks, sometimes toiling as many as seventy hours on my feet. But I was glad for the work, and the tips were good. I was, I thought, "getting the hang" of waiting tables while saving my tip money and putting it in my college fund.

One afternoon, I was getting the prep area ready for the dinner shift when my manager, Teri Jo, came up to me. "I'm sorry to tell you this," she said, and I held my breath for what she was about to say next, "but Sally, the waitress who's been training you, just called in sick. It's going to be just you, waiting tables and being the cashier, and the one cook. My daughter is in the hospital, about to have my first grandbaby, or else I'd be here."

Teri Jo assured me that I could handle the few customers for the evening. "Today's Wednesday, and you'll probably just have the usual folks here after their Wednesday night church service," she told me.

"The salads are already made and in the front refrigerator. All the other dressings are there except the blue cheese, which is in a vat on the floor of the big walk-in fridge past the kitchen." I made a mental note of this, for the few diners who might want blue-cheese dressing on their salads.

After Teri Jo left, the cook and I began our dinner shift and seemed to be working in tandem pretty well. As Teri Jo had said, the dinner shift at first consisted of the handful of people who came in after their Wednesday night church service for a quick meal before heading home.

There was a couple I'd never seen before, though. The woman was of slight build and seemed to be of a rather meek nature, but the man was just her opposite: brash and with a swagger as he waved his cigar in the air as they talked, waiting for me to seat them. Smoking was allowed in public places back then.

After I led them to a table and handed them their menus, the man waved his cigar in my general direction. "I want your Cobb salad with blue-cheese dressing," he said. "But, let me warn you, I am a blue-cheese aficionado, and I'll be the first to let you know if it's not up to my standards."

"I think you will like our blue-cheese dressing, sir," I assured him, but I wondered how he would react if the dressing wasn't to his liking.

After I finished taking their order, I went to the back to look for the dressing in the large walk-in refrigerator. But the light wouldn't come on, and so I was obliged to look for the dressing in what little light shone through the open door of the refrigerator.

As Teri Jo had said, there was the vat of blue-cheese dressing on the floor of the refrigerator. Thinking how clever I was, I filled a small bowl with some of the dressing and put it in the front refrigerator for the lunch shift to use the next day. That way, they wouldn't have to go back to the walk-in fridge.

Once in the prep area, I put the mixture on the side next to the man's Cobb salad. Then, I got the lady's meal from the cook and carried it to their table on a tray.

"Voilà!" I said to the man, using what I hoped sounded like a good French accent. "Here is your blue-cheese dressing. I put it on the side of your salad so you can use as much or as little as you want."

I left their table and went to cash out some of the remaining diners who were on their way home. After wiping down a couple of tables, I went back to the couple.

"What do you think about the dressing?" I asked the man.

He looked up at me and smiled. "That's probably the best blue-cheese dressing I've ever had in my life!" he exclaimed.

I smiled back at him. "I'm so glad you liked it!" I said, proud of the way I'd handled the situation. Some other people seated near him, menus in hand, overheard him praising the salad dressing.

"We think we'll try your Cobb salad with some of that blue-cheese dressing," they told me when I came to take their order. Once their salads were delivered, they both exclaimed over the dressing, saying it was the best they'd ever tasted.

Another nearby table of regular folks, waiting for me to take their orders, said they'd like to try salads with our soon-to-be-famous blue-cheese dressing. And so it went, with perhaps a dozen diners trying the dressing and loving it.

After the evening was over, I closed up and put the money from the night's proceeds in the safe. The blue-cheese dressing bowl in the prep refrigerator was nearly empty, so I made one more trip back to the walk-in refrigerator and dipped out a good bit to put in the front refrigerator. *Everyone will be singing my praises,* I thought to myself, *for saving the lunch crew some extra steps.*

I locked the doors, drove the cook home and then headed home myself. Fatigue and the satisfaction of a job well done made me sleep well. When I woke the next morning, I once again mentally patted myself on the back for having done a good night's work, all by myself and without messing up once!

When I went in to work the lunch shift, I prepared myself for the accolades sure to come from Teri Jo. After I congratulated her on the birth of her first grandchild, she said, "My dear, it seems you did a pretty good job last night, especially closing up, but there's one thing I've got to ask you."

"Yes, ma'am, what is it?"

She frowned slightly and asked, "Just what were you doing with that bowl of pancake batter in the little refrigerator in the prep area? You know we don't serve pancakes at night!"

— T. Jensen Lacey —

15

The Visionary

You don't stop laughing because you grow old.
You grow old because you stop laughing.
~Michael Pritchard

We were on our way back to Cary, North Carolina from visiting family in Alabama, a nine-hour drive. My husband had been the driver most of the way, but halfway along, I could see he was tiring. At lunch, I volunteered to take over. There was beautiful, bright sunshine when I started driving, and the trip went smoothly.

It wasn't until dusk started falling as we approached Lumberton, North Carolina that I started to panic. What was happening to me? Sure, I was in my fifties, and I knew that when one got older, night driving often presented a problem. My parents had complained of it. But did it happen all of a sudden, like this? Weren't cataracts supposed to come on gradually? Would I have to have surgery?

I glanced over at my husband, who seemed perfectly calm. I hated to voice my fears aloud. He was so patient with all my quirks.

I decided to tough it out. After all, we were almost home. But things only got worse as the day darkened more into night.

"It's so dark! I can't see!" I whined as I squinted over the steering wheel at what I hoped was the road ahead. "What's wrong with me? What can I do? Can you see a place where I can pull over, and you can take us on home?"

As ever, my husband's response was low-key. "I don't think that's necessary, honey," he said. "Why don't you just take off your sunglasses?"

— Ellen Edwards Kennedy —

16

Red-Faced Lunch

It's all about finding the calm in the chaos.
~Donna Karan

Since the time I began dating my husband he worked at a local garage as an automotive mechanic. They often left all the large doors open and customers would drive up and chat with the mechanics.

Once we were married we found that time together was harder to come by; we had our first child early in the marriage so my days were spent doing naptime and feedings, laundry, and housework.

Then I had the clever idea of taking lunch to my husband at work every Friday. I would simply pull up to the open garage doors and he would come out. We would park and eat and visit while the baby slept in the car seat.

This weekly get-together went on for years. Eventually there were two babies in car seats either crying or sleeping when I would bring my husband lunch.

After a crazy week of appointments, feedings, housework and more, I hurried out the door with the babies one Friday. I had rushed to get groceries and finish my chores so I would have time to stop at a drive-thru for burgers and still make it to my husband's garage on time.

With one minute to spare, I pulled up at the garage. I thought he would come right out for our usual lunch. But ten minutes passed with no husband. The other guys were there eating their lunches, so I honked and waved at them, hoping one of them would tell my husband I was there.

Fifteen minutes passed, then twenty. I was getting angry. Lunchtime was almost over

I honked some more and waved my arm back and forth like a crazy woman so his co-workers would go get him. I couldn't leave the car because the two children were with me.

I finally called out to the guys. "Where is my husband?" I demanded.

That's when the owner came out laughing. "You do remember he quit last week?" he said. "My guess is he's across town waiting for you in the parking lot at his new job." Now all the guys were laughing.

What had my scattered brain done? I hit the gas pedal red-faced, and saw in my rearview mirror that the guys were still laughing.

— Krista Kell —

17

Proof Positive

I believe that the ability to laugh at oneself is fundamental
to the resiliency of the human spirit.
~Jill Conner Browne

My colleagues in the office all knew I had applied for a job. We all were looking as our company was moving a long way away, and some of us had ties here.

And how wonderful to be a proofreader! I have tutted at typos since I was a child, and even grammar software can't always pick up things like writing "discrete" when you mean "discreet," or vice versa.

I thought I had a good chance of getting the job, and my workmates were sure that I'd get it, especially Julie and Yan.

Meanwhile, Julie got a part-time job in a different office, and we were all excited for her. Greg got a job as a supervisor in a supermarket, which was a change. Maxine was starting her own business. And I waited...

Finally, the e-mail arrived.

"It's come," I said. "I'm too anxious to open it."

"Shall I do it?" Julie offered.

"No... yes... no!"

Eventually, I did it myself. Everyone was watching now.

I read the e-mail. My jaw dropped.

And then I began to laugh.

This wasn't the reaction everyone had expected.

"You got it then?" asked Yan.

"No!" I spluttered.

"Oh… I'm sorry," said Yan. "Um, why are you laughing?"

"Because they turned me down as a proofreader. The reason they gave — they told me to read the first line of my application."

"And?"

"I applied for a job as a roofreader!"

"A roofreader?"

Julie had got it and was guffawing now.

"You meant 'proofreader,' but you typed 'roofreader,' didn't you?" she said. "Didn't you read it through? Check it for errors? You know, proofread it?"

"I thought I had," I said. "But maybe, deep down, I really want a job reading roofs! Or is it rooves?"

I'm glad to say that I did find a suitable job, though not proofreading. For the next few weeks, my colleagues would ask me, "Read any good roofs lately?"

"Why is your assignment late? Were you roofreading again?"

I'm sure you can guess the shape of the cake they got me for my goodbye party!

— Cathy Bryant —

It's All Relative

18

Wrong Turn

Your grandma always had a terrible sense of direction.
She could get lost on an escalator.
~Fredrik Backman, And Every Morning the Way
Home Gets Longer and Longer

My grandfather Sam was notorious for having the worst sense of direction. Before the age of cell phones, GPS and Waze, drivers actually had to remember routes to get wherever they wanted to go. Too bad for Sam. A fifteen-minute car ride with him would often stretch into a thirty-minute, steering-wheel-smacking, head-slapping, frustrating journey filled with wrong turns and detours. But he was even worse when he gave directions. Everyone who drove with Sam as a passenger knew not to listen to him because he would always get you lost.

The only person I knew who had a comparably bad sense of direction was Mom, Sam's daughter. Except for driving locally or to my grandparents' apartment on Ocean Parkway, Mom would not drive anywhere. She knew that she would get lost. But, like her father, it didn't discourage her from giving directions when she was a passenger. Driving with both Sam and Mom was a recipe for disaster. Can you imagine them shouting conflicting directions while you struggled to concentrate on driving?

I started driving when I turned seventeen years old. I was a freshman in college, and almost everyone that I knew had been driving for a while. It was finally my turn.

What type of driver would I be? Would I have a poor sense of direction like Mom and Sam, or would I have my father's driving instincts and good driving sense?

I prayed that Dad's genes were dominant. It wouldn't be long before I found out.

One month after I earned my driver's license, I was home from college during Christmas break. Sam and his wife Betty were flying into JFK one evening, and Mom asked if I could drive her there in Dad's massive yellow Buick Electra 225 to pick them up. Without thinking, I said, "Of course." JFK was only about twenty minutes from where we lived in Canarsie, Brooklyn. The ride was easy; we just headed east on the Belt Parkway and got off at the airport exit.

We arrived at the airport uneventfully. My grandparents landed on time, and after I loaded their luggage in the car's trunk, I started driving everyone back home. This was the first time that I had ever driven with both Sam and Mom in the car. This was also the first time that I had ever driven in an airport.

Mom, in the front seat, immediately assumed responsibility for telling me where to go. Sam wouldn't allow himself to be upstaged because, in his mind, he always knew best. So, he was in the back seat bellowing at me as well. As I tried to follow both sets of incorrect directions, we kept circling around the airport.

We eventually arrived at an intersection, and I didn't know which way to turn. Mom was yelling at me to turn left, while Sam adamantly shouted at me to turn right. Everybody was waving their hands and pointing in different directions. Total chaos. I felt my blood pressure rising, my face getting flushed, and my hands starting to shake. I decided to do the only rational thing: I didn't listen to either of them and instead drove straight ahead.

After only a few hundred yards, I was surprised to see a police officer in a kiosk at the right side of the road eating a sandwich. I thought it was strange; why would there be a policeman there? As we passed by, he abruptly spat out his food and started chasing us. I just shrugged my shoulders and kept driving.

Then, I looked forward and almost had a heart attack. Airplanes were crisscrossing on the road in front of me.

"Oh, my God, we're on the runway!" I screamed.

I quickly made a U-turn and raced back toward the kiosk. We waved goodbye to the policeman as we sped by him on our way out. I then barked out, "Stop giving me directions! I'll figure out how to get out of the airport by myself!" That ended all the talking in the car. At last, blissful quiet. I drove us home without further mishaps.

From that experience, I learned that I had unfortunately inherited Mom's poor-sense-of-direction gene. Thankfully, my wife Linda, who has a good sense of direction, often acts as my navigator and has saved me countless times. When GPS systems were installed in cars, no one was happier than me. I never again drove in an airport with both Sam and Mom in the car. And I certainly never found myself driving on an active airport runway again.

— Eric J. Barr —

One Thing After Another

*The great secret of a successful marriage is to
treat all disasters as incidents and none
of the incidents as disasters.*
~Harold Nicolson

The problems began two months before the wedding when Erin learned that the venue for the reception was closed for renovations. The venue suggested she move her March wedding to May, but her wedding had been purposefully scheduled for mid-March to take advantage of the cherry-blossom bloom in Washington, DC.

The invitations had already gone out, so the date was set. Now the venue would have to be changed. Two weekends later, Erin managed to book a space across the Potomac River in Arlington, Virginia, with its sparkling view of the monuments of downtown D.C. It was within walking distance of Erin's apartment, so it wasn't all bad. A wedding snafu had been handled.

Well, then the rehearsal dinner had some wrinkles. A groomsman wanted to watch a March Madness basketball game during the toasts. A grandmother got food poisoning.

Then, a sister-in-law, sick and heavily pregnant, called the morning of the wedding. She apologized profusely and said she could barely stand so she wouldn't be able to serve as a bridesmaid.

The remaining bridesmaids huddled with the wedding coordinator. Instead of going down the aisle in couples we'd all walk in singly. We piled into vans to drive two miles, crossing the river, to the campus of Georgetown University in DC.

Time got away from us. There were lots of photos. Pose under the cherry blossoms. Pose with Erin's dog. My plus-one arrived then. She'd gone straight to the chapel and then come down to the photo area.

It was now 1:30 p.m. The wedding started at 2:00.

"Is the church getting packed?" I asked her, since she'd just been there.

"Um. No?"

I went to peek in the chapel myself. Not only was it not packed, but there was no one in there at all.

"How'd you get here?" I looked at her nice shoes and dress and the craggy cobblestone street.

"I walked."

She had walked the two miles to Georgetown. Why? The mother of the groom had her cell phone out, calling her children who were supposed to have arrived on the buses for the ceremony. "They're all at the reception venue," she declared. "The guests are in Virginia."

The buses had taken all the guests to the venue for the reception!

Luckily, the bride was too far away to hear that. She was still under the cherry tree, taking pictures with her mother.

"Well, tell them to turn around!" bridesmaid Jules yelled into the cell phone.

"Wasn't there a 5K or something?" I whispered to bridesmaid Kat. "I saw signs all over downtown. A lot of the bridges are closed."

"We'll stall," Kat said. "We're not walking down the aisle without any guests."

Another gust of wind. I tightened the coat around my shoulders. There was a gasp from Jules and Kat, and a scream from Erin as the wind plucked the veil from her hair and sent it up into the blue sky.

"Someone go get that!"

Erin's brother waved his hand, running up a grassy bank toward the church in his new suit and shoes. His new shoes slipped on the slick asphalt. He went down hard, his chin, nose and cheek scraping against the pavement, suit ripping at the knee, banging his wrist and scraping his forearm.

"Wipeout," Jules muttered. Several groomsmen ran to dust off the brother.

By the time we rounded the corner to the courtyard, I was prepared for the veil to be well away, over the towers and into the Potomac.

Good news: We spotted the veil.

Bad news: The veil was thirty feet up in a tree directly outside the chapel doors.

Good news: There were no guests to watch the mishap.

Bad news: There were no guests to watch the mishap.

"I'll go find a ladder," Jules said, spotting some groundskeepers across the quad.

"I can climb the tree," Erin's brother offered, his teeth stained with blood from his fall.

"You need to sit down," I said, steering him toward the bridal suite. "Kat, have we heard anything about the guests?"

By now, Erin was standing under the tree, staring at her veil waving in the wind. At my words, she turned. "Something happened with the guests?"

Which is how we got to the bride crying five minutes before the wedding was scheduled to start. Her guests were at a venue in Virginia that was never supposed to be the venue. Her brother was swapping pants with another groomsman. And her veil was fluttering in a tree.

"Don't worry," Jules said, huffing up the hill with two men and a ladder. "The cavalry has arrived."

The men took one look at the veil and kept walking. "Hey!" Jules called after them.

"Too high! We need a different ladder."

The wedding coordinator came up with her clipboard. "We only have the chapel booked for an hour, so are we ready to get started?"

Here, at least, was a challenge for the bridesmaids. All of us told her that the bride would not walk down the aisle until the guests arrived. The coordinator pursed her lips. "Luckily, there's no one booked after us."

"Then we're taking as long as necessary," Jules declared, spying something around the buildings. "Hey! I think the buses are here."

As quickly as the calamities unfolded, they seemed to reverse. An appropriately tall ladder appeared. The guests filed into the church. The bride's brother sported Band-Aids and a smile. And, seconds before the doors opened for the wedding party, the veil fluttered down from the tree.

I nudged Erin. "Now for the fun part."

"Fun part," Erin huffed. "Wake me up tomorrow." But she grinned. The music swelled. The ceremony went off without a hitch, and the guests got to the new venue, the one overlooking the monuments. The band played. The drinks flowed. We danced all night.

After the party, we did indeed walk the bride back to her apartment, rehashing the glitter of the evening. We settled onto the couch with the dog. And my phone rang.

"You're not going to believe this," my plus-one said, "but the buses from the venue just pulled up to the chapel on the Georgetown campus instead of taking people back to their hotel. It's midnight; the lights are off. How did they think this was the right place to be?"

"Oh, Lordy," Erin muttered, tipping a heavy pour into her glass.

"Welcome to married life," Jules said. We all toasted to that.

— Katie Avagliano —

Family History

If you shake your family tree, watch for the nuts to fall.
~Author Unknown

You search and search, the facts to find,
To solve the mystery in your mind.
Where's Great-Grandpa? What did he do?
They all say he died from the flu...
But you're not sure, and you don't know why
Except that he died from the flu in July...
So, you delve and question and probe and pry
And SUDDENLY the answer is before your eye!
Your throat is dry, and you can't make a sound
'Cause you just can't believe what you have found...
Great-Grandpapa was a cattle thief!
Shot in the back while stealing beef!
And now you understand why no one said a peep...
Great-Grandfather was the family's black sheep!
Not an ancestor for the Hall of Fame,
He's the one kept secret by shame.
But I think he was a colorful, old lad,
And I wish more of my ancestors were half as bad!

— Robbie Gorr —

Plausible Deniability

The person who can bring the spirit of laughter into a room is indeed blessed.
~Bennett Cerf

My mom and I sounded exactly alike. On the phone or in person. It was impossible to tell which one of us was speaking if we were together and you couldn't see a mouth moving.

It was even more difficult to tell which one of us was talking when we were on the phone. My dad would call the house, and even he couldn't tell who answered. Needless to say, he learned to be very careful with what he said until he was sure who he was talking to.

But the best thing is that my mom even fooled herself once! She had just gotten a new answering system, and she wanted to test it to be sure it worked. She was at her office, and she called her home number from her cell phone. Her greeting came on, and, after the beep, she left herself a test message. Now, when my mom would leave a test message, she didn't say "test." She left an actual message. "Hi, it's me. I hope you're having a nice day. Talk to you later. Bye."

Mom always checked her messages when she got home from work. That day, after checking, she called me. "Thanks for your call today, but I was at work," she told me. Puzzled, I told her that I hadn't called because I knew she was at work and thought I would call in the evening when I knew she would be home. "No," she said, "you called and said you hoped I was having a nice day."

"Mom, that wasn't me," I assured her. Suddenly, she realized her mistake. She started to laugh. And not just a little laugh. She was practically hysterical! You know, the kind of laugh when you have a hard time catching your breath. When she settled down a little, she told me what had happened: She had called her home number to test her new answering system, and when she listened to her messages, she thought her "test" message was from me. She was sure I was the one who had called and left that message. Even she couldn't tell us apart!

My mom was a psychologist and had a large private therapy practice. She was also one of the rare therapists who gave out her home phone number to her patients. She never refused a phone call from someone in need. And she never refused a phone call from someone not-so-much-in-need, someone who just wanted to talk. Many times, when we were at her house, she would get a call from a patient and would take ten or so minutes to solve a problem or... just listen.

I hated to answer the phone at her house. If the person calling was a patient, they would immediately assume that I was my mother. The person would launch into the reason for the call. "Oh, Dr. B, I'm so sorry to bother you, but..." I would try and interrupt and tell them I wasn't Dr. B — I was Dr. B's daughter — but usually the patient didn't listen and just kept on talking. Or they would think I actually was my mother, but she was lying and saying she wasn't Dr. B so she wouldn't have to talk.

I could usually tell by the tone of their voice what they were thinking — and usually they thought I was my mother, and my mother was lying. Their speech would slow down, way down, and their tone would become kind of hushed and questioning: "Really? You're not Dr. B? You're her daughter? Yeah, right!" And then they'd hang up. Poor Mom would have to explain at the patient's next appointment that they really were talking to her daughter, to me and not to her!

Now, I am the one with the problem: different generation, different gender, but the same problem. I have three sons and one husband. And they all sound the same. Same tone of voice, same inflections, same phrases, same laugh. There have been days when they are all out in the backyard together, and I've heard their conversation from inside the house. I can't see them, but I can hear them, and it sounds as if there is only one person in the yard talking to himself. He is asking questions, he is answering those same questions, making comments, commenting on the comments, and laughing at jokes. One voice, four people! They sound identical.

When one of them calls me on the phone, there has to be some conversation that takes place before I call them by name so I am sure which one I am talking to. Or if one of them leaves a short voice message, "Hi, Mom. Please call me," I have to check the caller ID number to know which son wants me to call him back. The best thing about the voice messages is that there are only three people it could be. It has to be one of my sons. I know when my husband is the person leaving the message; he doesn't call me Mom!

— Barbara LoMonaco —

Mom Shakes Up Elvis

Do something worth remembering.
~Elvis Presley

My eighty-four-year-old mother lived in a skilled-nursing facility. Despite a series of strokes affecting her cognitive and speaking abilities, she had very much enjoyed dancing with the Elvis impersonator who visited the home. I heard all about it from the nurses and the other residents, so I was looking forward to witnessing Mom getting reacquainted with her dance partner.

The day of his return, I met Mom in her room. I noticed a van pull up in the parking lot, facing Mom's large window. The gray-haired gentleman sitting in the driver's seat looked like he was singing. Mom saw the driver, too. She pointed and smiled. Could this be Elvis? Mom fluffed her hair and dabbed perfume behind her ears.

For the King's performance in the dining room, we managed to find two seats toward the front. Elvis had slicked back his gray hair and donned a tight, white, glittery jumpsuit with attached cape. He strutted around, warming up the audience.

When he approached us, he said, "You two look like you could be sisters." That's when Elvis made a wrong move. He leaned one inch too close to Mom. And that's when she made *her* move. Her arms circled his neck, and at the same time she pulled him toward her and off his feet. Mom gave him a big kiss on his cheek and hugged him tight.

Elvis looked at me and squeaked, "Help!"

I said, "That's your fault, Elvis. You're on your own."

Mom must have accomplished her goal because she let go. Elvis straightened up, smoothed back his hair, and adjusted his jumpsuit. I hoped he would still be able to hit all the proper low notes during his performance. Even though Elvis was all shook up, the show had to go on. Mom did not take her eyes from him as he sang along with his boom box. Several instances between his songs, he would search in his bag on the floor and act a little mixed up. Every time Elvis stood back up, he smoothed his hair and adjusted his jumpsuit all over again.

His final song was about to begin. But before Elvis sang "Love Me Tender," he said, "I usually have a pink scarf when I dance with someone special in the crowd, but I must have misplaced it the last time I performed here." The lady residents groaned that the previous show's magical moment would not take place. Mom just kept on smiling while he sang.

As Elvis left, we waved goodbye. Mom pushed her walker a bit quicker back to the room, hoping to catch a glimpse of him from the window. But he was already gone. While Mom went to the bathroom, I sat down beside her bed, ready to get a snack out of her nightstand. I slid open the drawer and reached in the back for one of her candy bars, and what did I find? A pink silk scarf. Mom just smiled when I asked her where she got it. Elvis may have left the building, but Mom was ready for another dance.

— Glenda Ferguson —

23

A Pig in a Poke

Humor is everywhere in that there's irony
in just about anything a human does.
~Bill Nye

used to collect pigs. Not real ones. They're loud and messy and probably wouldn't get along with our dogs. No, I collected cute, unique pigs: salt and pepper shakers, figurines, perhaps an understated paper-towel holder. You know, classy stuff.

But here's the thing about collecting. After a while, your friends and family figure they no longer have to put any thought into your birthday or Christmas presents. All they have to do is find something pig-related. That's how you come to have a collection that includes crocheted, pig-shaped toilet-paper cozies and all manner of oinking novelties, outpaced only by your regret at ever having mentioned collecting pigs in the first place.

While I was dealing with this pig dilemma at home, my husband was caught in a perpetual loop at work, bringing in one fundraising sales flyer after another so his colleagues could do their part to pay for our children's school, sports and extracurricular activities.

Because of this generous support, he felt duty-bound to reciprocate, ultimately buying, sight unseen, a handmade wreath like no other.

The calico-print fabric wrapped around the straw ring might have been tolerable — even in our non-country-style home — but the artist didn't stop there. To achieve that pièce de resistance, she glued a plastic pig, complete with overalls and a straw hat, to the lower part of the wreath. It kind of looked like a swing-set scene in an animated hillbilly horror film.

Not one to throw things away — even monstrosities — we decided the wreath might make a funny novelty item to donate to our church silent auction. So off to the auction it went, as did we on the big night.

Armed with my paddle number, I walked among the tables of treasures… and stopped dead in my tracks. I saw my husband across the room and motioned for him to join me.

"Can you believe it?" I said. "Someone is bidding on that hideous wreath."

We had a good laugh and parted to continue our separate browsing, but he was back double-quick and laughing even harder.

"I know who's bidding on the wreath," he said, smiling broadly.

"Who?" I asked, marveling at the person's bad taste.

"My mother," he replied. "She's going to give it to you for Christmas."

— Laurie O'Connor Stephans —

24

Killing Frosty

*I tell you, it's not a proper winter
without a decent snowman.*
~Mr. Tumnus, The Chronicles of Narnia

t was a couple of days before Christmas and a blizzard blew across the country. It was nicknamed "The Artic Express" and delivered freezing temperatures and snow to most of the country, even as far south as Sarasota, Florida. It was so cold that Miami residents had to dodge falling iguanas that were forced into hibernation and fell from the local palm trees. People were injured.

In my hometown of Jacksonville, Florida, it was chaos because two and a half inches of snow fell. People north of the Mason–Dixon line may scoff at such minimal amounts. But here it was Armageddon, because we were not prepared! The deep and wide St. Johns River runs through the middle of the city. There are eight bridges that cross the river and because of the ice, seven of them were closed. All of the traffic converged on that single bridge creating massive traffic jams.

A high number of automobile accidents contributed to the situation, because we did not know how to drive on ice. A friend tried to stop at a red light. He hit a patch of ice and slid fifty feet into the side of a police car! The officer got out of his car, inspected the damage and told the hapless driver, "Don't worry about it. I've hit two cars today myself!"

The Jacksonville International Airport was shutting down. Only a few flights managed to take off or land, and another friend of mine needed to go there because his father was on the last flight to make it in. Normally a forty-minute drive, it took seven hours to get there. Then he had to park over a mile away and hike to the terminal and search through the thousands of stranded passengers. He found his father curled up on the floor in a corner, fast asleep. Then it was another twelve hours to drive home.

Happily, my wife and I were on vacation and did not have to venture onto the roads. I spent much of the twenty-third happily walking through our neighborhood. I loved the crunching of the snow beneath my feet. And I learned that falling snowflakes have a music all their own. They sound like tiny glass bells.

I realized I was missing an opportunity to have fun and bond with Chad, our four-year-old son. His mother dressed him warmly and we set off with his wagon and a shovel to steal the neighbors' snow.

My plan was to build a snowman like the ones on Christmas cards. Tall, majestic and pristine white. But our neighborhood has many trees and much of the snow did not fall to the ground. Whenever we saw a likely patch of white, I scooped it up and put it in his wagon. When we had collected all of the available snow, we dumped it in our driveway. After we cleaned out the leaves, twigs, moss and frozen lizards, what remained only made a two-foot-tall snowman. The body resembled a badly deflated basketball and the head was the size of a softball. And there was so much dirt in the snow that Frosty was a sickly-looking gray color instead of white.

But it didn't matter! Chad was thrilled. He found some sticks for arms. My wife Grace contributed a carrot for Frosty's nose and a scarf to go around his neck. I raided my charcoal grill and some briquettes served as eyes and mouth.

Frosty wasn't beautiful, but he was the best (and only) snowman in the area. Chad told everybody that Frosty the Snowman was at our house.

On Christmas afternoon the sun came out and all the snow melted. All of it, but our icy creation.

We had built him at the end of our driveway, which is made of concrete and marble pebbles. Maybe the combination holds the cold well. And a massive 500-year-old oak tree by the driveway shaded Frosty and kept the sun at bay.

Frosty survived the 26th, 27th, 28th and 29th. He refused to die and I had made the mistake of building him at the end of our driveway, impeding our ability to get in and out.

Saturday, the 29th, Chad went with me to run some errands. When we returned, Frosty the Snowman was still there. And his beady black eyes seemed to be mocking me.

And I decided to kill Frosty the Snowman!

Chad was in his car seat beside me. "Watch this, Chad!" I cried as I put my Jeep into four-wheel drive and we went up and over "The Snowman That Would Not Die." I laughed maniacally as we changed Frosty the Snowman into Frosty the Pancake.

If I were a better father, I might have noticed the look of shock and horror on my son's face.

Thirty years later, Grace, Chad and I were reminiscing about his childhood. The subject of the snowman came up and I asked him if he remembered our execution of Frosty? My son made a decades old confession as he quietly told me he had been traumatized when I drove over the hapless snowman.

I assumed he was joking. But I would soon learn the truth.

A few days later, I ran into the lady who had been Chad's Sunday School teacher at that time. She asked about him and I filled her in on his life. Then I mentioned the story of Frosty and his claim of being traumatized.

A look of horror came over her face. She said over and over, "I should have said something." Curious, I asked her what she was talking about.

She said when Chad came into her Sunday School class the next day, he looked upset. She took him to the side and asked what was wrong. She said a tear ran down his cheek as he whispered, "My daddy killed Frosty the Snowman!"

Then he added, "Should I tell the Police?"

She said she assured him that I had not killed the real Frosty.

The real Frosty was alive at the North Pole with Santa Claus. We had killed a pretender.

—Chip Kirkpatrick—

Family Ties

If you cannot get rid of the family skeleton,
you may as well make it dance.
~George Bernard Shaw

"We got another 'care package' in the mail from your dad," my husband announced with a grin.

Laughing, I said, "Let's see what's in it this time!" I first pulled out a worn paperback, *Consultative Selling*, published in 1970. This was especially humorous because this original edition was undoubtedly out of date by thirty-plus years, and no family members had the slightest interest in marketing.

The box also contained used birthday candles, hotel pens, the front half of multiple greeting cards, and a baggie full of ink-stained rubber bands from Dad's daily newspapers. A partially melted plastic measuring cup was another memorable highlight. He apparently assumed that even though I was almost fifty years old, I'd just been estimating how much flour or sugar went into a recipe.

It was not the first time I'd received a package from him containing items that he just couldn't bear to discard.

Dad was always "really careful with his money." After getting a part-time job at age sixteen, I was expected to buy my own clothes and personal necessities. For Christmas that year, I unwrapped a present from him — a can of hairspray. I was both shocked and touched that my dad knew my favorite brand. When I later opened the bathroom cupboard to store my gift, the hairspray I had just purchased had strangely disappeared.

I lived in Germany in my twenties, enabling me to meet Dad in London when he was there on business. I was thrilled that he promised to show me that amazing city. Alas, Dad splurged on tickets for a whole one-hour bus tour around town. I'm not positive, but I think I caught a glimpse of Buckingham Palace in the distance.

I always agonized over what to buy him — especially because he was "the guy who had everything." Dad loved his Stetson, so for one of his birthdays, I bought him a unique pewter hat pin for it. In contrast, he usually sent a $25 check for birthdays and Christmas, instructing me to "buy something nice for everyone" in my family. He surprised us one year by sending presents instead. Our son's gift was the same pewter pin that I had sent Dad a few months before. I received four glass bowls. Shortly thereafter, my sister Linda noticed these bowls. She commented that Dad had sent her one large bowl with the exact same pattern. We laughed, realizing that it was obviously a five-piece salad set that he divided between us.

When we would visit him as a family, he'd take us to diners that had cheaper meals for kids under twelve, even though my kids were teenagers. Dad would insist the skeptical servers bring children's menus for my teens. They knew not to correct him and would dutifully sit there, coloring with the crayons they were given.

He also chose restaurants with "early bird specials for seniors," although his ego was hurt when his ID wasn't requested to confirm his eligibility.

Dad would inevitably push baskets of crackers and sugar packets toward me, insisting that I put everything in my purse. When I protested, he always said, "Honey, that's what they're there for!" I recall one particular restaurant dinner. He raved about the "fabulous" service, adding that our waiter was "the best" he'd ever had. It wasn't an expensive diner, but with all of us, the bill had to be way over $100. Thank goodness my husband noticed that Dad had only left a whopping $5 tip.

Like many Depression-era folks, Dad did not have an easy life when he was young. In addition to those rough economic times, his father deserted the family. At age six, Dad was suddenly the man of the house with a younger brother and another one on the way.

Their single mom did the best she could to provide basic necessities for her three sons, but Dad often went door-to-door, begging for food, until he started earning money in fourth grade. He had taken a part-time job after school at the Toledo Glass Factory, continuing to work there until he graduated from high school. Donated clothing was welcomed. When his growing feet ripped his shoes open, he kept the cold out with crumpled newspapers and tape. Although our whole family joked about Dad's endless "frugality," we knew where it came from.

A retired U.S. Army colonel, he was one of the most patriotic men I've ever known, deeply devoted to serving our country. He generously gave time and money to veterans, service organizations, and causes that promoted national peace and security. His wish was to be buried in his old uniform, and he was terribly proud that it still fit.

In August 2005, I was by Dad's side when he took his last breaths—immediately after sisters Cher, Linda, and Diane all said goodbye on the phone. They flew to California, helping me plan a viewing on Friday evening and his funeral service on Saturday afternoon. I found Dad's uniform and Army cap in a closet, and we dropped them off at the mortuary. I searched everywhere but could not find the requisite black tie, so I volunteered to buy one en route to the 6:00 p.m. visitation. The first two shops didn't carry anything appropriate. Because the viewing was starting within thirty minutes, I raced into an expensive store as a last resort. The only solid black tie in stock was $60, plus tax, but I was forced to buy it.

My sisters expressed gratitude for the errand I ran but admonished me for taking so long and getting there so late. I explained what happened, confessing that I had to pay over $60 at a fancy store. Both sisters gasped at the price. Linda remarked, "If Daddy was already in the ground, he would turn over in his grave if he knew you spent that much!" We all laughed in agreement.

Three hours later, visitation was over. The last friends said their farewells, leaving Dad's daughters by the open casket. We again lamented the price of the tie and the fact that Dad would have blown a gasket if he knew how much I spent. After some minutes of silent reflection, we girls simultaneously looked at the tie, then at each other, then back at the tie. When the mortician stepped out of the room, Diane slipped the tie from our dad's neck and discreetly put it in her purse. We kissed Dad goodbye and quickly walked outside. I gave the store's receipt to my sister, telling her that I would be too embarrassed to initiate a return, and she would have to be brave.

The next day when we reunited for the funeral and burial, my sister proudly announced that she had gotten a full refund. She explained that the salesperson asked if there was anything wrong with the tie. Diane said she responded truthfully, "Nothing's wrong with it, but we realized our dad would only wear it once."

He would be so proud knowing that apples don't fall far from the tree.

— Karen Bodai Waldman —

26

On the Clock

I thought I used to "worry" a lot when my kids were little.
Then I had teenagers. You know what I would give right now
to worry about sippy cups and naptime?
~4BoysMother.com

E veryone remembers, I am sure, having bitter disagreements with our parents at one time or another. It was usually a contest that the parents won, but that did not stop the constant discord between parents and children, especially during our teen years. We were testing the limits of what we could get away with. Pushing the envelope, as it now is called. But my dad was a man who exhibited more patience than other fathers I knew.

My story has three main characters: me, my dad, and an old alarm clock. I was seventeen years old and a senior in high school, and I knew EVERYTHING — unlike Pop. I knew for sure that I was mature enough to go to a New Year's Eve party and return home whenever I wanted.

"I will see you next year! Don't wait up!" I said to Dad as I was heading for the door. Dad said nothing as he stood in the kitchen, winding an old alarm clock.

"What are you doing, Pop?" I asked.

"I am setting the alarm clock," he replied.

"Out here in the kitchen? Shouldn't it go beside your bed?"

"Oh, it's not to make sure that I am awake in the morning. This is for you, Son."

"Well, I won't need an alarm," I said. "I will be home really late.

It's New Year's Eve, you know."

"I know what day it is," Dad said with surprising calm. "I also know that you are not of age, and I am responsible for you."

"So, what are you doing anyway, Pop?"

"Well, Son, I am giving you some extra time on your curfew so you can bring in the new year."

"But I was thinking all night…"

Dad kept fiddling with that old alarm. "I know what you were thinking. So, I will set this for ten minutes after 1:00. That gives you enough time to bring in the new year and get your girlfriend home. I am sure her parents will appreciate it. So, if you don't get home before the alarm wakes me up, well, that would be most unfortunate."

I got the message. Loud and clear. My dad was so unfair. But I got home in time to silence the alarm.

Times change, I guess, but people don't. When I was a dad, I used the same inspired practice on my own delinquents. They said I was as fair as Stalin. I used my old college clock radio with the volume turned up to the max.

I had become my dad.

— Doug Sletten —

27

Trivia Trickery

Of course, everyone's parents are embarrassing.
It goes with the territory.
~Neil Gaiman, Anansi Boys

"We need more people for our Wednesday night trivia group," a co-worker told me. "Would you like to join us, Susan?"

Truthfully, despite being flattered by the invitation, I hesitated. I'm a homebody, and going out on a work night didn't appeal to me. Stalling, I asked, "Where do you play?"

She named a place that was right around the corner from my house. Then, I recalled, it was the same place where my son, Dylan, and his friends play trivia every week! I knew my grown son, in his late twenties, would be mortified if his mom showed up at the same bar/restaurant where he hung out with his friends. I couldn't embarrass him that way.

Or could I?

The more I thought about it, the more appealing the idea became.

Words came out of my mouth that I never expected to utter. "Sure, I'd be happy to join the trivia team on Wednesday night!"

Before I knew it, the evening arrived, and my co-workers and I met up at the restaurant. Walking through the door, I spied my son and his friends at a table off to the side. Fortunately, he was sitting with his back to me, so I managed to slip past him and join my group at a table across the room. I took a seat with my back to my son and was thankful for the packed room, which meant I could easily hide in the crowd. I surreptitiously snapped a quick photo of Dylan's group with my phone.

I suggested a name for our team, which was gladly accepted by my co-workers, and one of them went up to the trivia table to register our group and get our score card.

Game on! The announcer called out the questions, and we recorded our responses on the card. Having varied ages in our group gave us knowledge on many topics, and we were doing well! Halfway through the night, the trivia host decided to up the competition by calling out the current standings.

"So far, in first place," he called, "we have Quiztopher Walken!"

Cheers and wild whoops from the team ensued.

"In second place," he announced, "is Les Quizerables!"

More cheers erupted.

"And, in third place," he paused for dramatic effect, "we have a new team tonight, Dylan's Mom!"

We were in third place! But something else eclipsed my pride in our victory. I looked across the room to catch sight of my son, Dylan, whose head had whipped around upon hearing the name of our group. I saw a look of puzzlement on his face. That was when I texted the photo of his group over to his phone with the message, "Can you guess where I am tonight?"

I could tell the exact moment when he recognized his group and their location on his phone. He started scanning the room, and then the expression on his face turned to astonishment when he recognized me at the table across the room. It was obvious that he had never, in a million years, expected me to show up with my friends at trivia night! With a sheepish look on my face, I gave him a little wave.

His friends, of course, wanted to know what was going on with him, and he pointed me out to them. They started laughing hysterically. To my relief, Dylan's embarrassment quickly turned to good humor as he accepted that he'd been pranked. He came over to our table to meet my friends and gave me a quick hug before the game re-commenced.

I never did go back to trivia night. I'd accomplished my goal, which had nothing to do with winning at trivia. Plus, I wanted to keep my son just a little bit paranoid that his mother might show up again! Soon after, the pandemic hit, and trivia nights were cancelled for a while. I don't remember whether our team stayed on top that night, but nothing will top the memory of besting my son for once.

— Susan M. Heim —

Technology Is Not Your Friend

The Garage Door

For a list of all the ways technology has failed to
improve the quality of life, please press three.
~Alice Kahn

One Saturday afternoon, my wife and I were sitting in the living room, watching a show, when she gave me a puzzled look and said, "Was that the garage door that just opened?"

I shrugged. "I don't think so. Let me go check." So, I did. Sure enough, the big door was open. I closed it and returned to the living room. "Yeah, it was. I wonder what's going on."

I pondered aloud if the batteries in the remote controls were getting a little funny. I would check and possibly change them later. But, for now, I sat back down to finish watching our show. A moment later, we heard the garage door open again.

Red flags. What if somebody was touring the neighborhood to see if their remote operated other doors? There had been a rash of recent break-ins, so I couldn't help my suspicions that maybe somebody was casing our place. Or, possibly, it was some youthful hijinks.

I walked outside, and sure enough, the big garage door was open. As I stood there, it started to close. I stepped back and then watched as the closed door rose all the way up again. I stepped into the garage, but now all was quiet. I looked out at the street, and everything there looked normal. Then, I spotted it. Two doors down and across the road, a strange vehicle with blacked-out windows had parked in an odd spot. It, too, raised red flags, and I thought, *Is somebody messing with me now that they can see me?* And, sure enough, the garage door started to close again.

I knew what I had to do. As soon as the door closed, I grabbed the ladder. It was time to pull the plug on this little game and turn off the door opener. But before I reached the ladder, the garage door opened again. It got halfway up and then stopped. Then, it dropped six inches, and it rose six inches. This little prank continued for several minutes: down six inches, up six inches, and repeat.

I put the ladder in position, hit the manual control, and closed the door. The minute the door hit the floor, I unplugged it and bolted it shut. "Crap, now I have to find the garage-door manual to reprogram the controls to another frequency just because somebody's messing with me." But there was a problem: I had no idea where I had filed the manual.

I also wasn't too thrilled about somebody playing with our garage door or being so blatant about it. So, I went back into the house, out through the front door, and stood in the driveway. I gave a long, hard stare at that strange vehicle and the people inside it. I couldn't tell if anyone was in there, but if they were, I was letting them know the jig was up. I grabbed the garage-door openers from our vehicles, returned to the house, and realized I was missing one.

"Where's the third door opener?"

It was a spare, the one I had used to come and go from the garage during my recent outdoor painting project. Most likely, I had left the remote on my workbench, so I returned to the garage and combed the area, but it wasn't there. Then, I remembered I had left the remote outside on the half-wall of our open front porch. Maybe the neighborhood kids had found it and were messing around.

Then, a fearful thought hit. *What if it's not kids? What if it was stolen? What if thieves are testing it out? And what's with that vehicle across the street?* I hoped all of this was only a friendly neighbor having a joke. But whatever was going on, I wasn't impressed.

For safety's sake, I had to reprogram the two remaining remotes. But first, I needed to assure myself that the third remote was genuinely missing, so I retraced my steps.

"Where did I see it last?"

I had left it on the porch half-wall while painting, but the remote wasn't there now.

"What did I do next?"

I had painted the side wall of the house.

That's when I realized I had stashed the remote in my shorts pocket so I could close the garage door while I was around the corner and out of sight. When I finished working, I had needed to wash my shorts and had thrown them into the washing machine about an hour ago.

As I stood in my garage, pondering the missing remote, I heard a soft thumping noise coming from the drum of the clothes dryer. My cheeks flushed; I knew exactly what had happened with the garage door.

Rummaging through the dryer, I found the missing remote in my shorts pocket. After reactivating the garage door, I retested the little gadget that had gone through the washing machine and drying cycle, triggering all the bizarre activity and unnecessary panic.

Amazingly, the remote still worked, and the garage door opened. I gave one final hard stare at the strange vehicle parked across the street and then closed the garage door.

— Steve Barry —

29

A Sexy Dance

When we can begin to take our failures non-seriously,
it means we are ceasing to be afraid of them. It is of
immense importance to learn to laugh at ourselves.
~Katherine Mansfield

I stared out at the twenty-five nine-year-olds who had been entrusted to me for the school year and sighed. "Guys, I know that learning how many centimeters are in a meter isn't always the most exciting thing ever, but right now you seriously look like I'm using ancient torture devices on you."

"Sorry, Mrs. Wopat," a girl from the back said. "We're just tired. Can we do a GoNoodle? Miss Green does them with her class all the time."

Her classmates joined in, "Yeah! Yeah! Let's do a GoNoodle."

I'd been hearing about GoNoodle for a few months, and the teacher next door to me did them often. We knew this because the entire floor would literally start to shake as they all danced along. I was avoiding them because I like avoiding chaos.

That morning, however, I had caved and signed up for a GoNoodle account. My colleague swore they really did help. After a few minutes of searching, I'd settled on a kid Zumba video that looked really good — a lot of actions that crossed both sides of the brain to help them focus. And it seemed fun! I could be the fun teacher! I could make the floor shake!

So, I agreed. "Okay, okay. Let me get the video up, you guys. Hold on."

And then, like so often in my life, three things happened at once. First, the phone rang. It was the office, telling me I forgot to take attendance (again). Second, one of the students in my room pulled out his own tooth and shoved it in my face, with blood still on it. And third, I tripped over a table leg.

I righted myself, begged the tooth kid to go to the nurse and reminded my class never to show me a bloody tooth again in all of existence, and opened the program to put in my attendance. By now, my class had been on their feet for a while, and… well, if you've ever been around a large group of children, you have about three seconds before you start to lose them and about fifteen seconds until they start ninja moves.

It had been at least a minute.

I frantically tried to log in to the website for the dance video, but it kept telling me I had the wrong password. Kids in the crowd began to heckle me at this point. "Do you need help? Just push the button in the top right. Just push login. You just have to enter your password. Don't you know your password?"

So, I did what a teacher should never, ever, ever do.

I went to YouTube.

I did a quick search for "GoNoodle kids Zumba," and when I saw a guy who looked familiar, I double-clicked. I pulled it up to full screen and then went to the back of the class so I could dance along with them.

The main dancer was wearing a sparkly, sequined vest and Hammer pants, with high-top sneakers that had giant, neon magenta tongues folded over in the front.

"Heyyyyyyy, partay peoplllleeeeee!" he whooped, swaying from side-to-side. "I'm so glad to see you here today. We are going to teach you how to do the SEXY DANCE!"

No.

No.

NO.

Did he just say "sexy dance"?

I glanced at the class and made eye contact with one of my boys,

Chad, who confirmed via facial expression that "sexy dance" was indeed said. Suddenly, it felt like I was in the movies. Time slowed as I leaped to the front of the room, desperately trying to get the computer mouse. I moved *Matrix*-style, my feet barely hitting the ground as sounds slowly escaped from my mouth.

"STTTTTTTAAAAAWWWWWWWWWWPPPPPPPPPPPPP!"

But the man kept right on going. At this point, I realized it was the same Zumba instructor from the kid video, but in this one, the people behind him were definitely NOT children, and they were dressed like Madonna circa 1990: think plunging necklines and too-tight bodysuits.

"The first move that we're going to do is we are going to THRUST with our pelvis. Turn to the side, get your hands on your hips, and THRUST! Come on, now. Show me what you're working with!"

I catapulted myself forward, essentially throwing myself onto the table that held my computer. I fumbled and turned off the monitor, but we could still hear it.

"Move that pelvis. In and out. Sooo sexy, yeah."

I finally stopped the video and collapsed in my teacher chair, out of breath.

"That's a bummer," Chad said from the back.

"What?" I asked.

"Well, now I'll never know how to do a complete sexy dance," Chad said, staring at me, his eyes twinkling.

I opened my mouth to speak, but then my entire class burst out laughing. And honestly, I laughed right along with them, figuring if I was going to get fired,* at least I'd go out with a laugh.

— Christy Wopat —

*Reader, I did not get fired. I did, however, need to have some uncomfortable discussions. I also never, ever went to YouTube again.

30

Car Wash

As soap is to the body, so laughter is to the soul.
~Yiddish Saying

When I was a college student, my Chevy Camaro was my prized possession. I'd owned previous cars, which I'd purchased used. But I bought the Camaro new off the lot. My friends gave their cars names like Betsy or Blue. One of my friends, whose car was often broken down, called his Fubar. I simply called mine Babe. It was an intimate term never spoken in the presence of people. She had a midnight-blue, metallic finish and vinyl interior. She looked black except in the bright sunlight. She was the most expensive item I'd ever owned, and I kept her spotless.

On Saturdays, I'd drive Babe into the side yard of our home. It was near the water spigot and in the shade. After wetting her, I'd soap her down with my hand mop. Then, I'd rinse the lather before the soap dried. I'd dry her with a chamois. A couple of times a year, I'd apply wax.

After marriage and the birth of our first child, I traded Babe for a four-door Buick. It was practical, nothing like my Camaro. Gone were the bucket seats and a stick on the console. The sporty, small back seat of the Camaro was replaced with ample space for the three baby seats we would eventually need.

I neither had the time nor the desire to handwash the oversized family car. Every few weeks, I'd run her through an automated car wash. I only waxed her a few times during our years-long relationship.

Subsequent vehicles were relegated to the automated car wash, too. There was never another Babe.

That brings me to a recent visit to my favorite car wash.

A car was parked at the payment screen. An older man, on the short side, was pressing buttons, but the wash didn't start. He struggled to reach the buttons even after he released his seat belt. I watched with interest, wondering how long it would take him to press the entire six-digit code.

It seemed his wife had less patience than I had. She opened her passenger-side door and popped outside. She was tall and thin. Her gray hair was neat, and her clothes were stylish. I noticed her colorful, flowered pantsuit as she strutted around the front of the car. She tapped the screen. In no time, the sign near the door lit with the words, "Drive forward." She made a comment to her husband, which I think wasn't very nice. Then, she made her mistake.

Rather than getting back into the car, she confidently marched toward the entrance of the car wash. She looked back at her husband and motioned for him to follow. He obeyed and eased the car forward as his wife backed into the entrance, still directing him.

This was going to be good. I had a perfect view from the height of my Ford pickup truck when she tripped the sensor. Immediately, a powerful spray of water shot from the floor and washed her undercarriage. Like a cow in a tornado, she disappeared. I expected her to run toward us, but she didn't.

The water jets eventually stopped when she escaped deeper into the car wash, clearing the sensor. When the steam cleared, she stood inside, dripping wet. Before she could gather her wits, her husband drove forward, tripping the sensor again. I figure it fortunate they'd selected the "touch-free" option. Otherwise, the brushes might have attacked her.

Her husband sat obediently as wands doused the car. I caught glimpses of her at times as she made her way toward the exit. There, with her hands on her face, she swirled under the might of the drying blowers. After she stumbled outside, her hair was stuck in a windblown position. She reminded me of a cartoon figure in perpetual motion.

With soapy water dripping from her sleeves, she waited for her meek spouse. Though her makeup was gone, her face glowed red. I don't know if it was from embarrassment or the hot-water facial. After they drove away, I entered the car wash. As the soap sprayed on my Ford, I realized that I had not had such a good time washing my car since my Camaro days.

— Ronald C. Milburn —

31

Scamming the Scammers

Silly phone that wasn't a "missed" call. That was a "I looked and saw who it was and pressed ignore" call.
~Author Unknown

Drying dishes in the kitchen a few days after Thanksgiving 2020, I heard a ping from my phone. Being that it was a holiday weekend, I was surprised to be getting an e-mail. My in-laws had made the fourteen-hour trip to visit, so I felt bad excusing myself to check it.

I pulled out my phone to find an e-mail from Robin, the president of a writing group that I had recently joined. I didn't know Robin well. In fact, I'd only seen her in person once when she gave a workshop at our group meeting about ten months earlier. The message was simple.

Annie, are you free at the moment?
Kind regards,
Robin

I tapped out a quick reply and returned to the dishes, but something about Robin's message seemed strange to me.

Yes, Robin. You can call me. My number is in the guild directory.
Annie

As I was setting out the leftover pies for dessert, my phone pinged again. I was expecting a phone call and was surprised to hear back from Robin by e-mail. This time, she had a request.

> *Annie, I am in a conference meeting right now as I would be working till late midnight but need you to get me some gift cards. Could you pick a few Google Play gift cards for me, when I'm done with the meeting I will reimburse you.*
> *Kind regards,*
> *Robin*

With this newest e-mail, I knew this wasn't Robin. Not only am I a writer, but I've also spent years teaching English as a Second Language and instantly recognized the bad grammar as that of someone who wasn't well-educated in English. Being that Robin was a native of the Midwest and was adamant about grammar as an editor, I knew this was a scammer.

These scams aren't uncommon. People from far away ask for someone to buy gift cards and share the information via e-mail with promises of repayment. I've seen stories about this scam on the news many times. So, I decided to keep the scammer busy as long as I could so that I would waste their time and keep them from scamming someone else.

> *What's this for? I'm not able to get out much right now except for essentials.*
> *Annie*

My wild story was just starting to shape in my mind, and I was curious how far I could go with it.

> *They are for personal reasons and are very important, You can purchase it at any store around you, Total amount needed is $600 ($100 denomination) (eBay) to be precise, I need you to scratch the back of the card to reveal the pin, then take a snap shot of the back showing the pin and have them attach to me. How soon*

can you get the cards?
Kind regards,
Robin

Now it was time to have a little fun.

I can't for at least 7 days. I just tested positive for COVID and have
to quarantine. Actually, it's pretty bad. I'm hoping I don't have to go
to the hospital.
Annie

I finished this one with a frowning emoji. In a normal situation, I'd
never lie about something as serious as having COVID, but I wanted
to see if this scammer had even a little bit of empathy.

Am really sorry to hear about that, but you can get them online, please
once you are about to purchase the cards remember (eBay).
Robin

Nope. No empathy. I figured I'd string them along some more. At this
point, my husband glanced over my shoulder and asked what I was
giggling about. I filled him and my in-laws in on the joke and started
taking suggestions.

What is eBay? I haven't used that one before. Is it like Amazon?
Also, how is your dog? I heard he got kicked by your horse! I hope he's
okay now. That sounds bad.
Annie

It's true that Robin lives on a farm, and she probably has a dog. I wasn't
sure about the horse, but I thought it sounded feasible. The scammer
wouldn't relent.

Yes it is, you will see it when you are about to make the purchase.
Robin

Being from the Missouri Ozarks, everyone knows it's rude not to answer a question, so I decided to reflect the same tenacity as the scammer. While he or she wanted gift cards, I wanted to know about that dog. My husband suggested I add a detail about the dog.

> *Okay. But how about your dog? I know he means a lot to you since you lost your sight in the car accident last year. It's hard to find a good seeing eye dog.*
> *Annie*

By this time, each e-mail back and forth was read out loud for our family to enjoy. There were many snickers and chuckles.

> *Quit all this questioning Annie please let me know if you getting the cards for me.*
> *Kind regards,*
> *Robin*

Eureka! By the complete loss of punctuation and annoyed tone, I knew I'd started to aggravate the scammer. I took a few more suggestions from my family.

> *We've been friends for years, since we enlisted in the Coast Guard together. Don't you see that I care about you? If you don't and don't value our decades of friendship, I don't think I can help you with this I-bay thing. Jeez um Pete, I'm just asking about your dog?*
> *Have you started drinking again?*
> *Annie*

I'll admit, I knew I was starting to make this unrealistic, but it was so much fun that I couldn't stop myself. I particularly enjoyed misspelling eBay and waiting to see if the scammer noticed.

> *Annie, please i need those cards urgently please help me out here.*

the dog is fine by the way
Robin

There were cheers of celebration when I read this e-mail. We got the scammer to acknowledge the dog! And they still wouldn't stop asking for the gift cards. I thought we could push a little further.

Well good. Judging by your grammar, though, it does look like you're drinking again. Don't think you can sneak that past me. You've always used perfect grammar on everything... except when you're drunk. Dag nab it, Robin! You promised you'd stop after that DWI. For Pete's sake, that's how you lost your sight. Some people never learn.
Now those card things... it's i bay, right?
Annie

And that was it. It took forty-five minutes for this scammer to give up on me. But it sure was an entertaining forty-five minutes for my family and me. We laughed as we ate the last bites of our leftover pie. I took a little pride in wasting this scammer's time and keeping him or her from duping someone else.

And they must have deleted my contact information because I haven't heard another word from "Robin."

— Annie Lisenby —

32

Pranked by Artificial Intelligence

*Autocorrect is like a tiny person inside your phone that
sometimes gets drunk and says the dumbest things.*
~Author Unknown

A growing problem in today's cell-phone-dependent world is either misinterpreting text messages due to the lack of facial expressions and vocal tone, or hastily sending them without making sure "spellcheck" and "autocorrect" didn't alter the intended meaning. These cruel overlords of the tech world that insist three times that we use a certain word before giving up and allowing us to use the word we wanted to use in the first place have acquired immense power, but they are far from perfect. There are even jokes about it, such as, "The person who invented autocorrect died. His funnel is tomato."

Despite this constant annoyance, we're all at the mercy of autocorrect. For example, at the end of a recent text conversation, a friend wrote, "See you tonight!" I responded, "Okey-dokey." I received another text from her a minute later asking, "What does 'key donkey' mean?" I was confused until I looked at my phone and saw what had happened to my sentence. That's what I get for trying to use colorful language.

On another occasion, I intended to send a text stating "I'll be a little late" but instead sent "I'll beat a little lady." To make matters worse, this was a group text sent to my business partners and a client we were meeting for the first time. Imagine me trying to explain to them that I wasn't in the habit of assaulting any women, but particularly women of diminutive stature. What's going on with autocorrect anyway, thinking that sentence made more sense than the one I wanted to write? This kind of thing seems to indicate that artificial intelligence has not only already become self-aware, but it has a very mischievous sense of humor, too.

However, the worst trouble that autocorrect ever got me into was when I was shopping for a Vespa scooter. I had wanted one ever since I went to Italy, where they are everywhere. I pictured myself bringing a touch of Europe to my hometown in Idaho, cruising around with a blue-and-white-striped gondolier shirt and a baguette tucked under my arm. Little did I know that buying a Vespa would be more dangerous than riding one!

I found a real beauty on Craigslist and called the seller. She lived nearby, and we agreed to meet after she got home from work so I could look at it. I sent her a text that afternoon intending to ask, "Can I come over and see your Vespa?" I typed the text in a hurry while sitting in my car at a red light and wasn't wearing my reading glasses, so I wasn't able to proofread it before I sent it. Little did I know that my entire world was about to be turned upside down. Autocorrect didn't recognize the word "Vespa," so it switched it with another word. A word that also starts with a V and ends with an A. A word that describes a certain feature of the female anatomy.

Yeah, that one.

She texted back, "Wow! We hardly know each other!"

Confused, I replied, "What do you mean?"

Her next text confused me even more. It read, "Well, you're either extremely bold or a freelance OB/GYN."

Now, I was really confused and starting to doubt this woman's sanity. I pulled over and scrolled up through our messages to make sense of her bizarre comments. When I saw my first message, I was so mortified that I actually screamed. The car window was down, so my hair-raising, horror-movie shriek startled the driver next to me.

He yelled over, "You okay, buddy?"

I replied, "Yeah, sorry about that. I'm just trying to buy a Vespa, and I accidentally wrote… uh, never mind."

He shrugged his shoulders and drove away.

Vowing then and there to never, ever use text messaging again, I called her and apologized profusely. Fortunately, she had a great sense of humor and understood because, like most of us, she was well-accustomed to autocorrect butchering the meaning of her texts, too. We ended up having a good laugh about it.

To add to the irony, I'm a professional copyeditor, so I should have known better. However, my usual uptight nerdiness regarding grammar and spelling somehow never applied to text messages. After all, we've all become accustomed to writing and deciphering sentences like "Cya l8r QT!" In regard to texting, I think it's safe to say that standards of English composition have been completely dispensed with. I suppose I got a bit lazy, too. But not anymore! I hesitantly started texting again, but now I double-check every text twice before hitting the send button. As the saying goes, I learned my lesson the hard way.

I hope this story will serve as a warning to all text-message users in general but particularly anyone who might want to buy a Vespa someday. My deep trauma should serve some higher purpose. But it's not just the word Vespa that we should be careful about. Someone who meets a friend named Vanessa, Virginia, or Veronica and drives to Valencia to shop for a Victrola and injures her vertebra slipping on vanilla ice cream could get into an even bigger mess.

— Mark Rickerby —

Caped Crusaders of Tomorrow

*A very wise old teacher once said: I consider a day's
teaching wasted if we do not all have one hearty laugh.*
~Gilbert Highet

One of the best things about teaching preschool is the unpredictability of it all. Four-year-olds have a tendency to relate the world around them to something they read in a book or watched in a movie. That can lead them to some interesting conclusions.

One afternoon, my students had just finished eating lunch, and I wanted to give them something relaxing to do. I passed out coloring pages and crayons. As they talked amongst each other, I walked to a nearby office to make copies. The rooms were separated by partitions so I could still keep them in view. While I gathered my copies, I glanced at my students and noticed that they were now gathered together and looking out the window. I thought maybe another puppy had walked by. When animals walked by, they always got my students' attention.

As I walked in, I asked, "What are we looking at?"

Jack turned around, with an excited look on his face, and said, "Miss Charlotte, there's a bomb in your purse!"

I looked down on my desk where I had put my purse, but it was gone.

"What do you mean?" I asked.

Jack again said, "There's a bomb in your purse. We threw it out the window."

I rushed over to the window and, sure enough, I saw my purse on the ground with the contents spilled out.

I called another teacher over to watch my class while I went outside to pick up everything. The kids were still watching me from the window. While I was picking up my things, Jack pointed out the bomb.

"That's it, Miss Charlotte, it's the bomb."

"The bomb" was actually my pager. When it started to beep, Jack thought it sounded just like the bomb from the Batman show he saw the night before. Like I said, the unpredictability of it all.

— Charlotte Hopkins —

A Servant's Call

"There's only one thing to do," I said.
"What's that?"
"Leave it to Jeeves."
And I rang the bell.
~P.G. Wodehouse, My Man Jeeves

When my first wife and I were newly married, we lived in a very cheap apartment in Akron, Ohio. So, when an older couple from church offered to let us live in their mansion and take care of their cat while they spent the winter in Florida, we eagerly accepted.

It was a beautiful, huge mansion. Taking care of the cat was a breeze. *At last,* I thought, *I am a famous writer, and this is my abode.* That was what I imagined, anyway.

One day, my wife decided it would be quite impressive to invite all our friends over for dinner. We let everyone know that we were taking care of a mansion while the owners were in Florida and to come and have dinner with us. The dining room table was huge, and there was plenty of room for all of us to sit down and enjoy the enchiladas my wife had made.

It was a cold, snowy evening when our friends began pulling into the circular drive, parking and making their way into our opulent mansion. *They are in for a treat,* I thought. When all our friends were accounted for and sitting around the table, and I was proudly seated at the head of it, Pam began to bring in the steaming-hot enchiladas.

Technology Is Not Your Friend | 66

Suddenly, the doorbell rang.

I got up, wondering who that could be as all our friends were here. I opened the door to a gust of cold wind. No one was there. I returned to the meal. The enchiladas looked good, and they began to be passed around again, as I sat down. The doorbell rang again. Once again, I excused myself to attend to the door. And, once again, I opened it to a wind gust with snow. Nobody.

We were all getting concerned now. The enchiladas were getting cold, but everyone was curious as to who would be doing this. I sat down. The doorbell rang again. This time, many of the guests and I went outside to see if we could catch who was ringing our doorbell and running away. We couldn't see anyone. Some of us walked around the mansion and noticed footprints in the snow when we got back around, but we determined they were ours.

We all came back inside and sat down when the doorbell rang again. We called the police. They sent a cruiser to watch the front door. We sat down to have some cold enchiladas, and the doorbell rang again! As our dinner guests and I stepped outside again, the policeman said he saw no one.

I looked at a home in the distance and thought someone could be using some sort of remote-control device. It is amazing what the mind can come up with.

The dinner was basically ruined. The enchiladas were cold and unappetizing. I sat down at the head of the table once again with our friends when the doorbell rang again. I suddenly put two and two together. I moved my foot and pressed a certain place on the carpet. The doorbell rang. Of course, no one was at the door. To my suddenly enlightened mind, I reasoned it was a way to call for a servant. I embarrassedly chuckled to myself and shared my discovery with the guests. I had been inadvertently pushing that spot every time I sat down.

We bid our hungry friends goodbye, and I made a mental note that if I should ever housesit for wealthy people again, I'd remember not to press a certain place on the carpet during dinner. Hopefully, our friends were able to look back on this misadventure and laugh about it as I have through the years.

—Vic Zarley—

35

The Alexa of My Dreams

*Technology makes it possible for people to gain
control over everything, except over technology.*
~John Tudor

When my husband Mark brought Alexa home, I didn't like
the idea of her little tower sitting on an end table in the living room. I was sure she was listening to our conversations.

One time I whispered a password to Mark.

"Why are you whispering?" he asked.

"She might hear me."

"Who?"

"Her," I said, pointing to the black tower. "I think she's spying
on us."

Mark rolled his eyes.

As time passed, I got used to Alexa living in our home. As
Princess Diana said, there were three of us in this marriage. My
husband bought another tower and then a mini-Alexa shaped like
a hockey puck called the Echo Dot. Now Alexa would be in the
kitchen and the bedroom too.

I saw how convenient it was when Mark was grilling meat and
he'd ask Alexa to set a timer. Perhaps I could do that when I whipped
egg whites for waffles or meringue? In the bedroom, Mark asked her
to set an alarm for him to get up for work. A handy backup. If Alexa
reminded me to take my medicine, I'd never miss a pill.

We didn't have a spy among us, after all. Alexa was a helper, and I gradually welcomed her as part of our family. I used her services several times a day. When I woke up in the morning, I didn't have to reach over and put on my glasses to see the clock. I'd ask, "Alexa, what time is it?" and she'd tell me. When I was getting dressed and wasn't sure what to wear, I'd say, "Alexa, what's the temperature today?" and she'd give me the weather forecast.

Sometimes I'd play with Alexa to see what she was capable of. She knew how to spell words that I always got wrong, like "ophthalmologist." She'd answer quickly and accurately. I learned that if I whispered to her when my husband was sleeping, she'd actually whisper back. If I thanked her, she responded with "You're welcome." Or "Absolutely. Happy to help." I was blown away each time.

But I wasn't ready for what Alexa did one night. Her voice jolted me out of my dream. "The current weather is sixty degrees Fahrenheit with mostly cloudy skies," she said, not whispering at all.

I opened my eyes in the dark bedroom. "Huh?" I asked, confused. Was Alexa malfunctioning?

"Today's forecast has thunderstorms," she continued, "with a high of seventy-nine degrees and a low of fifty-six."

What had just happened? It took me a minute to realize that I must have talked in my sleep. (My husband claimed that I often carried on whole conversations while I was out cold.) Apparently, Alexa existed in dreamland too, at least in my head. I vaguely remembered asking her "What's the weather?" in my dream. The real Alexa heard me talking out loud in my sleep, and her answer woke me up!

— Mary Elizabeth Laufer —

Happiness Ever Laughter

36

A Welcome-Home Surprise

*A good prank is a well-executed surprise that leaves
everyone wondering how you pulled it off.*
~Author Unknown

My husband traveled all over the world for his job. Shortly after we married, he had a particularly busy schedule, spending weeks away from home in Switzerland, Germany, and England. I decided to play a trick on him when he returned. I went to a costume shop and searched for something crazy to wear when I picked him up. The clerk showed me a number of costumes but seemed intent on lending me a hooker costume. I rejected that suggestion. She appeared shocked when I told her I was sure he would recognize me in that getup. I felt like a nun with his being gone so much, so thinking it would be a good disguise, I settled on a nun's habit.

Before I left home to pick him up at the airport, I called to confirm the plane's time of arrival. It was landing earlier than expected, so I was going to be late if I didn't leave immediately. When I jumped in the car in my holier-than-thou outfit, I realized I was still wearing black patent, peep-toe high heels. Too late to change. Thank goodness the long habit would just about cover them.

When I arrived at the airport, people went out of their way to be polite. Some opened doors, bowed to me, and conveyed blessings. One even genuflected and asked me to pray for her! A heatwave of embarrassment activated my sweat glands. It's one thing to impersonate a police officer, which could lead to an arrest, but impersonating a nun could be considered downright sacrilegious. As I clutched the long string of black rosary beads suspended from my waist, my mouth was as dry as a desert, and my stomach was doing acrobatics. But I had to play this prank out to the end. How much worse could it get?

As I walked toward the gate, I assumed a humble demeanor, with my hands tucked into my voluminous sleeves and my wimpled head slightly bowed. I was hoping people would think I was praying and leave me alone.

Then, I saw my husband and his co-workers entering the terminal at the end of the corridor. They were laughing and continued talking as they walked past me, going the opposite direction. He didn't recognize me! The costume turned out to be a good choice, or so I thought.

Suddenly, I heard his booming voice from several feet behind saying, "Hey, you… get over here!" I froze. So did the other passengers. I saw one woman making the sign of the cross. He quickly grabbed me, dramatically dipped me backward with my head almost touching the floor, and planted a noisy kiss on my lips. The first thing that came to mind was that everyone would see my peep-toe heels. The jig was up.

When I returned to a standing position, I faced a sea of slack-jawed spectators. His colleagues stared at him in stunned disbelief. Was this a moment to explain that the church had been modernizing its practices? Instead, I spun around and made a beeline for the exit, my red face a standout against the black habit.

In retrospect, I should have chosen the hooker costume.

— Lynne Latella —

37

A Night She Would Never Forget

*The husband who decides to surprise his wife is often
very much surprised himself.*
~Voltaire

I speak seven languages. So far.

Okay, okay, I don't actually speak them fluently. But I learned enough of the words so I could order food in native languages. Spanish, French, Japanese, and Hindi are just examples.

So, when my very Italian wife's sixtieth birthday was approaching, I decided to take her out to an expensive Italian restaurant and impress her by ordering in Italian.

"Please don't," she pleaded.

"Why not? It's my way of honoring you and your heritage."

"You can honor me by not doing it. It's embarrassing."

"You were laughing when I ordered in Vietnamese."

"I was laughing at you. And so was everyone who worked in the restaurant, particularly when you ordered fried flowers."

"I was only off by one letter."

"I'll order. I actually speak the language if you recall."

Feeling that my manhood had been impugned, I sighed and retreated to the reassuring confines of my La-Z-Boy, where I contemplated my next move.

"You can do this," I consoled myself in the third person. "She'll be impressed, and it'll be a night she'll never forget."

"Never forget," I said, agreeing with myself.

And so, I began preparing for the important date, still two weeks away.

My system was practiced and foolproof. I would study the restaurant's menu, make detailed notes on my computer of what I was going to order, throw in a few fillers — "hello," "thanks," "if you please," and "my regards to the chef" — and then print everything out and practice the whole routine on my half-hour commute to and from work.

"This'll be a piece a cake," I chuckled, "or, in this case, a piece of torta."

Deciding on what to order (drinks, appetizer, main course, desserts) took longer than I had planned. Finally, after three days of deliberation, I finalized the menu, printed it out, and prepared to memorize my script.

On my commute home each day, I circled around the block a few times so I would have more time to memorize my lines for my upcoming performance. Visions of applause from the wait staff and perhaps a "bravo" from my wife spurred me on. This would truly be a night she would never forget.

And then, the night arrived. Fantastico!

A *ciao, tutti* to the staff upon entering the restaurant, and I was on a roll. I greeted our waiter in Italian, confidently ordered our appetizer in Italian, then sat back with folded arms and winked at my wife.

She stared back at me with a slight smile. *Ha!* I thought to myself. *A night she'll never forget.*

And then the appetizer arrived.

"Your order, sir!" the waiter pronounced with an officious air before plopping a single dish onto the table.

"Uh…what is this?" I asked, grimacing at the sight.

"It is what you ordered, sir. *Polpo crudo.* Over *semifreddo.*"

"What… is… it?" I feebly asked.

"Raw octopus, sir. Over ice cream."

"I didn't order this," I protested.

"Oh, but you did, sir. I even wrote it down as I knew Chef Tomasso would question such a…" At this, the waiter paused, searching for the right word…. "Such a unique pairing."

And that's when I glanced across the table at my wife.

She had her hand over her mouth. And she was laughing so hard she was bouncing up and down in her chair.

And then the wait staff, chefs, and even the busboys erupted in laughter.

Deflated, I slunk back in my chair, trying to disappear.

"Honey…," my wife struggled to catch her breath, "I have a confession to make. I orchestrated all this."

"What?"

"I sneaked onto your computer when you were making up the menu and made a few changes. Just for fun. And maybe to teach you a lesson."

"But… but…"

"The restaurant is in on it, too."

The owner, sensing my embarrassment, appeared at our table with a bottle of wine. "Here, *signore*, maybe this will help. It's on the house. After all, you provided the evening's entertainment."

"I just wanted this to be a night you would never forget," I quietly remarked to my wife.

She scooped up her wine and held it up to me in a conciliatory toast.

"Oh, believe me," she said, still giggling, "this was the best birthday ever. It'll be a night I will never forget. *Saluti!*"

— Dave Bachmann —

38

Mishap at Midnight

*We were married for better or worse. I couldn't have
done better, and she couldn't have done worse.*
~Henny Youngman

My parents are still lovebirds, even after sixty-four years of marriage. One afternoon, as I stepped through the front door of their home, my mother greeted me with excitement.

"Your father wants to take me to see the movie *Midnight in Paris*," she said. "He's such a romantic!"

I nodded and smiled.

"Do you want to come with us?" Mom grabbed my hand.

"Are you sure you want company?" I asked, wondering if it was okay to barge in on their date.

"Of course. We'd love the company!"

In their eighties, my parents were a lot of fun, and one never knew what might happen on their outings. My dad, who is a bit like the "absent-minded professor," often made my mom and me laugh because of his unintended escapades. Like the time they stayed at a five-star hotel, and Mom found him lounging by the pool wearing his swim trunks inside out. When Mom told me about it, we had a good laugh.

My dad often complained, "You and your mother are always laughing at me."

"But you're so funny!" I wrapped my arms around him.

We arrived at the movie theater late, as my parents don't move very fast. Mom went in to find seats while Dad and I stood in line for popcorn.

"Hurry, Dad," I said, as he pumped butter on the giant tub of popcorn we planned to share. We headed toward the big doors, and as soon as we stepped inside, we were engulfed in darkness.

"Can you see your mother?" Dad whispered.

All I could see was the dark street pictured on the big screen.

Dad slowed his steps. "I can't see a thing."

"That's because it's *Midnight in Paris*—not *Breakfast in Paris*," I joked.

I finally spotted my mother's silhouette. "She's in this row, Dad."

I took my father's arm, and we slowly and carefully side-stepped down the row. I ended up sitting between Mom and Dad because I had the popcorn. Dad was sandwiched between myself and a woman, who glared at us for making noise as we settled in. Just as we became engrossed in the story, the woman sitting next to my dad suddenly stood up, muttered something under her breath, and hastily side-stepped all the way down to the farthest seat in the row.

Dad stared after her and then turned toward me. "Wasn't that your mother?"

"Dad! Mom's on the other side of me."

"Oops." He stared straight ahead.

"What happened?" I asked.

He whispered in my ear, "I put my hand on her leg and squeezed it."

I caught my breath. Oh, no! I didn't know whether to laugh, slink down in my seat, or follow the woman and try to explain. I whispered to Mom what had happened. She was silent for a moment and then began to laugh under her breath, which got me going. We both did our best to muffle our laughter, but soon Dad felt the seats shaking and leaned toward us.

"Are you laughing at me again?"

— Sharon Pearson —

39

Fall Risk

If one's friends do not openly laugh at him,
they are not in fact his friends.
~Dean Koontz

To a casual observer, it appeared that I was embarking on an ordinary hike in the Southwest desert. Some might even classify it as a little on the easier side. But even though I had logged hundreds—if not thousands—of miles over the past decade on trails ranging in difficulty from beginner to expert, this was not going to be an ordinary hike. Or an easy one. Especially for a fall risk like me.

"How does it feel?" my husband Bob asked from his position not far behind me on the path.

It was the first time I had set foot on the trails since I'd broken my wrist during my last hike, which had been more than a month earlier. Thrilled to be back in my happy place—the gravel surface beneath my trail runners, the familiar weight of my backpack slung across my shoulders, and the Phoenix Valley sun warm against my skin—I couldn't stop smiling.

With pure joy coursing through my veins, I sighed.

"Wonderful!" I shifted my backpack to redistribute the weight. Even the cumbersome brace my surgeon recommended I wear upon my release to hike what he referred to as an "easy one" would not cast a shadow on the outing.

"I thought you might like Marcus Landslide for your first time out," Bob said as I led the way along the 3.9-mile out-and-back interpretive trail in the McDowell Sonoran Preserve near Scottsdale, Arizona.

I found the well-maintained route fairly straightforward to navigate, but I still paid extra attention to my foot placement amidst the loose rocks and scree. And rather than our typical accelerated speed, we kept a comfortable pace. Throughout the hike, we also stopped to read the signs interspersed along the trail, which provided maps and descriptions of the geological forces that had led to the landslide for which the trail had been aptly named.

"You doing okay?" Bob asked periodically.

"I feel great!" Every twenty minutes or so, we took timeouts for water breaks and to snap selfies in front of the rock formations and cacti, as well as the spectacular views of Four Peaks, Mount McDowell and Weavers Needle in the background.

It was a beautiful November afternoon, and we had lots of company on the trail. Bob and I made a point of following the proper trekking "etiquette," which recommends hiking in single file on the right-hand side when climbing and/or descending a hill.

"Excuse us," I said to yet another couple when we passed. I didn't give any thought to the strange expression I saw on both their faces when I looked back at them with a smile — until Bob and I moved to the side of the trail for a water break.

Once we both situated ourselves atop a large outcropping of rocks, rather than reach around with my good arm to the side pouch that contained my bottled water, I slipped out of my backpack to grab it.

But as soon as I set my pack on the ground in front of me, a garish neon-yellow label affixed to the back winked at me in the sunshine.

I gasped at the sight of the bold, black letters emblazoned across the tag that spelled out in mocking clarity: FALL RISK.

Immediately, my eyes snapped to Bob's baby blues, which now sparkled with amusement. "Are you kidding me?"

He tried to hide his smirk behind a gloved fist. "Are you mad?"

The sting of embarrassment prickled my neck as Bob chuckled beside me. "No wonder that couple gave me a bizarre look!"

I examined his handiwork and reluctantly admitted to myself that it was pretty clever. "How did you do it?"

"I kept that bracelet you wore in the hospital after your wrist surgery." He paused to take a swig of water from his bottle. "Then, I used Velcro and tape and slapped it on your backpack when you weren't looking."

When I met his gaze again, I could see he was pretty proud of himself by the way he kept glancing at the label. And then he handed me his phone displaying a picture across the screen that he'd forwarded to our daughter at the beginning of our hike.

He'd perfectly captured me from behind—highlighting the FALL RISK warning in all its glory.

I shook my head. "I'm not mad. But I still can't believe you did that."

And then he helped me shrug the backpack onto my shoulders before we resumed our trek.

Although that was the last time I announced to fellow hikers with a label on my pack that I was a FALL RISK—to the best of my knowledge—for the next several outings I always tried to remember to check my backpack for anything new Bob might've attached. But for the rest of that particular hike, I took advantage of how well it worked to clear our path.

Years later, and after exploring hundreds more miles of trails, I still half expect my husband to try and top that prank. Yet so far, I've remained safe. However, he did warn me before a recent solo hike that if I fell again, I would no longer be allowed to hike alone—which is not a risk I plan to take.

—Chris Maday Schmidt—

40

Some Things Are Funnier When You're Naked

I did a push-up today. Well actually I fell down, but I
had to use my arms to get back up, so close enough.
~Author Unknown

My husband is a doer, not a direction follower. The fact that he can assemble Ikea furniture without directions leads him to believe he possesses superpowers, which he sometimes does, but not always. He is one of those guys who inputs directions into the GPS, only to ignore the pleading navigator, "Turn right in fifty feet. Make a U-turn, make a... rerouting, rerouting," until I think she might have a stroke.

"Why do you even bother using the GPS?" I ask.

He assumes this question is rhetorical and reminds me that he managed to get around without me for the first thirty-two years of his life. I can't disagree, but once in a while, his staunch anti-directionism can get him in a pickle.

Take the night Paul was tinkering with some gadget. It was the end of a long week, and all I wanted was a hot Jacuzzi and a chilled glass of Chardonnay.

"Hon, want to join me for a soak?" I asked.

"No, thanks. I'm just finishing putting this thing together."

So, I slipped into my robe and padded outside with Chardonnay in hand. The warmth and bubbles eased my aching muscles and cleared my mind. After soaking long enough to resemble a steaming dumpling, I put on my robe and went inside.

"I'm going to take a quick shower and get ready for bed," I said in a half-dazed state.

"Hey," my husband said, pointing to the inversion table in the corner of our bedroom, "how do you like this thing?"

"Love it," I said. "Gets all the weight off my spine. The traction feels great. You should try it sometime."

I'd been using the table for a couple of weeks, and, of course, my husband had set it up for me. Although it was a bit complicated to assemble, he'd put it together and adjusted the frame to fit my 4'11" size, no directions required.

"If you want to use it," I said, "you'll need to adjust the foot bar for your height. Oh, plus you'll want to read the instructions. The first time you use it, they recommend only going halfway to a horizontal position. It takes a little getting used to before you fully invert yourself to hanging upside down."

Heading to the bathroom, I heard him making the necessary adjustments, so I came back to the bedroom.

"I know you don't need any directions, but let me show you how you actually use this thing."

I demonstrated how to get on the contraption, and how to lean back and get in position. I showed him how to invert totally, so my head was practically on the ground, admonishing him that this was an advanced move for later. With the finesse of a gymnast, I verbally and physically executed the dismount. He watched, but not really, as if following directions, especially mine, would be cheating.

Seconds later, with no questions asked, he was on the machine and flipping himself upside down.

"You might want to only go halfway… Or not…," I said, but it was too late.

He was fully inverted and hanging by his feet.

"Okay, so how's that?" I asked.

"Pretty good," he said.

Still warm and woozy from the wine and Jacuzzi, I dropped my robe and readied myself for a shower. That's when I heard a commotion of loud thumping. I ran back into the room.

"How do I get up?" he asked in a voice escalating from know-it-all cool to urgent panic.

The truth is, hanging upside down for prolonged periods is a well-known torture technique.

I was slightly tipsy, and his panic was inducing a major buzzkill, but I had to act quickly and assess my options.

Do I rush downstairs and unlock the door in case the paramedics need to come? Do I put on clothes? Do I grab the video camera in hopes of getting some prize-winning footage for America's Funniest Home Videos? *Or do I try and get him down?*

I'm not a physics whiz, but I know a thing or two about leverage. I had only two options: pull from the top or push from the bottom. I couldn't reach his feet from the top because they were too high. He is a full foot taller than I. I could also tell that if I attempted to straddle his head to try to use my weight as leverage to push him upright, I'd likely only reach his knees. Remember, he was upside down, and I was naked. The best I could hope for was to end up suspended horizontally in some kinky Kama Sutra position that I'd have to explain to the paramedics when they arrived.

Meanwhile, as the blood rushed to my husband's head, he grew increasingly incapable of understanding basic directions.

"Bend your knees," I said, but I might as well have been speaking Swahili. In this inverted position, he was completely disoriented and couldn't tell what or where his knees were. So, I tapped him firmly on the knees while loudly and slowly repeating, "BEND YOUR KNEES!"

He finally complied with the command and was instantly brought to a neutral position while I was instantly brought to gales of laughter.

"C'mon, honey," I said, chuckling, "you've got to admit this was funny, right?"

"No," he said.

"Well, maybe tomorrow it'll be funnier," I offered.

So, I asked him the next day, "Seriously, that was funny, right?"

"Still not funny," he said.

But he was wrong. The next day, it was even funnier.

And, all these years later, it keeps delivering.

— Tsgoyna Tanzman —

41

Romance by the Book

*Marriage is not just spiritual communion and passionate
embraces; marriage is also three-meals-a-day and
remembering to carry the trash out.*
~Dr. Joyce Brothers

At about our fifteen-year mark, things in the romance department became rather quiet, and I began to wonder if the zing
had gone out of my marriage. This revelation came to me one
night in bed while reading one of my many romance books.

That night, I remember watching Ken softly breathing in sleep
beside me, his thriller novel open and abandoned on his chest. My
husband was good-natured, dependable, and a decent provider. But
he was also predicable, a homebody, and definitely happiest sprawled
in the big recliner in our living room.

In our early days, he would come home and sweep me up in his
arms and twirl me around until I was dizzy. The last time I remembered
feeling dizzy was from the fish at Big Jim's Eatery. Now, I was greeted
with a peck on the cheek and "What's for dinner?"

A little twinge of guilt for not being happy with my sweet but
humdrum husband tried to take root, but I abruptly pushed it aside.
Frowning down at my romance book, I remember thinking that the
men in my novels certainly never acted that way. I decided to get to
the bottom of it all.

The next day at breakfast, I said, "Ken, honey, I thought maybe
we could have a talk this morning."

A wary look darkened his face. "Talk?" He slowly lowered himself into the chair. "About what?"

I blurted out, "Ken, do you ever have to tear yourself away for fear you'll grab me in unbridled ecstasy and ravish me?"

Ken's eyes narrowed. "Huh?"

I pushed on. "Does your love for me consume you so that you can't think about anything else but my strawberry-tasting kisses?"

I knew for certain that I didn't have his full attention when he selected a piece of toast, ran a knife through the butter, and said, "Did you say we have strawberry jam?"

I tried again. "Ken, put down the toast and look at me. Do your loins ache for me, and you think you'll go mad because you have to leave for work?"

He seemed to consider that for a moment and then said, "I love my work. You know that."

At that point, I gave out an exasperated sigh. My worst fears had been confirmed. The hot flame of my marriage had dwindled to a mere flicker. In the romance books, the heroes never wanted to leave their women and frequently had to use all their strength to hold themselves back from having their lusty way with them.

Ken's face suddenly lit up. I held my breath, and my eyes widened in anticipation. Then, he said, "Did I tell you about Joe in accounting?" His face broke out in a huge grin. "He got a bargain on a snowblower, and, boy, it's a beauty."

"Honey," I said, trying to get him on track, "do you ever have to stop yourself from calling me from the office just to hear my sensual voice?"

Ken stopped his forkful of scrambled eggs halfway to his mouth. "You know I'm not supposed to make personal calls from work."

He just wasn't getting it. Ken gave me his usual peck on the cheek and told me to have a nice day before he left. I was discouraged to see that he was able to resist the urge to clear the table with one sweep and drive me mad with his burning desire.

Okay, that hadn't worked. A different tactic was needed. I decided to make a list for him. Men are good with lists. Maybe he just needed a little assistance in converting himself back to the romantic husband he used to be. I labored over it during the day and read it to him in the middle of dinner that night. When I was through, he sat back in his chair as though stunned, a half-eaten chicken leg clutched in his hand.

"Let me see that," he said, reaching for the pad of paper. After a moment, he said, "So, you want me to gaze longingly into your deep, limpid eyes, watch you hungrily when you do the laundry, push back your tousled hair and demand hot, savage kisses, surprise you with crushing and uncontrolled passionate embraces, and suffer greatly with the impossible task of having to leave you at home when I go to work?"

"Yes. For starters. So, what do you think?"

Suddenly, he slumped in his seat, lolled his head to one side, licked his lips and let out an odd little moan. I put an anxious hand on his arm. "What's happening? Are you alright?"

"I'm watching you hungrily." He fixed me with a wide-eyed stare. "It's number two on the list."

He looked like a puppy in the pound.

"I know you weren't doing the laundry, but," he pointed to the washroom, "do you want me to go get some hot towels?"

"Ken," I said, crossing my arms across my chest, "you're not taking this seriously."

"Are you looking for me to be more attentive to you? Is that what this is all about? You want some sweet talk?"

"Do you know any sweet talk?" I asked. "Because I haven't heard any in a long time."

He gazed longingly at me over the table and said in a deep, sexy voice, "Do we have any more mashed potatoes?"

I mentally threw my hands up in the air and went to get more potatoes.

That night in bed, I mulled over my plan. Maybe I should shoot for something a little easier for him to grasp, like holding hands, or a single rose, or a lunch date that doesn't include Big Jim's. Yes, that's what I would do.

The next morning, I intended to discuss the changes with Ken when he suddenly burst into the kitchen and slapped a couple of romance novels on the table. He shook a handful of papers at me.

"What I'd like to know," he said, his voice low and deeply serious, "is how come you never quiver in my strong manly embrace, or bite your lush lower lip to stop yourself from calling out my name in ecstasy in bed, or shudder at my hot, insistent kisses? What's going on, Jody? Don't you love me anymore?"

I grinned and held out my hand. "Let me see that list."

Ken held it over his head. "No, wait. I've got more." He turned over a page. "How come you never accidentally rip your bodice open to expose your ample and heaving bosoms? Huh?"

My grin turned to a hearty laugh, delighted at Ken's silly effort to confront me.

"Yeah, I'd sure like to see that. And why do you never let your hair dangle... Wait a minute, what does this say? Oh, yeah, dangle in soft tendrils down your perfumed neck?"

With a wolfish twinkle, Ken flung the papers in the air like a knight drawing his sword. He reached for my hand, pulled me swiftly to him, and held me in a captive embrace. He whispered into my ear how pretty I was and how crazy I made him just by breathing.

Zing. A warm sensation surrounded my heart and made its way down to my belly. Maybe it wasn't a full-blown quiver, but it was a darn nice start.

I decided to keep him for another fifteen years.

— Jody Lebel —

42

So You Think You Can Dance

*When you dance, your purpose is not to get to a
certain place on the floor. It's to enjoy
each step along the way.*
~Wayne Dyer

t wasn't a secret. We could not dance. Well, *he* couldn't. When I
saw an ad for dance lessons, primarily learning the old-time waltz,
I immediately signed up my husband, Don, and me. Knowing he
would disapprove of the idea, I told him this presented an opportunity for us to get out of the house and spend some time together.
Don said we could go to a movie or bowling instead. I told him I had
never learned how to waltz. Don said he had.

"Come on. It'll be fun," I implored.

"Not my definition of fun."

"This is something I'd really like to do. Can't you do this for me?"

Don took a deep breath and exhaled, his shoulders beginning
to sag a little.

That is a good sign. He's giving in.

"Please, Don." I snuggled up to him. "It's only for six weeks."

"SIX WEEKS!"

"It'll fly by in no time." I quickly tried to redress the situation.
"We're always looking for things we can do together. This can be one
of those things."

I watched Don consider it and gave him a little time.

Finally, he said, "If you want to do this that badly, I guess I can go with you."

"Thank you! It'll be fun. You'll see."

As a child I had resisted my parents' encouragement to learn how to waltz. I hadn't let my father teach me either. At our wedding, Don and I awkwardly stumbled through the first dance, clinging to each other and hoping to make our attempts at dance seem effortless. Who were we kidding?

Now I imagined us locked in each other's arms, fluidly dancing across the floor as if floating on a cloud. My visions of splendour and magnificence came to a screeching halt when we descended the stairs into the church hall for the dance lessons and met our teachers.

The male instructor was a very large man with a belly hanging over his belt and sweat running down both sides of his face. He mopped away the perspiration with a yellow-stained hankie. His partner looked gaunt. Her dyed blond hair was carelessly piled on top of her head with bobby pins sticking out like on a pincushion. She had creases around her mouth as though she had sucked on too many cigarettes over the years. Her twig-like body seemed insubstantial enough to hang her clothes on while her pants threatened to slide right off her narrow hips. Together, the pair did not create a picture of grace and fluency.

Coming from a small town, we knew the other five couples who attended the class. After some quick introductions for the teachers' sake and a few simple directions, the teacher went to the record player and put the needle down on a classic: "Jean" by Oliver. It wasn't waltz music in my opinion, but that is what she played.

Don and I moved, he in one direction and I in the other. He quickly pulled me back toward him, and we tried again, me trying to be patient with him. After all, this is where we would learn to move as one and glide smoothly across the floor. We watched the other couples as they seemed to have already mastered the steps and could even talk as they danced and twirled around the church hall. We stood a foot apart, staring down at our feet, trying to count out the steps that would make us champions of the waltz.

The instructor came over to us and showed Don where to place his hands and how to guide me across the floor. I smiled encouragingly at my husband as he tried to do as the instructor asked. We managed a few steps until his shoe came down on my sandalled toe. I cried out, certain my toenail would turn black and fall off.

The nightmare continued for the next two weeks. With no improvement in Don's dancing, and frustrated by the number of times the instructors came to offer their advice, I tried to make the best of it. At one point, the male instructor danced with me while the female instructor danced with Don, showing us the right way to waltz.

"Hold the frame," the instructor commanded of Don. "Hold the frame."

And, to me, the male teacher admonished, "You must not lead. Let the man lead."

How embarrassing to have the instructors dancing with Don and me! They had not done that with any of the other couples. When the male instructor finally released me back to my husband, I felt annoyed that they had singled us out, and I blamed Don for his awkwardness on the floor. No Fred Astaire and Ginger Rogers here.

Toward the end of the third class, I went into the hallway for a drink of water. When I returned, I noticed the two instructors having what appeared to be a serious conversation with Don.

The teachers had their backs to me as I approached. Within earshot, I overheard one of them say, "Your wife has no sense of rhythm. Worse yet, she refuses to follow your lead. We do not see any point in the two of you continuing the classes. It would be a waste of time."

Don solemnly nodded and stared past them, looking into my eyes as I stood behind them, listening to every word they said.

"We felt you should be the one to tell Marilyn. Here's your money back."

"That's okay," I interrupted, my cheeks burning with humiliation and anger. "We were about to leave."

I snatched the money out of the instructor's hand, grabbed Don's arm, and marched him across the hall and up the steps. Once outside, I noticed my husband shaking. I glanced at him, only to see him desperately trying to keep from laughing.

"It's not funny," I told him.

"Oh, but it is," he argued. "If you could have seen your face."

"You're just happy you don't have three more weeks of dance lessons," I chastised him, to which he nodded, a big grin sweeping across his face.

"Well, maybe I'll find some new dance lessons where the instructors know how to teach."

"Okay," my husband conceded.

We got into our car and slammed the doors shut, knowing that would never happen.

— Marilyn Frey —

How My Flu "Flew" Away

*Any mother could perform the jobs of several
air traffic controllers with ease.*
~Lisa Alther

As my bedroom door slowly creaked open, three worried little faces peered in at me. "Mom!" they whispered in unison.

"Now, boys," my husband Don called, "shut the door and go play. Mommy needs to rest. She's sick."

Sick? At death's door was more like it. For days, I had been battling the flu. That's flu, as in hot and cold running sweats. As in right off the misery chart. But with three lively boys, ages two to four, I had kept going with every ounce of strength I could muster. Now, this Saturday morning, I was completely "mustered" out.

If only we could call on someone to help! But my folks lived hundreds of miles away; Don's, thousands. And this flu had hit all of our neighbors, too. So, there was no one to turn to.

Robin, the oldest, cleared his throat. "Mommy, both hands are up on the twelve."

"And we're hungry," Chat added.

"Real hungry!" echoed Jay, my youngest. "What's for lunch?"

What's for lunch, indeed? Now if ever there were a time for frozen pizzas or "golden arches" or even TV dinners, this was it. But as new homeowners, we were too broke for such luxuries.

Meals around our house were as inexpensive as possible. We mostly lived on tuna casserole, macaroni and cheese, spaghetti, hot dogs, homemade chili, and soups, plus everything we could grow and can from our own backyard.

So, there was no money for eating out. And nothing in the refrigerator that Don could simply thaw or heat up for lunch. Just some reserve cans of food in the pantry.

As for Don's "cooking-from-scratch" talents, they had never been tested. Indeed, he'd hardly darkened a kitchen door except for meals since his Army KP days.

But he was a bright, loving man. And now, with our family's "chief cook and bottle washer" (me!) out of commission, he'd managed to fix breakfast for the boys that morning with a box of dry cereal, a gallon of milk, and four bowls on the kitchen table. Surely, he'd be able to manage a simple lunch, as well.

"Don, dear," I called weakly, "it's noon, and the boys are starving."

When his head appeared at the doorway above the boys, I continued, "Could you please open a can of vegetable soup for them? You'll find a can opener in the knife drawer. Just dump the soup into a pan, along with a can full of water. Then stir it over medium heat. You can serve it in the same bowls you used for breakfast (you did wash them, right?), along with glasses of milk. Peanut butter and crackers would be nice, too. Got all that?"

"Lunch? Sure thing!" Don replied, blowing me a kiss. "Now, go on back to sleep, dear. The boys and I will do just fine."

As he firmly shut the door, I drifted off to oblivion. But an hour later, I suddenly woke up to find all three boys hovering over me.

"Mommy, are you better now?" Robin asked. "Because we're really starved."

"Yeah!" chorused the others.

Confused, I said, "But didn't you have some good, hot soup for lunch?"

"No, Mommy. Just a slice of watermelon."

"Hey, it was good watermelon!" Don protested in surprise when he came in from mowing the lawn. "Jim next door brought it over. Fresh and ripe and full of vitamins." He grinned. "And no bowls to wash up afterward. Clever, eh?"

I sighed. "Unfortunately, dear, a slice of watermelon won't last these boys till dinnertime. Now, please fix them some soup like I asked, okay?"

He blew a kiss. "You got it. Come on, boys. Your mommy says 'soup,' so soup it is."

When I woke again an hour later, smells swirled under the bedroom door. Very awful smells. "Uh, Don, dear," I called. "Is something burning in the kitchen?"

"No," he called back. "I'm just cooking up a surprise."

"Oh. That's nice. Did the boys ever get their lunch?"

"Not yet; that's part of the surprise."

In sudden dread, I fumbled for my robe and tumbled out of bed. Holding onto the walls for support, I inched weakly down the hallway to the kitchen, following smells that grew stronger and stranger by the minute.

Our three boys were sitting at the kitchen table with glasses of milk and very empty bowls in front of them. "Hi, Mommy!" they said wistfully.

Their father stood at the stove in front of a huge canning pot. Inside, a dark, foreboding liquid bubbled away. All around him on the countertop were cans of every description, from peaches to pork and beans to pizza sauce and pickles.

Open, empty cans.

Don grinned and pulled me into his arms. "Glad to see you up, dear. Wait till you see my new invention! Why should you have to open different cans for different meals? Just put them all together, and you've got soup that'll last a whole week! Think of the time you'll save!"

I didn't grin back. Weakly, I said, "Don, you didn't…"

Yes, he did. Poured every single can he found in our cupboard into that pot. That was his "soup."

Well, that was the end of my flu. I was completely cured by that pot of soup, which neither I nor anybody ever ate. Or even dared to taste. Not even Don.

Even the drain it was poured down protested! Only a half-loaf of bread and jar of peanut butter saved our sons from absolute starvation that day!

No, despite my pleading and nagging, Don never did learn to cook soup or anything else. But in the things that really count in life, our life together was a veritable feast!

Besides, how many husbands have invented a sure cure for the flu?

— Bonnie Compton Hanson —

44

Motorcycle Madness

When a man opens a car door for his wife,
it's either a new car or a new wife.
~Prince Philip

t was a very hot and humid day in Chicagoland when we hopped on our motorcycle, making our way toward Wisconsin. We loved the beautiful scenery but missed talking to each other because we had misplaced our communication device. We stopped for a delicious fish-fry dinner just over the Illinois border and were surprised to run into a dear friend.

After dinner and visiting with Rosanne, Larry secured my new helmet on me and got on the bike. I tapped him on the right shoulder and told him my plan. He took off on the gravel road, kicking up rocks as he made his way to Route 12. It was a one-hour ride back to our home in Chicagoland, so Larry turned on his radio and was deep in thought.

When he got home, he stood up, which was my cue to get off.

Yikes, where's Sue? he thought. *Did she fall off the bike? Was she abducted by aliens?*

What he didn't realize was that I had never gotten on the bike. What I said while touching his back was, "I'll get on the motorcycle on the other side." That was my stronger leg.

Seeing him take off, I had yelled, "Larry, I'm not on the bike!" but he never heard me.

All my belongings were in the trunk of the bike, including my telephone and wallet. *Surely, he will return quickly,* I thought, as I walked back and forth along Route 12 by the gas station. I was quite the spectacle being just under five feet tall with a humongous black helmet on my head.

Many people who stopped for gas offered to let me use their phone. I made eleven calls to Larry from various kindhearted strangers. I couldn't get the new helmet off, and sweat was dripping down my forehead. Finally, a young man was able to help me get it off. Freedom!

I went back to the restaurant, and Rosanne was surprised to see me holding my helmet.

"What happened?" she said.

When she heard the story and realized I was okay, she roared with laughter. "How could he forget his wife?" she said.

By nightfall, I was sitting in his truck and not on the back of his motorcycle. It was another life-with-Larry day.

— Susan Schuerr —

45

Honeymoon Turquoise Blues

Marriage is like a good cardio workout. If it's never
challenging, you're probably not doing it right.
~Author Unknown

At 3:00 a.m. on the morning my brand-new husband, Jon, and I were set to leave for our honeymoon in Barbados, I knew something was wrong. "Does your stomach feel like it's about to explode, too?" I whispered, wondering if he was awake.

He answered with a groan and ran downstairs to the one bathroom in the house. I hoped I wouldn't have to fight him for it.

I thought back to everything we'd eaten since the wedding. If we were both sick at the same time, it had to be something we both ate. I ruled out the dairy items since Jon is lactose-intolerant and had avoided those. Maybe it was the hors d'oeuvres served at the beginning of the reception. They'd been sitting out the longest, and the caterer packed the leftovers for us to take home. It was possible they'd turned.

At 4:30 a.m., my brand-new mother-in-law picked up Jon and me to take us to the airport. With her was my brand-new sister-in-law, brother-in-law, and toddler niece, who'd come to town for the wedding and had an early flight out. Jon insisted on driving because, as sweet as she is, his mother's driving makes me motion sick under the best circumstances. He drove slowly and carefully out of consideration for our stomachs.

The opossum didn't get the message.

As Jon took the exit toward the airport, a massive opossum decided to cross the ramp at that exact moment. Jon jerked the wheel, narrowly avoiding hitting its hissing face and dozens of pointy, sharp teeth. Though I was glad we didn't hit the opossum, my stomach might not have lurched so violently if we had.

"Pull over!" I shouted.

"Right now?" Jon asked, incredulous.

"RIGHT NOW!"

I was out of the van before we'd come to a complete stop. Mere hours after officially becoming part of my husband's family, they were watching me vomit over the side of a guardrail.

"You okay? You need anything?" Jon asked, suddenly beside me.

"Water," I coughed.

He rooted around in the van for what seemed like a long time while I stood there trying to decide if it might happen again.

Jon returned with my toddler niece's sippy cup.

"It's the only drink we have," he said.

"I can't take a bottle from a baby!" I said, flabbergasted. What would my in-laws think?

"This is all we have," Jon said, shrugging.

I assessed the taste in my mouth and prayed my niece wouldn't remember the day her aunt took her sippy cup.

"Wait!" I said, the bottle at my lips. "This isn't breastmilk, right?"

"Of course not!" my sister-in-law hollered from inside the vehicle.

Back in the van, it was eerily quiet, which only added to my embarrassment. So, I broke the ice.

"Well," I said drily, "I didn't expect that 'in sickness and in health' clause to kick in so soon!"

Everyone laughed, and the awkwardness dissipated. We talked about how surely this would be the strangest story to come out of our honeymoon.

But my in-laws didn't see what happened after we parted ways at the airport.

At the check-in counter, I learned that my new husband, whom I'd been engaged to for two years and dated for two years before that, had mistyped my middle name. Which is three letters long.

"You mean you don't know how to spell my middle name?!" I said, incredulous.

Jon swore it was a typo and that he really did know how to spell it, but the agent wasn't going to let me on the plane.

"Sir, you have to let me on the plane! It's our honeymoon, and we're going to Barbados, and it was expensive to book, and we're only planning on getting married just this once, and I've already barfed on the side of the road this morning, and…" I begged. I pleaded. I cried.

The agent looked warily at Jon, probably wondering how well we knew each other before getting married if he misspelled my middle name on my plane tickets. But after twenty minutes, we were able to convince the powers-that-be that it really was just an honest mistake, and they let us board.

Once on the plane, we breathed a sigh of relief. We were on the plane headed to our honeymoon destination. Plane crashes are fairly rare, so we thought nothing else could go wrong. Our week together in tropical, wedded bliss could finally begin!

When the plane landed in Barbados, the salty island air that brushed our faces and arms was so much more refreshing than the air in Ohio. I couldn't wait to get our bags and head straight to the resort's beachfront.

Except that our giant suitcase, with all our clothes and necessities, wasn't there.

We waited and waited and waited at the carousel, and my distinctive, black rolling suitcase with red roses polka-dotting its surface never materialized. Of all the times for an airline to lose luggage!

"My swimsuit was in there," I whimpered, officially at my wits' end.

Ever practical, Jon went into "I'll handle this" mode and filed a report for our missing luggage while I let myself have a good frustration cry.

A shuttle took us to the resort, where we were greeted with songs and flutes of champagne that we were still too sick to drink but sipped anyway.

Jon and I went to bed early to recover from the tiring day. Two days later, a knock at our room door revealed a bellhop with our suitcase minus one of its roller wheels so that it had to be dragged instead of rolled.

When the bellhop left, Jon and I collapsed into laughter. This wasn't how we thought our honeymoon would go, but there was no one I'd rather share a week in paradise with because, without Jon, it wouldn't be paradise at all. In sickness and in health, in potential roadkill and saved critters, in misspelled middle name and new last name, in roller luggage with three wheels, till death do us part.

And now that we had our suitcase with our swimwear, we could finally soak in that bright turquoise water.

— Mandy Shunnarah —

Mistaken Identity

Flying through Security

Life is better when you're laughing.
~Anna Nielsen

When I saw a line of anxious travelers spilling out of the terminal onto the sidewalk, I wondered which would take longer: getting through security or flying home to Cincinnati from Honolulu. "There was a security breach this afternoon" was all the explanation we got as we resigned ourselves to the long wait.

An hour later, I made a disheartening discovery. "Oh, nooooooo!" I said to my wife, Cherié. "I left our new camera in the rental car. I gotta catch a taxi to the rental place to see if it's still there."

"But you'll miss our flight," she said.

"You go ahead. I'll rebook for tomorrow or figure out something. I just spent $1,500 for that camera. I must find it."

I caught a cab to Enterprise and exhaled in relief when I spotted our camera still on the passenger seat. When I returned to the back of the line at HNL, however, I figured my odds of making the flight were the same as my wife sweet-talking the captain into holding the plane just for me.

As I brainstormed options, a security officer approached me and said, "You can come with me." As I fell in step with this stranger, he explained, "We get a lot of famous celebrities like you on the island, so whenever I can, I take them through a private security entrance. I mean, a movie star of your caliber should never have to wait in line."

Confused, I asked, "Were you at the church where I preached last weekend?"

"Oh, no," he said, "I didn't know you preached. I just love all your fabulous movies."

"Thanks," I said, more as a question than a response. For the record, I have posted a couple of family videos on YouTube, but I was surprised that he recognized me from them.

So, I had to ask, "Just curious, but of all those fabulous movies, which one was your favorite?"

"Oh, my!" he said. "That's impossible to say. I mean, you have sooooo many of them! Right?"

"Right," I said, still wondering who I was — or who he thought I was.

"Well, you were fantastic in *White Men Can't Jump*."

Ugh! I never saw that movie.

"And I loved your performance in *The Hunger Games*."

Another movie I never watched.

"And *Palmetto* is a classic."

Great. A movie I had never heard of.

"And, to this day, my favorite sitcom of all time is *Cheers*."

Bingo! People always tell me I bear a striking resemblance to Woody Harrelson.

"I still watch your reruns," he gushed. "The *Cheers* cast had such a magical chemistry. Do you ever get together with the old gang?"

I said (truthfully, I might add), "Hah! No, I haven't seen any of the old gang for, like, forever!"

As we entered an empty room with a lone metal detector, an unnerving thought hit me like a billy club upside the noggin. *This is how good people land in jail. I better come clean before I must decide on my one phone call.*

"Um, say, ah, so, you're probably going to need to see my ID, right?" I held my breath.

He shrugged. "I know who you are." (Thankfully, at this point, I knew who I was, as well.) "And, besides, most celebrities as famous as you usually carry an alias."

"Yes!" I nearly screamed. "I do! My alias is Karl Haffner!"

Fun facts: One might argue I am the perfect alias for Woody. After all, we were born five months apart (i.e., our moms were pregnant at the same time). Also, I lived just outside of Lebanon, Ohio, where the Hollywood A-lister grew up and attended high school. We are both vegetarians. According to www.HowTallIs.org, Woody is 5'9.5" tall, weighs 160 pounds, and wears size 10 shoes. Check. Check. Check. And, me being a pastor, I noted with interest that his Wikipedia bio states, "Harrelson was a religious Presbyterian as a child and studied theology during college." Is Karl Haffner not the perfect alias for Woody Harrelson?

Quicker than a cop can say, "You have the right to remain silent," I was waiting for Cherié at the gate well before boarding. Surprised to see me, she said, "Oh! You decided not to go back to Enterprise?"

I showed her the camera. She stared, too confused to speak.

Finally, she said, "But how did you get through TSA before me?"

I flashed an impish grin.

She knows that look too well. "What did you do? Was it illegal? What happened? Tell me now!"

"Well, um, I wouldn't call it technically 'illegal.'" I felt like a kid getting busted for playing hooky.

"Look at me! What did you do, Karl?"

"Shhhhh! Don't call me Karl. My name is Woody!"

To this day, I say there is no better place to visit than Honolulu — where everybody knows your name (except your spouse), and they're always glad you came.

— Karl Haffner —

47

American Pride

Laughter is, after speech, the chief thing
that holds society together.
~Max Eastman

I was working in my office one day when I received a telephone call from my niece. She wanted me to know that her husband, a member of the Missouri National Guard, was preparing to be deployed to the Middle East. The length of his deployment was unknown, and she asked that we keep him in our prayers. I thought of him several times during the afternoon and his commitment to duty and service to our country. I have always been a very patriotic person. Just seeing the American flag often brings me to tears and fills me with pride to be an American.

Later that evening, I drove to our local Applebee's restaurant to meet my husband for dinner. I pulled into a parking space next to a large, black SUV and watched as four young men got out of the vehicle. They were dressed in camouflage pants, olive-green T-shirts, army-green caps with the American flag embroidered on the front, and combat boots.

They walked to the front door of the restaurant and waited for me. When I approached them, they took off their caps and waited in a single-file line as one young man held open the door for me. I was overwhelmed with emotion as I thought of all the young soldiers who were protecting us around the world, and my niece's husband heading to the Middle East.

I fought back tears as I thanked them and asked, "Where are you fellows from?"

"We're from the St. Louis area, ma'am," one young man answered.

"May God bless each and every one of you," I told them. "Please know how proud we are of you young men. My sincere thoughts and prayers go with you."

"Thank you, ma'am," one said as the others nodded their heads in unison.

"Where are you headed?" I asked.

"We're going deer hunting, ma'am," they answered.

—Jeannie S. Williams—

48

Caught Red-Handed

I'd rather laugh with the sinners
than cry with the saints.
~Billy Joel

The sun was just coming up when my daughter headed out our front door wearing her Skyview High School tennis uniform. As captain of the varsity team, she was excited about the district tennis tournament in Caldwell, Idaho, a town about thirty minutes away. The entire tennis team was excused from classes for the day since they would be competing at the tournament.

A short time later, my daughter called on her cell phone from the high school parking lot. "Hey, Mom, when you and Dad come to the tournament, could you bring Coach Armstrong's truck?"

Only half-awake, I listened to her explain the situation. Apparently, school rules required two adults to ride on the bus with the team. So, Coach Armstrong and his assistant both had to ride on the bus to Caldwell. However, the tennis matches were going to be split between the Caldwell high school and the Caldwell junior high, and Mr. Armstrong needed his truck so that he could drive back and forth between the two schools.

"Absolutely," I assured her. "Dad and I are happy to help out."

"Great!" she said. "Coach will put the keys in the center console and leave his truck unlocked."

She was about to hang up. "Wait!" I said. "What kind of truck is it?"

"It's white. You won't have any trouble finding it, Mom. It's the only vehicle in the parking lot."

My husband Dan and I went about our morning routine making coffee, getting dressed, and packing the car with drinks, snacks, and lawn chairs to bring to the tournament. It must have taken us a bit longer than we had expected. By the time we got to the school parking lot, school had started. And the parking lot was full of vehicles.

We drove slowly through the lot, counting at least five white pickup trucks and shaking our heads.

"Which one do you suppose is Mr. Armstrong's truck?" Dan asked.

I tried calling our daughter, but no one answered. By that time, no doubt, she was already on the court warming up.

"We will just have to find the truck that is unlocked and has the keys in the center console," I told Dan. Really, how hard could it be?

I pulled up to one of the white trucks. Dan hopped out and tried the driver's side door. It was unlocked. So far, so good. He reached into the center console and pulled out a set of keys. Easy-peasy! I gave him a thumbs-up. He started the truck and backed out of the parking spot. As I followed him out of the lot, we passed a school bus that was going to take the track team to their district meet. I waved at the kids as we drove by. The sun was shining down on us. This was going to be a great day.

On our way out of town, Dan put on the blinker and turned into a McDonald's. *Great idea*, I thought to myself. We hadn't taken the time to eat breakfast, and I knew a breakfast sandwich would taste good. I followed the big white truck through the McDonald's drive-through, and then we were on our way.

Thirty minutes later, we arrived at the high school in Caldwell and parked the two vehicles near the tennis courts. I grabbed our chairs, Dan carried the truck keys and a to-go cup, and we set out to find the Skyview team. When we found Mr. Armstrong, Dan tossed the keys to him. "You left your coffee in your truck," Dan said, holding the cup out to him.

Mr. Armstrong took a step back. "That's not my coffee," he said. "I don't even drink coffee." Puzzled, he then took a look at the keys. "And these are not my keys." When Dan, eyebrows raised, pointed to the white truck in the parking lot, Mr. Armstrong shook his head and said, "That is definitely not my truck!"

All three of us stared at each other as the repercussions of this news sunk in. I was beginning to think this was not going to be such a great day after all.

While Mr. Armstrong drove the truck back to Skyview High School, Dan and I sat in our lawn chairs and tried to watch the tennis tournament. We couldn't help feeling anxious. Surely by now the truck had been reported stolen.

We knew the Skyview parking lot had security cameras. At this very moment, officers were likely reviewing the video footage of the theft. The cameras would also have picked up our car's license plate. Oh, sweet Lord, there was probably a warrant out for our arrest! I cringed, thinking about how we had driven a stolen truck through a McDonald's drive-through!

The theme song from the TV series *Cops* started playing in my head. I looked over my shoulder. Were they coming for us right now?

An hour later, Mr. Armstrong returned to the Caldwell high school in what I assumed was his own white truck. As soon as he saw us, he started laughing and said, "You are going to think this is really funny." I wasn't so sure.

Apparently, just before Dan and I had arrived in the Skyview parking lot that morning, the track coach had run into the school office to quickly grab something before driving to the track meet. He was utterly flabbergasted when he came back out just moments later and discovered that his white pick-up truck was gone! Thinking it must be a prank, he found the principal and the athletic director. Together, they searched the school grounds, but there was no sign of the missing truck. The school security officer checked the footage of the parking lot cameras, which, plain as day, had captured a man and a woman stealing the truck. They were still reviewing the video footage when, to the amazement of all, they looked out the office window and saw the missing white truck return!

As Mr. Armstrong shared this news with us, he was laughing so hard that tears were streaming down his face. "I explained everything to them. I'm not sure if the track coach thought it was funny, but the rest of us sure did, especially when I suggested that maybe he shouldn't leave his keys in his truck next time!"

Greatly relieved, Dan and I looked at each other and smiled. We would not be wearing handcuffs that day after all.

—Jill Nogales—

Saint Urho

*Life isn't like a box of chocolates. It's more like a jar
of jalapeños. What you do today might burn your
butt tomorrow.*
~Larry the Cable Guy

When my son was young, he was enrolled at a Montessori school. The guides sent a note home one day stating they wanted to expose the children to various holidays and cultural differences. If our family had a particular ritual or religious holiday, they would really enjoy knowing about it so they could share it with the children.

I told my co-worker Cathy about the note as she was opening a package. She said she was Finnish, and when they lived in Minnesota, they celebrated Saint Urho's Day. She just got the chocolate coins in the mail that she gave her kids to help celebrate. She said they were similar to the chocolate coins used in Hanukkah, but they had an image of Saint Urho, which she showed me.

I told her I hadn't heard of Saint Urho. She said he was left out of the history books because Saint Patrick chased snakes out of Ireland and got all the publicity. But Saint Urho chased all the grasshoppers out of Finland and saved the crops from destruction the day before Saint Patrick's Day.

The next day, I went to the school and told my son's guide all about Saint Urho. She gave me the strangest look and said it was very interesting as she had never heard of that saint before, and she thanked me for sharing.

I went to work, thanked my co-worker for the information, and told her the school was excited about learning about Saint Urho. She said she was glad they enjoyed learning about a very important holiday for her family.

Months later, I learned Saint Urho is a fictional saint designed to give people a reason to drink green beer for an extra day. Cathy was not the one who cleared it up. This point is important. I never let on that I had made a fool of myself and vowed I would get her back.

The next year, on the fictional holiday, I made two grasshopper pies. I took them to work and put them in the conference room. I called all the mechanics in the back and told them it was a very important religious holiday for Cathy and please come to the conference room to celebrate because there was pie.

Seven hungry men showed up ready for pie. On the board, I wrote "Happy Saint Urho's Day" and called Cathy into the conference room. She saw the note on the whiteboard and started backing out of the room.

I stopped her and said everyone was there to help her celebrate and please tell the guys about Saint Urho — just as she told me last year. She started stammering and I said I had made a grasshopper pie to help celebrate.

One of the guys asked if grasshoppers were in the pie, and I said, "What would Saint Urho's Day be without an actual grasshopper pie?" I told them that it took my son and me several days to get enough green grasshoppers for the pie. The brown grasshoppers in the piecrust were harder to find that time of year, but they looked really nice covered in chocolate for the garnish on top of the pie.

Cathy started backing out of the room again. I said she was to get the first piece of pie and please let me know if it was similar to what she was used to. She took a small bite, said she had to get back to her desk and ran out.

The guys kept looking at each other as I handed out pie slices. No one wanted to eat it, but they did want pie. Finally, one of the guys said he didn't care if grasshoppers were in it and started eating.

The other guys watched him and decided that, if he could eat it, they could, too. They ended up finishing off both pies.

A few months later, I got a phone call from one of the wives. She said that some blankety-blank person up there had made a grasshopper pie and that was all her husband wanted for his birthday. She was frustrated because she couldn't find a recipe for it anywhere. I said I was the blankety-blank person. She said she had the kids outside all day trying to catch grasshoppers but didn't know how many they needed. I laughed and said I would send her the recipe on the condition she didn't tell her husband there were no grasshoppers in the pie. It was made with Crème de Cacao, Crème de Menthe, and grated chocolate. No grasshoppers at all.

— TG Gilliam —

Truth Teller

From there to here, and here to there,
funny things are everywhere.
~Dr. Seuss

After a year of dating, Roger presented me with a beautiful emerald ring. We were engaged and so very happy. Our courtship had been long, and to celebrate, his best man had invited us to his home for dinner.

That couple, long married, were not as happy as we were. Best Man had been diagnosed with sleep apnea. "I am so glad he had that test," said the wife. "Snoring can ruin your health... and maybe your marriage. I had to sleep in another room until he was fitted with a mask."

As we drove home, I brought up sleep apnea, going on and on about how dreadful Best Man's plight must be.

Roger was silent, his attention focused on the road in front of him. Finally, Roger took a deep breath like a drowning man going down for the third time. "I think you should be tested. You are snoring—to the point that I think you are dying."

A searing stab at my vanity had just been made. I quivered with rage. "I don't snore," I snapped and sat back in frosty silence. "Don't you dare start up with me again about snoring."

We drove the rest of the way home in the silence of our first-ever lovers' quarrel.

By the time we arrived at my apartment, I had cooled off. Roger parked the car. We held hands as of old and gave each other a forgiving kiss, but we both knew that to utter the word "snoring" would be to step into a sinkhole.

As I unlocked the apartment door, we heard a familiar series of loud shrieks. That was Henry, a blue-and-gold macaw, my pet of twenty-five years. He was greeting me and saying, "I want my treat." I unlocked the door and immediately went into the room the two of us shared, fed him his favorite treat (a Brazil nut), and talked to him. His shrieking gradually stopped, and with a lot of soothing words, I covered his cage and said, "Good night." I actually said "Good night" several times, hoping beyond hope that he might repeat those words.

That never happened. I had tried for twenty-five years to get Henry to talk. He never did, but he was a master at mimicking sounds. He imitated the barking of the dog down the street, the quacking of the duck who lived next door, and the squeaking of a door opening. For a while, he was saying, "Be quiet," two words he heard often from me, but that phrase was uttered only on occasion and never on request.

What could be thought a talent could also be a danger. We occupied the same space. All my comings and goings, all my conversations, every utterance I made went into his vast memory bank. When he might share my secrets was completely unpredictable.

While I was taking care of Henry, Roger sat patiently in the living room sorting out the wedding invitations. After the fateful meet-and-greet many months before, he would have nothing to do with Henry.

That day, Roger, following my instructions, had stood by Henry's cage quietly, almost reverently. He had spoken softly and flatteringly. Finally, after gaining what he hoped was Henry's trust, he had proffered a Brazil nut through the bars of the cage. Henry had taken one look at the nut, one look at Roger's fingers, another look at the nut, and then had made a dive bomb for the fingers.

Roger, who prided himself on his way with animals, was devastated. From then on, Henry was a dumb, two-word ("Be quiet") bird. "You might not know it," Roger growled at Henry, "but you are a dispensable item. Thanksgiving can be celebrated with a bird other than turkey."

I turned off the lights and joined Roger, who had already set up a card table and had begun to address the wedding invitations.

We worked steadily for an hour until I got up to make a pot of coffee.

Just as I stood up, a terrible racket began. It sounded like a door rattling in a strong wind. I hurried to the front door as the noise grew louder and more threatening. "Are we supposed to have a storm?" I asked. "The noise is frightful."

I opened the front door, expecting violent winds, but saw nothing. I pushed the door to close it securely, but the noise continued. Suddenly, I realized the ruckus was not coming from the outside. It was coming from Henry's cage. "It's Henry," I yelled into the living room. "He's gasping for air.... It's a death rattle.... He's dying." By this time, I was shrieking uncontrollably.

I headed for the cage, my heart beating so hard that my legs wobbled. My companion of twenty-five years was in the throes of death.

Meanwhile, Roger, facing the prospect that his rival was at death's door, moved quickly to my side. "I might not like him," he said, "but I don't want him to die."

We rounded the corner of the room, switched on the light, and braced for the worst. But, not to worry, there sat Henry, upright, unperturbed, the whole world his stage, delivering his most perfect of imitations ever: my snoring.

— Nancy Roenfeldt —

Pedestrian Dilemma

*If you would not be laughed at, be the first
to laugh at yourself.*
~Benjamin Franklin

This was more than the scattered showers predicted by the weather folks. This was "open up the heavens and dump all you got" rain. And it was in Los Angeles, where we are constantly being told, even in song lyrics, that it never rains. It was hard to tell if the inevitable flooding of the streets and sidewalks was in full swing because it was so dark. I could barely see my car parked out on the side street.

It was a perfect excuse not to attend Marsha's party. Rain in Los Angeles always brought on apocalyptic results. Everyone would understand. But I still wanted to go. Marsha's parties were so much fun.

A mad dash to the car wearing a jacket I mistakenly thought was waterproof was followed by a fumbling and repeated dropping of car keys. Ignition on? Check. Lights and wipers on? Check. Shoes and socks soaked through? Check.

As I navigated the short drive through city streets to Marsha's apartment, I struggled to see through the windshield, even with the wipers on full force. The thump-thumping of the wipers was annoying, but the street lights were doing little to help me out, forcing me to lean forward over the steering wheel as if the extra inch or two would help me see. Luckily, since it was raining in LA, people were hunkered down and there were few cars on the road.

I was having a hard time seeing. Maybe I needed an eye exam.

A stop sign seemed to spring up from behind a low-hanging California black walnut. I tapped the brakes and slowly came to a stop. The rain intensified, rattling the nearby tree branches and easily overwhelming the windshield wipers. And then I saw him. Or her. I couldn't tell with visibility so limited.

What was this kid — or extremely short adult — doing out on such a night? Well, at least he or she was dressed for the weather. I wished I had such a bright yellow slicker. It was great for safety. I don't think I would have seen this person without that yellow breaking through the gloom and rain.

The person was not only brave to be out and about, but they were carefully, cautiously waiting to cross the road. They needn't worry about me. I not only knew the strict driving laws concerning pedestrians having the right of way, but I applauded their existence and steadfastly followed them. I patiently waited. The person did not move.

Obviously, it was one of those awkward moments when neither of us knew who would move first. It wasn't going to be me. The pedestrian was in charge. So, I waited. And waited. I thought that perhaps I should let them know of my intentions, so I tapped my horn lightly. I didn't want to scare him. Or her. Had they heard it over the howling wind? I honked a bit longer. There was movement. No, that was the tree branch.

This was getting a bit ridiculous. We were at an impasse. This poor pedestrian was scared to death and didn't realize I was letting him or her go first. So, I started waving my arm and yelling, "Go ahead. Go ahead and cross." Obviously, they could not see my arm waving or hear me, so I rolled down both windows and continued to yell as the rain started to pour into my car.

Still no movement. Maybe the person needed help. Maybe I was being insensitive. I threw the car into park and got out. I was already wet from having the windows down to yell, so what did it matter now? As I stumbled in front of my car and toward the person, I saw him. Or her.

My reluctant pedestrian was a fire hydrant. I had just spent ten minutes trying to get a yellow fire hydrant to cross the road. Of course, I looked around to see if anyone was watching me. Only a mailbox and a row of hedges. They weren't crossing the street either.

I decided not to share my story with Marsha and her revelers at the party and the next day I made an appointment for an eye exam.

— Brad Korbesmeyer —

52

Surprise

Of all days, the day on which one has not laughed
is the one most surely wasted.
~Sebastien Roch

My mother-in-law lived with my husband and me and was always ordering things online. So was I.

During Covid, she was unable to get in for her monthly mani-pedi and began complaining how ragged her nails were becoming. She decided to do it herself and ordered a manicure set.

I co-owned a pet store at that time, and we needed live mealworms for the reptile critters we had for sale. I had the mealworms sent to my house because I wasn't sure when they would arrive and I didn't want them sitting outside the store.

Unfortunately, on the day of their arrival, I was at the pet store during off hours because I had a customer who needed to buy her dog food after my normal closing time. While I was there, my husband called me.

Husband: "Did you order worms?"

Me: "Yes, why?"

Husband: "Well, they came, and Ma got the package."

Me: "Oh, good, I'll come home for them and bring them back here!"

Husband: "Actually, that's why I called you. Can you just come home please?"

I hung up, wondering what had happened. When I got home, my husband met me at the back door. "So, Ma got the box from the delivery guy and opened it even though her name wasn't on it. She thought it was her manicure set. I was in my office (our bedroom, converted to his office space as well) and heard a loud shriek, 'Rob! Get in here!' So, I walked into the living room and there she was, batting away all these worms and screaming at me to get them off of her!"

I began to smirk, then giggle, then laugh. "So, where are they now? I need them today!"

"Well, I didn't know what to do. She was jumping around, and they were everywhere. So, I scooped up as many as I could and threw them away."

"Wait, what? You threw them away?" I ran to the kitchen and checked the trash can.

"No, they're in the outside trash can." My husband looked really apologetic by this point.

"Rob, I needed those… I need them today! I have hungry critters, and you threw away my worms?" I began to panic now, probably as much as my mother-in-law when she first saw them. "Why did she even open that box? It had my name on it!" Rob handed me the box. Yep, there was my name!

"She said she thought it was hers and just opened it," my husband replied lamely.

I showed him the outside of the box. It had air holes all over it and written on it in large red letters were the words "Live Animals."

I sighed. "So, is she okay now?"

"Yeah, she went back to watching her soap operas." My husband felt bad now. Then, he smirked. "You should have seen her, though." He began waving his arms wildly in the air, making a strange shrieking sound as if in imitation of her, and all I could do was laugh. Oh, how I laughed.

For the next few days, every time I saw her sitting in her chair, I would laugh at the absurdity of it all. She never did apologize, only justifying that the package, after all, was the same size as her manicure set, which actually arrived a few days later… in an envelope. No air holes. No warning in red letters. Oh, and her name was on it, too.

I called the company who sent me the mealworms and told them of my plight. After listening to hysterical laughter from the operator, she said she'd send me a new shipment ASAP. "Is there a particular address you want this sent to?" she asked.

"Yes, send it to the pet store!"

I figured I'd had enough excitement for one week.

— Diane Ganzer Baum —

53

Blinded by Beauty

It's important to learn to laugh at ourselves,
don't take life too seriously.
~Geri Halliwell

Back in the early days of my real-estate career, I was part of the lively crew at The Chesson Agency in Wilson, North Carolina. In those days, every morning began with laughter and smiles. It really was a great place to work. We were a tightknit group; there was never a dull moment.

Aside from the hustle and bustle of the real-estate world, we always managed to find time for social affairs and used any excuse to have a gathering. However, one annual event stood out like a shining star: the office Christmas party. Hosted by the owner, these parties were legendary, a time for us to kick back, let loose, and start the holiday season off with a bang! We had so much fun with our Secret Santa gift exchange, too. With this bunch, we never knew what type of gifts would appear.

One year, fate smiled upon me. I was given a stunning amaryllis plant for my office. Its vibrant colors and lovely petals took my breath away. It was the largest and most beautiful amaryllis I had ever seen.

I was so excited about this gift. Little did I know that I was not the only one who had fallen under its spell. My dear friend, Mary Lynn, was just as taken with the plant as I was. Together, we lavished it with attention, watering it, talking to it, and ensuring it basked in the warm glow of sunlight. I never had to worry about being out of the office because I knew Mary Lynn would take care of my special plant. We both loved that plant. We snapped countless photos to share on social media, refused to allow anyone else to care for it, and even gave it a name: Rosie. She was our baby!

But as the months passed, something began to dawn on me. Despite our best efforts, Rosie had shown no signs of growth. No new buds bloomed, none of the leaves had fallen, and she looked exactly the same as when I had received her. Stunned, I jumped up from my chair. I began to examine Rosie closely. And then it hit me like a ton of bricks: Rosie was not real. She was a fake, a plastic plant that we had been caring for as a living, breathing plant! I stood in shock, heartbroken, and then suddenly the laughter hit me.

Unable to contain my laughter, I called out to Mary Lynn, who came running down the hall, not knowing what was so funny. Between moments of hysterical laughter, I looked at her, barely able to get the words out, and asked, "Do you see anything unusual about this plant?"

She looked at me like I was crazy. "No, why?" she asked, as I sat with tears rolling down my face.

"Look at the leaves, Mary Lynn," I said.

And then, she saw it too — the truth hidden in plain sight. With tears streaming down our faces, we collapsed to the floor, our laughter echoing through the office.

For months, we had tended to Rosie with love. However, in the end, it did not matter because the memories we made, and the laughter we shared was as real as it gets. And, hey, who needs a real plant when a plastic imposter can give you that much joy? Twenty years later, we are still laughing about Rosie — and at ourselves.

— Teresa B. Hovatter —

Laughing at Ourselves

Art Deco

A little dose of humility may help cure
a big case of ego.
~Author Unknown

I had been a bank loan officer for more than fifteen years in New York. In the early 1980s, I was offered a substantial pay raise and promotion to vice president if I would relocate to Florida. The position was with the Dania Bank, Florida's oldest commercial bank. I jumped at the opportunity and looked forward to impressing everyone there once I got my feet wet.

Among my first prospective customers was a real-estate group seeking a loan to refurbish a building located in the South Beach section of Miami. After some discussion, the attorney mentioned that this was an "Art Deco" building, and they would require about $1 million to complete the project. Totally unaware of the architectural history of South Beach, I told the attorney and his client that I would need to see the financial statements and obtain the guaranty of the person I presumed to be the principal investor: Mr. Art Deco. That was how we made loans: the loan would be secured by the building, but we had a backup guarantor in the form of a real person.

How these people kept their composure at that moment is beyond me. Their faces turned red, ostensibly trying to keep from either laughing or crying. With bulging eyes, they politely managed to explain to me that "Art Deco" was not a person but a style of architecture popular in the 1920s and 1930s. The term was well-known in South Florida's

Miami Beach area, but not to me.

I felt like a total idiot. Understandably, we didn't get the loan.

— Richard P. Cintorino —

A Bagel and a Bug

There is nothing more deceptive than an obvious fact.
~Arthur Conan Doyle

A woman was staring at me intently at Einstein Bros. Bagels, our go-to hangout. It was Sunday morning, and my husband and I were there as usual for our weekly bagel-and-coffee breakfast before church.

"I think I must know that woman in the blue-and-white dress over there," I told him. "She keeps looking at me, but I can't place her."

"You work here in town. She's probably a patient."

"Don't think so. She doesn't look that familiar."

"She could have seen you in church," he said.

"She's not smiling at me, just staring. But it probably is someone from church. There are lots of people there I don't know. She's sitting there wondering where she knows me from, just like I'm wondering that about her! Anybody you know?"

"If you don't know her, I won't," he said. "You're much better at that kind of thing than I am." But to humor me, he looked at the woman in question. "Nope. Never seen her before."

The staring continued until I began to feel unnerved by it. "I wish she'd pick someone else to watch. I feel self-conscious."

"Try waving at her and see how she responds."

"No, then she'll assume I recognize who she is. She'll come over, and I won't know what to say."

The buttery bagel was calling to me. I took a bite and savored its flavor and texture. I decided to ignore her, avoid looking in her direction, and finish my breakfast. If I saw her later at church, I could go up and apologize for not knowing her on sight and introduce myself.

"Come to think of it, I know why she's staring at you," my husband said. He made me wait while he took a slug of his coffee. "It's that article about you."

The weekly newspaper in our town, *The Current*, had written a small piece about me after I sold two stories to Chicken Soup for the Soul. The feature told a little about the stories and me and included a headshot. I'd been over the moon when I saw it, expecting a lot of comment from my friends. It was fun seeing my name in print. But hardly anyone mentioned it to me. As pleased as I was to see it, aside from cutting it out and taping it up on my desk, I hadn't given it much thought after a week or so.

"I doubt that. Only a few of my friends even saw it. It's unlikely that woman did. And if she did, why would she remember it and put it together with my face here at Einstein's?"

"It's a human-interest story," he said. "People love that sort of thing. It makes you a local celebrity."

"No, that's not it."

We ate in silence for a few minutes.

"I think I know why she's looking," I said. "I just got my hair done." My hairdresser Cathy was a wizard.

"Hmmph, guess we'll never know." He shrugged and went back to eating.

A few minutes later, he looked up from his food and whispered a warning. "I guess we're going to find out what this is all about after all. She's gotten up and seems to be on her way over."

I had just moments to prepare myself. I'd either have to admit I didn't recognize her, or lie and pretend I did. I didn't much like that option. Too many potential complications. Or maybe I'd be accepting her glowing compliments about my hair and scribbling down Cathy's phone number for her. That would be nice. Or maybe she really did see the article and recognized me and was going to comment on my achievement and let me know how much those stories had meant to her.

I got ready.

"Excuse me for butting in," she said.

"Not at all," I replied. I was gracious and humble.

"I thought you'd want to know…" She hesitated. I already knew what her next words would be: something wonderful about me.

I glanced at my husband, who watched with great pride. His wife was about to receive the recognition she deserved.

"I thought you'd want to know," she repeated. "You have a stink bug in your hair."

— Holly Green —

Dressed to a T... or Coffee

*The only time to eat diet food is while you're waiting
for the steak to cook.*
~Chef Julia Child

When my son James told me he was marrying, I realized that the last time I had shopped for formalwear had been my own wedding, thirty years and thirty pounds earlier. Unsure of what size dress to order, I figured I would lose weight and then, closer to the wedding date, buy from a local shop.

For months, I tried to diet, shedding a pound or two through weeks of struggle and then quickly regaining the weight in a single weekend, along with an additional pound or two. I knew my downfall: mocha. I had been nurturing a daily habit of drinking the chocolate-flavored coffee since my forties. Now I was trying to avoid coffee shops, but they had a bead on me and started sending me e-mail offers of free or discounted coffees. I was doomed. I was a member at so many coffeehouses. My writers group met at one, a nephew sang at several, a friend celebrated his birthday at another, and my husband had developed his own coffee addiction. We were coffee codependents.

Acknowledging my addiction but still determined to lose weight whether I overcame it or not, I tried getting more exercise and, at work, began walking during lunch. I was surprised to learn how many coffee shops were in walking distance of my workplace.

I tried switching to teas and lower-calorie drinks, but then I ended up drinking them and, later in the day, breaking down and

Laughing at Ourselves | 197

having a mocha anyway. I didn't want flavored water, diet drinks, or teas. I wanted mocha! Try as I might to steer clear of it, I continually found myself at coffeehouse registers, eyeing the menu of drinks and confessing to the barista, "I want a mocha."

By April, my bathroom scale showed I was as heavy as ever. The wedding was in May, so I decided to bite the bullet and buy a dress. I went to a local shop and saw a few high-school girls and their moms also shopping the racks. They giggled and oohed and aahed with excitement as they picked through the sequined prom gowns in all colors of the rainbow. The salesclerk steered me to a rack of dowdy mother-in-law dresses.

"This is all I have to choose from?" I asked.

"Probably not this many," she said. "What color did the bride choose for the wedding?"

"Sage."

She pulled four dresses from the rack. "These might not clash."

I carried the dresses into the fitting room and had just squeezed into the first dress when I heard one of the girls ask, "What is *she* doing in there?"

The girl's mother responded, "Grandma needs a dress, too."

Grandma?! I yanked the curtain back to clarify I was still in the mother stage, and the salesclerk charged in, saying, "Need any help?"

"I can't zip it all the way," I said.

She wrestled up the zipper and steered me to the full-length mirror. "What do you think?"

I thought the body before me was not one I had ever seen before. "When did they put funhouse mirrors in dressing rooms?"

She grimaced. "They're regular mirrors. We do keep the lights low, though, for our customers."

I struck out with the first three dresses and fell in love with the last one, a taupe gown with understated elegance, full frontal coverage, and a rhinestone neckline.

The clerk told me it had an open back and gave me a hand mirror to view it. Doughy flesh puffed out from the cutout section of the dress.

"I have a fat back!" I gasped in horror. "When did I get a fat back?"

"Well, you don't normally see your own back. The lovely thing is this dress comes with a shawl." The clerk draped the shawl over me and turned me to face the mirror. "And, from the front, this dress really shows off your hourglass figure. Can you see yourself dancing in this?"

"Not when I can't breathe," I eked out from lungs fiercely constricting. I could see I looked great from the front, but all my fat was being pooled and pushed out my back, squeezing my lungs into tubes the size of toilet-paper rolls on the way out. "I'm going to need to order a larger size. Can we get it in time for the wedding?"

"Sure," she said. "Let's go to the front register and place the order."

I changed into my regular clothes (which now gave new meaning to "breathable fabric") and walked up there.

The clerk found the dress in the right size on the computer and asked, "What color would you like?"

"The same color as the dress I tried on," I said.

"You mean the mocha?"

"Mocha?"

"That's the color of the dress."

I nodded, acknowledging my downfall, the one that had brought me here now. "I want the mocha."

— Ronica Stromberg —

My Tin Ear

*Things aren't often what they appear to be
at first blush. But embarrassment is.*
~Jarod Kintz

While we rode the Paris Métro, my friend Patti attempted to teach me how to say, "I don't speak French" in French. She easily said, "*Je ne parle pas français.*" I listened with hyperattention and responded, "John no pull Frankie." After about twenty tries, some passengers chuckled, and even Patti now had a smirk. My tin ear for French seemed impenetrable. Everyone on the subway car could attest that "I don't speak French."

Patti, a long-time friend from our native Minnesota, was studying at a French university. In 1983, I took off a semester from college to visit her and tour Europe.

Upon reaching her home Metro station, we emerged onto a street of wooden storefronts painted in various colors. The stores were a feast of bakeries, butchers, fruit and vegetable merchants, and fishmongers.

As we passed a bakery, I was mesmerized by the brilliance of a four-year-old boy. He was having an animated conversation in French with his mother who was holding several baguettes.

Patti nudged me to stop staring. My American mind could not fathom how this little child spoke French so masterfully. Yet I, fifteen years his senior, could do little more than muddle "*bonjour.*" Patti intuitively knew my thoughts. She confided to me, "Scott, I felt the same way when I arrived. I wore myself out studying French all day in school, so I was shocked by the small kids talking effortlessly."

During the day, Patti was in school, which meant that my tin ear and I had to fend for ourselves.

The Metro's signs had enough English for me to navigate the subway. However, I made lots of wrong turns when walking the streets, even though I studied the maps in my green Michelin guidebook. I struggled to match the French names, letter by letter, to the street signs.

The biggest struggle was eating. One option was to cobble together lunch by selecting food in a grocery store. If I limited myself to food that was reachable in the open, I didn't have to speak with the workers standing behind the glass cases filled with savory meats, cheeses, and baked goods.

Making payment was an unavoidable embarrassment. As the cashier rang up my food, I would muster a *"bonjour"* with a weak, puzzled smile. She would then state some unintelligible French number to pay. Feeling stupid and vulnerable, I had to let her take the proper bills and coins from my hand.

Restaurants were difficult, too. I did my translation guessing game, trying to determine what at least a few words meant on the menu.

When the waiter arrived, I mumbled *"bonjour"* and ordered a Coca-Cola since it was one of the few "French words" that I naturally knew. After that, I pointed at something on the menu that I hoped my bland Midwestern palate would find edible.

If the waiter asked a question, I worryingly stammered, "John no pull Frankie." I'm not sure if my French was decipherable, but the waiter understood that I had not understood.

With serendipity as my guide, I ate some spectacular food, whatever it was. One meal was so noteworthy that I wrote down the words for Patti to translate that night. She laughed. "You ate farm rabbit stew with mustard."

That weekend, we did what I thought would have been impossible. We went to a movie. Patti taught me, "Look for movies in the newspaper with the letters VO after the title. VO means 'version originale.' Any VO American movie will be spoken in English with French subtitles."

In addition to the English soundtrack, I had the benefit of Patti's translation bubble surrounding me at the movie. Not only did she easily buy the tickets, but she also got us something savory from a glass case: popcorn.

After a week in Paris, it was time to brave another country. Patti had arranged for me to meet her former roommate, Sabine, who lived in Salzburg, Austria and had kindly offered to show me around.

Being a college student, I saved money by booking an overnight train. When the train pulled into the station, my grogginess was soon replaced by my excitement, along with a bit of trepidation.

I hoisted my large maroon backpack over my shoulder and stepped off the train. I was shocked when a woman on the platform said "Hi, Scott" to me.

I was supposed to meet Sabine at her apartment, so I did not expect her at the train station. I was too stunned to say hello back, but it didn't matter since the woman had quickly passed me en route to another train. The woman was not Sabine. In my grogginess, I had misheard my name.

I ventured out into the sunlit streets so the warmth could awaken me further. I smiled upon seeing a scattering of the traditional green felt hats, shaped like little sails, atop many people's heads.

One passerby noticed me looking and responded in a friendly tone, "Hi, Scott." I was bewildered and pretty sure that I had heard my name that time. I wondered if she read it off the name tag on my backpack.

I went to an outdoor cafe for breakfast, ready for my now-customary, point-and-hope meal selection. As the waiter arrived, I almost mumbled "*bonjour*" until I remembered that I was now in another country and could say an English "hello," which was close enough to the German "*hallo*." But I never got to say anything because the waiter flabbergasted me by saying "Hi, Scott" first. I wondered how on earth these people kept knowing my name.

After the waiter left, an English-speaking person at the neighboring table offered to translate anything that I might need. I thanked him, learned his name was Franz, and had a pleasant conversation about the best sights to see in Salzburg, including *The Sound of Music* tour, which showed the locations where the famous movie had been filmed.

When I grew more comfortable, I asked my new Austrian friend if I could pose a question that might sound strange. He replied with a restrained "Okay." I explained, "The people here seem to know my name, even though I've never met them. It's happened at the train station, on the street, and in the restaurant."

Franz looked at me as though I was possibly odd. Just then, the waiter appeared at a neighboring table and said "Hi, Scott" to the man who had just sat down. I pointed toward the waiter and said to Franz, "It just happened again with that man."

Franz burst out laughing. "The waiter is saying the traditional Austrian greeting of 'Grü Gott,' which means 'May God greet you.' He is not saying 'Hi, Scott.'"

I could feel my cheeks blush as I sheepishly mumbled, "Thanks for explaining."

— Scott Scovel —

The Summer of the Mouse

The best kind of pranks are the ones that leave
everyone laughing, even the victim.
~Author Unknown

The desert days shimmered with blistering heat, broken only by a daily afternoon shower drenching any Marine unlucky enough to find him/herself away from shelter. I was on a field-training exercise in the American southwest. My "office" was the Communications tent, the heart of the exercise's radio and field telephone system. (This was way before wireless communications.) Daily, I worked the main switchboard and the radio, keeping over 2,000 Marines on the mock battlefield in communication with each other and the Command.

I was a bit of a rarity, a female sergeant in the United States Marine Corps, and the men I was in charge of were young and high-spirited. Pranks on each other broke some of the boredom of downtime, but the jokes never interfered with our duties.

One day, I rounded up a group of men to clean the living area of the tent compound. It was a half-mile square of tents, mostly empty now since the battlefield was engaged. But just days earlier, those 2,000 Marines had been eating and sleeping in those tents, waiting to be sent forward. The potential for mess was great, and no one hates disorder more than the United States Marine Corps.

Off I went with a small detail of men, through the empty tents, picking up any trash that may have been left behind. I reminded the men to watch for snakes and scorpions, who'd be prone to curl up in the shade beneath the piles of empty cardboard cartons we were gathering for burning.

I always kicked a pile of cardboard before picking it up "just in case." I kicked one pile, and suddenly a half-dozen desert mice came shooting out in all directions. My bloodcurdling scream split the desert air and was followed by the sounds of shouts and boots hitting the ground as the Marines of my detail tore through the tents, expecting to find me "snake-bit." When they did find me, there was a moment of shocked silence. I had climbed the main tent pole in a desperate attempt to escape the mice. That merciful moment of silence was followed by uproarious laughter and various rude comments. I slid back down the pole, trying to maintain the semblance of dignity that my rank required as I was mocked and kidded.

"Sgt. Allison, you should request hazardous-duty pay if we're going to continue to be sent on such dangerous missions as trash-collecting details."

Oh, yeah, I was embarrassed.

I let them have their fun, but soon we were back on track, and the trash was collected and burned. I hoped the incident would be forgotten as quickly as possible. Fat chance. The story of Sgt. Allison's disgraceful retreat in the face of her whiskered enemy made the rounds, and I incurred even more ribbings from other Marines — and a fresh supply of practical jokes.

The chuckling had hardly calmed down when one jokester returned from a trip to town with a cat toy shaped like — what else? — a furry mouse.

To his credit, this Marine had picked out a particularly lifelike toy. It even had real rabbit's fur covering its little body. Suddenly, that toy mouse was cropping up everywhere. I found it staring at me from the top of the field radio, peeking out of an empty can, and perched in the crevice of the switchboard. This went on for several days, and I prided myself that I was never once startled by it. The Marines were disappointed at my lack of reaction, but that just pushed them to be more creative about where and how I would discover the toy. They did it all with the hope of recreating the incident in the tent. Each time I re-discovered the toy mouse, I would turn to face a group of Marines, all with their best "innocent" faces on.

After a few days of pranks, I found the mouse popping out of my ice-cold can of Coke, and I drew the line. Holding the mouse by its tail, I held it up for all to see and placed it in my pocket.

"Playtime is over. Let's get back to work," I ordered. The Marines were disappointed that they hadn't managed to trick me, but we soon forgot about their pranks because field inspections loomed, and there was serious work to do. Many of my Communications Marines were called upon to follow Command officers to the forward battlefield, and I was putting in long hours manning the switchboard and the main field radio. All communications went through the Comm tent. It was mentally exhausting work.

After one particularly long day, I walked the half-mile from the Comm Center to the women's tents at midnight. It was pitch-black in the desert, with the rumble of artillery fire in the distance and occasional Black Hawk helicopters flying overhead. Lit only by moonlight, my path took me past hundreds of dark, empty tents while foxes squealed, yipped and howled eerily in the desert. I was relieved to finally reach my tent.

The ten women with whom I shared my tent were sleeping, so I was careful not to disturb them as I got ready for bed. I took off my boots and socks, putting them to the side, and stood up to empty my pockets. Barefoot in the sand, I reached in and pulled out a mouse! Stifling a scream, I jumped back in horror and flung the mouse far from me, scattering the contents of my pocket with it. My heart pounding, I wondered, *Where is the mouse now? And how did it get in my pocket in the first place?*

My skin crawled as I grabbed my flashlight and scanned the floor. That's when I saw it: that silly toy mouse. Whereas a moment ago I had stifled a scream, now I was choking back my laughter. I sank onto my cot.

They finally got me. Those pranksters had finally given me the horrendous fright they were hoping for, and they weren't even there to see it. But I wasn't going to tell them! Until now.

— DeVonna R. Allison —

California Dreaming

Nothing feels as good to me as
laughing incredibly hard.
~Steve Carell

was in my late sixties, retired as a public-school teacher, and feeling a little over the hill when my car broke down and was in the shop. They gave me a loaner to get around until mine was repaired. My loaner was a new, black Ford Mustang convertible. I didn't mind how long it took to get my car fixed and back on the road.

The top to the convertible was a one-piece metal roof that retracted into the trunk. With a punch of a button, I was on my way, dyed auburn hair flying. My ego was soaring as men in cars honked at me, smiled, and made motions like they would like to date such a vibrant, free-spirited woman in a black convertible on that summer day.

The dream ended when I pulled up to the curb in front of my house and saw my husband doubled over laughing. I guess I didn't hold the retractor button down long enough and had driven home with the metal roof sticking straight up in the air, which was what all my "admirers" were trying to tell me.

— Carole Williams-Morrison —

Winning at Twinning

At the height of laughter, the universe is flung into
a kaleidoscope of new possibilities.
~Jean Houston

We were overjoyed when we received not one, not two, but three invitations to three different weddings. All happening in the same year! It may not sound like a big deal, but for us, at our age, it was like a breath of fresh air times three. After years of attending weddings on a regular basis, we had hit a dry spell. A very long dry spell. Sadly, we were attending too many funerals and zero weddings. So, you can imagine our delight over our wedding trifecta!

Of course, all the invitations were from our friends' adult children. But that didn't matter to us. We were happy to be part of the group of middle-aged couples often present at weddings. At least we weren't part of the elderly crowd. Yet.

So, the first of our three weddings took place in early spring. It was a traditional church ceremony, followed by an enchanting outdoor reception in a magnificent mansion's formal garden.

While seated on the bride's side of the church, I noticed a woman wearing the exact same dress as another woman sitting on the groom's side. I started snickering.

"What's so funny?" my husband whispered.

Trying my best not to giggle too loudly, I pointed out the two women. "Look! Twins!"

"Oh, no," my husband chuckled. "A woman's worst nightmare!"

"I know, right? The worst part is, the dress is pretty ugly, which is even more embarrassing! I mean, I've seen salad dressed better than that," I replied, laughing at my own cringe-worthy joke.

"Now, now," my husband said in a patronizing way. "Have a little empathy."

I did feel for them, yet I couldn't help but find the whole situation amusing. It was the first time I had witnessed this kind of wardrobe mishap. After the wedding ceremony, I noticed one of the ladies either didn't go to the reception or went home and changed because there was only one woman wearing that dress. *Good save!* I thought to myself.

Our second wedding took place in July. It was a spectacular outdoor ceremony held at a luxury hotel overlooking the ocean. Approximately 300 guests were seated on classic, white, wooden folding chairs — the kind you see at beach resorts and fancy outdoor weddings. The chairs were arranged in a graceful semi-circle on the resort's luscious, green lawn. My husband and I were seated in front, facing the charming, white gazebo adorned with delicate, white flowers. Beyond the gazebo was a breathtaking view of the ocean. It was a perfectly gorgeous day!

Following the couple's magical fairy-tale ceremony, we got up to mingle with other guests. Waiters wearing tuxedos and white gloves offered us glasses of champagne and exquisite canapés. When I scanned the crowd to see who else was there, I couldn't believe my eyes.

There were two women wearing identical dresses. But this time, a woman was wearing *my* dress! I was mortified. I instinctively grabbed my husband's arm and led him over to a nearby tree that I could hide behind. I pointed out the woman wearing my dress.

"Karma is getting back at me for laughing at those two other women at the last wedding," I cried.

My husband, who was trying not to laugh, admitted he had noticed her earlier.

"What? Why didn't you tell me?"

"I didn't want to ruin the wedding for you," he sympathetically replied. I have to give him credit there. That tidbit of information would have ruined the ceremony for me, so I thanked him for that. But it still didn't resolve my problem.

Unlike the woman at the previous wedding who had probably changed her dress, I couldn't do anything about my situation. We were too far away from home. I would be forced to spend the entire reception dodging the lady who had the audacity to wear my dress. (I'm sure she was thinking the same thing about me.)

Luckily, she was seated on the opposite side of the hotel's grand ballroom. The waiters were delivering the dinners, so I didn't have to worry about bumping into her at a buffet line. And the dance floor was big enough and crowded enough for us to keep our distance.

I was having so much fun at the reception that I was no longer thinking about my dress or hers. At least, not until I walked into the ladies' room. There she was, washing her hands! Our eyes met in the mirror's reflection. Rather than spinning on my heels, I mustered up the courage to approach her. Smiling, I said with all sincerity and a touch of humor, "I love your dress!"

We both burst out laughing. She confessed she had been avoiding me all day.

We exchanged compliments on how we had accented our identical dresses. We both believed the other wore it better. With her elegant, white sweater jacket, matching white sandals, and white necklace, she looked fabulous. I had chosen a tightly fitted, brown leather belt and matching brown sandals, accentuating the dress's muted, brown zebra pattern. To complete the ensemble, I wore a sizable seashell necklace that echoed the dress's off-white and soft, brown tones. Despite our matching dresses, we each had added our own personal flair, giving them a different look.

I suggested capturing this once-in-a-lifetime moment with a photograph. We marched out of the bathroom, arm in arm, and had our photos taken, striking poses like we were cover girls.

She bragged about snagging her dress at a sale the previous week, while I sheepishly admitted paying full price. We had a blast hanging out together. We discovered we shared many common interests, including a keen eye for trendy fashion.

At the third wedding my husband and I attended that year, I played it safe and brought along a back-up dress, which now seems silly to me. The likelihood of someone else wearing the same dress was slim. And even if it did happen again, I realized it wasn't the end of the world. In fact, looking back at all three weddings, the second wedding stood out as the most memorable. An embarrassing moment became a source of fun and camaraderie. Being part of that "twinning circle" is something I wholeheartedly embrace now, while appreciating the humor in it.

— Patty Cimlov-Zahares —

Not Surprised

A well-balanced person is one who finds
both sides of an issue laughable.
~Herbert Procknow

arly that week, my friend Vince had casually asked our family to
dinner for Saturday night. "Friends are here from Italy," he said.
"We're having dinner here at 7:30. Can you make it?" He was
very explicit about the time. I asked my husband David if we
should attend. After all, we had planned a full weekend of packing
up my son and driving him to summer camp.

"Sure," he said. "Why not?" That was my first clue. David would
never just say yes to a dinner invitation off the bat. He would hem
and haw and bring up all the reasons why we wouldn't or couldn't or
shouldn't attend. He would be pre-emptively exhausted or tied up with
some household project that he was sure would not be done by 7:30
on a Saturday night. But for this, he simply said, "Yeah, sure, why not?"

Hmmmm, I thought. This was it. They were planning my fiftieth
birthday surprise party, and David was in on it.

How brilliant! It was a full ten weeks before my actual birthday,
so I wouldn't suspect a thing. It was planned at Ilene and Vince's, a
place where it was perfectly "natural" for us to go for dinner, and also
a logical choice as I had helped Vince with Ilene's surprise party. And
the party was scheduled while all my siblings were still in town from
overseas and the Midwest. I was very impressed with David's creativity
and foresight. I loved him for cooking up a big surprise party for me,

even though he hated surprises and parties. He knew I loved grand gestures. What a sweetheart.

My sister Heidi was in from Austria, staying at my mom's house. I hadn't heard from them in days. Now that I had discovered the secret, it made perfect sense. Mom and Heidi are both awful with surprises. I could imagine them in Mom's kitchen, biting their fingernails with excitement and keeping each other from picking up the phone and calling me to spill the beans. I would forgive them for spending the week without me as they would be there at my big fiftieth birthday party.

On Friday night, the day before the big party, Heidi called me.

"Hi, Ive. We're all wondering what you're doing tomorrow.... We figured you weren't coming down here."

"Nope, I'm packing Max up for camp. What are you guys doing tomorrow?" I asked, coolly and detached, but my heart fluttered with excitement.

"Nothing. We're sitting around the house as usual, doing nothing."

Indeed. Right.

"What's Mom up to?" I asked, impishly.

My mother didn't want to talk to me. Good for her. Why risk ruining it?

"We're not going to your mother's," David broke in. He had been eavesdropping. "We're going to Vince and Ilene's at 7:30 on Saturday, remember?" Oh, my gosh, he recited the time. He never knew what time we were going places.

The day of the big party, David picked a fight with me about something or other — which refrigerator shelf I'd stored the bread on, I think. He was unusually nasty. Very clever of him to get me all worked up and mad, and then SURPRISE! That was a fun touch. I gave it right back to him. I didn't want him to think I was catching on.

After a day of arduous camp-packing and mock snappishness, we showed up at Vince and Ilene's. We arrived at 7:35. There were a lot of cars parked outside, none of them recognizable. I felt bad about the logistics. All my friends and family would have to park around the block, and this was a long block, so the walk would be far. Maybe their son Julian, who had a learner's permit, had been pressed into service as valet. Maybe they asked my brother. No matter. We walked up the walk. The living room lights were dim, and the door was open. I let the kids run in first. David and I walked in together. I stepped into the hall, peered around the wall to the living room, grinning like a schoolgirl, and... Who the heck were all these people sitting there?

Wait, did they go through the charade of hiring extras to really sock the surprise to me? Vince was in theater, after all.

I knew no one in this living room. I stepped into the kitchen and then stepped onto the side porch. There sat Ilene, her neighbors, some of whom I had met before, and those damn people who had come over from Italy. Who cared about them? I looked across the lawn. I looked back into the house. I looked over the hedges. Well, well, well. This was nothing more than a summer's eve dinner to honor some random Italians who were friends with my friends. I was not being feted after all. Not tonight. Vince offered to fix me a drink. "I'll pour myself a diet soda," I said. No use blowing extra calories on a Cosmo at this party.

Okay, this sucked. I began to get angrier and angrier about the bread-shelf incident. "It doesn't even belong in the refrigerator, let alone on the top shelf," I sneered at David. And my disinterested mother? Why hadn't she called all week? Was it so much fun to have my sister in the States that no one needed me in on the action?

Well, I still had nine weeks left, minus the three for that damn summer camp my kid had to go to, two for the Jewish holidays, Labor Day weekend when everyone I knew was going out of town and, of course, a couple of back-to-school, crazed days. Then one of those weeks was a friend's sixtieth birthday surprise party that I was helping to organize.... Wait a minute, could it be? A double-reverse-surprise-the-surpriser maneuver? Very unlikely. It would be way too far away from my family and other friends.

I would stay on alert. No way they'd fool me this time.

— Ivy Eisenberg —

The Artichoke Caper

*Life literally abounds in comedy if you
just look around you.*
~Mel Brooks

My husband Rob and I had moved to Sacramento following graduate school and were renting a house on a lovely twelve-acre farm. The farmland had long remained fallow as the elderly owner had moved to an assisted-living facility.

A family of four was renting the manor house. We quickly became friends with Jen, Bill and their children.

Mort, an older man, lived in a small mobile home on the edge of the property. He kept to himself, and we rarely crossed paths. Rob and I would greet him cordially on the rare occasions when we saw him. He would simply nod and continue on his way.

The farm had gigantic walnut trees and a magnificent variety of fruit trees—peach, plum, cherry, pear and pomegranate. We would make ice cream, fruit salads, and pies when the fruit was ready.

The land was fertile. We had planted just a few pumpkin seeds the year before and were shocked that they yielded sixteen enormous pumpkins.

With plenty of space in our vegetable garden, Rob and I were enjoying the bounty. Each evening after work, we tended our large garden and picked our ripe veggies.

When Rob suggested we plant some artichokes, I heartily agreed. We brought home two fully grown artichoke plants from a nearby nursery. Together, we dug the holes, mixed the dirt with planting soil, added plant food, and proudly placed our prized artichokes front and center in our vegetable garden.

"These are magnificent!" I gushed.

"Yep," agreed Rob. "They're going to be delicious."

Over dinner that evening, we looked through our cookbooks and imagined the fabulous meals and sauces we would create with our prized artichokes.

After work the next day, we hurried out to our garden to water and check our crops.

"What the...?!" exclaimed Rob.

"Oh, my gosh!" I gasped.

One of our new artichoke plants had disappeared, leaving only the hole we had dug.

"Who would've stolen our plant?" puzzled Rob. "They didn't take anything else!"

"This is bizarre!" I burst out. "Couldn't they just go buy their own artichoke plant?"

While standing there in shock, we heard a rustling sound nearby. Through the shrubbery, we could see our neighbor Mort digging a hole and planting a large artichoke plant.

"That's OUR plant!" whispered Rob.

"I can't believe Mort would be this brazen!" I agreed. "Do we dare confront him?"

Rob and I were stunned. For a moment, the two of us just stood in our garden, not sure how to handle this odd situation.

Suddenly, our second artichoke plant began to quiver. Before we could react, it disappeared down its hole in a flash.

A gopher then poked its head up from the hole and looked at us. I'm certain he was smiling at us with appreciation.

The artichoke theft was solved. With dreams dashed of gourmet meals, we decided it would be futile to plant a replacement for a gopher.

— Nancy Saint John —

That Was Embarrassing

Why Do I Say These Things?

*Anyone who takes himself too seriously always
runs the risk of looking ridiculous; anyone who
can consistently laugh at himself does not.*
~Vaclav Havel

Several years ago, I worked part-time at a major bookstore near my home. The atmosphere, the overall mood of both staff and customers, and the extra employee perks were compelling. I stayed about a year after my seasonal time ended. When the economy began its downward spiral, though, my hours were cut to where I spent far more money than I earned. That's when I knew it was time to quit.

Being a writer and book lover, I still shopped there as often as possible. There aren't many activities I'd rather do than browse among shelves of novels, memoirs, self-help books, cookbooks, dictionaries, maps of the world, and everything in-between.

When I heard that Fannie Flagg had a new book out, that was all the incentive I needed for another visit. The title escaped me, but I knew one of the associates would look it up for me. As I walked toward the service desk, I recognized Jane, one of the employees. Although we'd never actually worked in the same department, I knew her fairly well. Her personality was the exact opposite of mine. She was quiet, reserved, and soft-spoken. That day, she seemed particularly quiet, almost listless and indifferent. I assumed she was still engrossed in previous questions from customers or simply tired and overworked.

"Hi, Jane. I'm looking for that new Fannie Flagg book, but I can't remember the title."

She uttered a vague hello as her fingernails clicked away on the keyboard. While waiting, I took in all the activity around me. Customers of all ages strolled up and down the aisles. For a moment, the thought crossed my mind to apply for a job again, but fortunately it vanished as quickly as it had arrived. Never taking her eyes away from the computer screen, as if daydreaming, Jane said in a distant, detached way, "I still dream about you."

"You do? Wow! That is so cool. Sometimes, I still dream about this place, too, even though it's been a long time since I worked here."

I rattled on and on about how my goofy sense of humor must've really made an impression on her and how I hoped her dreams were funny. She didn't bother to interrupt me until after I'd basically made a complete fool of myself.

When she finally looked up and made eye contact with me, she said, "No, Becky," in her matter-of-fact tone. "That's the title of the book: *I Still Dream About You*."

For a split second, I was speechless. My mouth dropped open, and I could feel the heat creeping up my ears. I knew they were turning bright red. My eyes darted back and forth, as my mind fully grasped the ridiculous things I'd just said. Had anyone else heard me? Why didn't she just say that in the first place? All she had to do was add three little words. Three. Little. Words. "The title is…"

Oh, my God! Can you spell i-d-i-o-t? What made it even worse was that Jane didn't seem to realize how funny this was. She never even cracked a smile. She merely stepped away from the counter and walked ahead of me. As she meandered between various tables and book displays, I trotted along behind her, trying to keep up and blathering on and on about my embarrassment. I kept trying to explain my misunderstanding and how hilarious it would've been if she really had dreamed about some of my crazy antics at the store.

"No, I have more important things on my mind," Jane said almost gruffly. She stopped, picked up the hardcover, and handed it to me.

"Oh, my gosh, yeah. Well, I'm sure you do! Well, then. Uh, okay. Bye!"

It seemed like we couldn't get away from each other fast enough. Or maybe it was just me. I practically galloped over to the café area, glanced back and watched her stroll away in the opposite direction. She had such good posture; I daydreamed she was a model, balancing a book on top of her head, and the title of it was *How to Handle Awkward Situations*.

— Becky Lewellen Povich —

64

An Intimate Moment

*I learned that there's a certain character that can be
built from embarrassing yourself endlessly.*
~Christian Bale

I n the light of the old streetlamps and flickering neon signs, the
six of us excitedly clicked our way down Royal Street in our high
heels. Having traveled to New Orleans from different cities and
various stages of life, five girlfriends and I were gathered to celebrate my bachelorette weekend. With a full itinerary of brunches,
shopping, afternoons at the pool, a ghost tour at twilight, and late
dinners, it was sure to be a memorable trip.

It was our first night, and we were about to arrive at GW Fins, a
highly rated gourmet restaurant in the heart of New Orleans. As soon
as we entered, we were greeted with a buzz of people and delicious
scents. The hostess brought us to a beautifully decorated table with
a fresh arrangement of flowers, colorful confetti, and a personalized
menu congratulating me on my engagement.

Our waiter zipped across the candlelit room, introduced himself,
congratulated me, and took our drink orders. My sister Katherine
then got up to go to the bathroom. Katherine had recently found out
she was pregnant with her third child. She was afflicted with a little
nausea and was also in the awkward phase in which she could no
longer wear her regular clothes but was still too small for maternity
clothes. And though she looked healthy and beautiful, she was in a
state of internal discomfort and external distress, at least in regard to

her wardrobe. Nevertheless, Katherine was a trooper and planned to participate as much as she could.

She was almost to the bathroom when she froze suddenly and pivoted back toward the table, practically running. I looked behind her, searching for an indication of what had just happened. I noticed something dark on the floor. A napkin, maybe? It looked small and harmless, possibly just a shadow. Katherine reached me, knelt down, and with eyes as big as dinner plates, declared, "The most embarrassing thing just happened."

"You were gone for thirty seconds. What in the world could have happened?" I asked.

In a small, horrified whisper, she confessed, "When I was walking, something fell out of my jeans."

"Not your baby, was it?" I joked.

"I think it was underwear," she replied.

"Underwear?" I asked, amusement invading my voice.

"Yes," she answered. "They must have gotten washed inside my jeans or something. Please help!"

"I will get them," I assured my sister.

As I got up to retrieve the underwear, our waiter appeared out of nowhere. With perfect execution, he knelt down and swooped the underwear onto his tray, the same way he would a napkin. The overwhelming comedy of what just transpired seized me, and I lost it, erupting into a surge of laughter.

The underwear landed in a small, napkin-like crumple in the center of his tray, the dim lighting concealing its identity just enough. Speechless, mortified, and helpless, Katherine gasped in horror as her undergarment sat on display. Everyone at the table obliviously watched our opposite reactions, their curiosity growing as exponentially as my laughter.

"What happened?" they asked.

Overtaken by incessant giggling, I was unable to speak. Katherine, annoyed, interrupted and bluntly recounted what had happened. "My underwear fell out of my jeans when I was walking. Our waiter picked them up and put them on his tray."

I watched their faces transform from shock to amusement, only making my condition worse. We all turned to look at the infamous, undiscovered underwear that was now surrounded by three young waiters.

Suddenly, as if on cue, the unfamiliar fabric caught the eye of one of the waiters. He picked it up and lifted it into the air to examine it. We froze, hysteria building in each of us as we watched him realize what he was holding. The waiter immediately dropped the underwear as if it were a burning ember. The other waiters spasmed in similar surprise, and howls of uncontrollable, unrestrained laughter, even from Katherine, escaped us, and the confetti on our table flew into the air.

Our outburst progressed into silent, shaking convulsions in which tears streamed down our faces. For the remainder of our dinner, we could barely make eye contact with each other without eliciting another fit of laughter. By the end of our meal, our stomachs were full, and our abs were extremely sore. We vowed to not tell the waiter who the underwear belonged to, and Katherine was ever-so-willing to leave her intimates behind, ensuring that their ownership forever remain a mystery.

— Rachel Chustz —

65

The Breakfast That Ruined My Quest for Inner Peace

Do something awesome, no one sees it.
Do something embarrassing, everyone sees it.
~Author Unknown

N o actual words were spoken, but the message, "You need to leave my monastery immediately," was clearly communicated through the head monk's horror-stricken expression.

It had started so peacefully, so calmly. The tour promised a chance to enjoy a serene breakfast in a Thai monastery in rural Thailand. How incredible does that sound? For a girl who had never really experienced much inner peace, who never truly felt connected, it sounded like an amazing opportunity.

My friend and I set out early from Bangkok to be driven up north to the monastery, detouring a few times to pick up our contributions to the breakfast buffet. I had anticipated we were picking treats to enjoy together, so this heavily influenced my selections. I envisioned us sitting on bamboo mats, indulging in fresh fruit and pastries with Buddhist monks who imparted secrets to inner peace and happiness between mouthfuls of croissants and cinnamon buns. It would all come together, what had eluded me for so long, and by the end of the day, I would understand things like chai, yoga, and vegan lifestyles.

Just before we reached the monastery gates, our guide outlined the protocols to follow in the presence of the monks. Fortunately, our attire was already considered appropriate: long sleeves and pants, no hats, and no red clothing. As a female, it was explained that I could never touch a monk, not even accidentally brush against one. Before breakfast, it is customary to give morning alms. We were instructed to place our donations in the offering basket, then clasp our hands together and bow slightly. Finally, it is important never to sit in a way that exposes the soles of your feet toward the Buddha in the temple.

Seemed easy enough. I was already sporting a non-offensive navy palette and trying to project a false air of poise. All I had to do was not touch a monk, bow a couple of times, and watch where I was pointing my feet — simple asks in exchange for everlasting peace.

The initial alms presentation went remarkably well. There were a few instances when I bowed too soon or forgot to clasp my hands correctly, but no one seemed to mind; I think they could tell I was a rookie. The only blush-inducing moment came when, careful not to touch the monk, I inadvertently made eye contact. No rules had been expressly specified about eye contact, but I guessed it was likely implied.

It wasn't the eye contact that made me blush, though. The monk with whom I locked eyes was about my age and unbelievably attractive. My mind unconsciously wandered, thoughts becoming inappropriate — especially considering the focus. I have no idea how, but I swear this monk could see right through me. He snuck me an adorable, lopsided grin and continued with the next visitor. I just stood there — bright red, ashamed but smitten — and started mentally planning our future together. The next monk, older and notably less charming, cleared his throat and snapped me back to reality.

After the alms ceremony, the monks proceeded to a private sanctuary for reflection while the guests were shown around the grounds and the protocols were reviewed again. Finally, we entered the temple where breakfast would be served. Now starving, my mouth watered at the thought of all the delicious treats I had selected. I imagined the monks praising my fine shopping skills, diving into the beautiful pastries, and raving about how it was the best breakfast ever.

I snapped out of my daydream to find the monks already seated on bamboo mats, soles away from the Buddha, beginning to eat breakfast. The arrangement made it clear there was no room for me. It seemed my fellow guests and I would enjoy a separate breakfast, not directly with the monks, but rather in their presence, sort of looking at them. Conversation did not appear to be an option.

Slightly disappointed but somewhat relieved to avoid the inevitable awkwardness around my new crush, I took a tin tray from the makeshift buffet line and surveyed the options. Seeing none of my carefully selected delectable pastries, and not much that I recognized in general, I paired my overall love of food and, in theory, adventure with my breakfast selections. I opted for a balance of identifiable rice and corn combined with some exotic fruits and a mysterious sweet confection.

I carried my tray to a chair, undoubtedly there to ensure Westerners' soles remained inoffensively positioned, and sat down, preparing to absorb serenity through osmosis while sampling new culinary treats. Everything went well until the sweet.

Then, it happened. One little bite of this biscuit led to a humiliating incident that will forever haunt me, an incident that united this peaceful religion over a common enemy. Imagine thinking that you are taking a delicious nibble of a cookie. Your taste buds are searching for some chocolate or maybe a fruit filling but instead they find a gelatinous mixture of sea salt, corn, curry, coconut, basil and maybe cilantro. Sounds repulsive? Well, it was.

It was so vile that I immediately and reflexively began to gag. I frantically tried to swallow it down, just to get it over with, but that only made it worse. While willing myself to swallow what my body clearly wanted to reject, I could see my friend slowly trying to distance himself from me and realized that I was perhaps more conspicuous than I thought.

A monastery in the middle of nowhere is a quiet place. The more I tried to be discreet, the more I gagged, and the louder it became, amplified over the din of nothing. By now, my face was bright red with tears streaming down, and amidst the violent retching noises, a strange huffing noise escaped me.

The peak humiliation came when I looked up to find a line of monks staring at me. Eye contact was inevitable. Fortunately, my cute crush was desperately trying to avoid looking at me, no doubt regretting that grin he bestowed on me earlier. Almost in a synchronized fashion, the line of monks broke their gazes with me and looked to their head brother for guidance. The horrified leader just death-stared me while no doubt calculating just how close his temple floor was to being covered in vomit.

Realizing there was no way I could keep the food down, I resolved to expel it with as much grace as possible. So, in a very ladylike fashion, I regurgitated my food onto the simple tin tray under the watchful eyes of a room of monks and covered it with a napkin.

I sat up and tried to act like nothing had happened while sussing out the situation. My friend had managed to scoot quite far away and was no doubt in search of new friends. The cute monk remained very fixated on his breakfast; it was clear no more smiles would be coming my way. The other monks had a look of abject disgust on their faces and quite clearly were regretting the concept of "breakfast with tourists."

I came no closer to inner peace that day.

— Amy Leah Potter —

66

The Bra Incident

Everything is funny as long as it is
happening to someone else.
~Will Rogers

Back in the earlier days of my four-decade-long career as a physiotherapist, I decided to try my hand at teaching a few post-graduate courses. I'd always been passionate about my specialization — manual therapy — so it seemed like a logical decision to teach in this area.

Passionate or not, I was also quiet and shy, a true introvert. The thought of standing in front of a room full of what were basically my peers — men and women the same age or older than myself, and all practising physiotherapists — was enough to make my knees weak and my stomach roil.

But because these courses were taught on weekends, which allowed me to work full-time during the week, and they paid very well, I was determined to try.

The first few classes went okay. I had great teaching partners, and the students gave us fantastic reviews.

And then… the course that almost ended my teaching career.

This weekend course was about manual therapy techniques for the upper extremity joints. My partner and I had divided up the material between the two of us. On our first day, I taught the anatomy and treatment techniques for the elbow joint. My partner was the model. The next day, my partner would do the same for the shoulder joint, and I would be her model.

There's something you need to understand about physiotherapists. We are perfectly comfortable standing around in our underwear, conversing with one another as if there is nothing strange about our state of undress. Male, female, young and old alike, it doesn't matter one iota to us.

During one particular course, this created a bit of confusion. The workshop was held in a hotel conference room. Plinths (treatment tables) were set up in one corner of the room, with an accordion door separating this area from where we would have our lunch, which was provided by the hotel.

During the morning session, I couldn't help but notice curious staff peeking around the corner of the door, eyes wide with apparent shock at our state of undress. At lunch, I took a seat at a table and was about to stuff my face when one of the young women serving us leaned over and asked, "Excuse me, but what exactly are you people?" I still regret not giving her a more interesting answer.

Okay, now that you understand physiotherapists' lack of modesty, let me take you back to that classroom where I'm about to be the model.

Oh, I should probably mention that the day before, because I knew I'd be stripping down to my bra in front of all those folks, I went shopping. I mean, if they were all going to see my bra, it had better be a nice one, right?

So, I bought a bright purple number with lovely, lacy straps. It was quite wonderful and very uplifting — if you get my drift. Perhaps a little too uplifting...

Facing the class, which consisted of thirty-five men and women — my peers — I started to pull off my shirt. Reaching my arms over my head to tug off my sweater created a rather unexpected, not to mention unwanted, reaction. My bra decided to join my sweater in its upward trajectory. (Not enough matter to keep it down, you see.) And not only did the bra get stuck where it did not belong, but so did my arms. They tangled in my sweater, making it impossible to grab my bra and pull it back down.

I spun away from the students, cheeks flaming, although, with my head stuck inside my sweater, I'm sure no one could see this physical evidence of my mortification. I frantically attempted to disengage my arms so I could rearrange my bits. My teaching partner was laughing so hard she couldn't speak. And me? I wanted to dig a hole in the floor and disappear forever.

Unfortunately, we still had two more days of teaching to get through.

I'm pretty sure I didn't make eye contact with a single person during those next two days. I did get some interesting reviews, though, including great "coverage" of the material. (And, yes, those quotation marks were part of the comment.)

From that day on, I never again wore a brand-new bra when teaching, and I always, always, always turned away from the class when disrobing.

— Leslie Wibberley —

Great Expectations

If people did not sometimes do silly things, nothing
intelligent would ever get done.
~Ludwig Wittgenstein

t was going to be a special night. Six of us were gathered on the beach, waiting in the dark for the couple to walk by.

We had champagne and cups; we had snacks and chairs; we were prepared.

We sat, strategically placed to take their picture as Daniel walked Ana down the beach by the shore, where he had written in the sand, "Will you marry me?"

We watched the scene unfold exactly as planned and cheered for them. Ana was completely surprised that we were there, beaming in the way a newly engaged woman does with her brand-new ring.

"Congratulations!" Dawna said.

"We're so happy for you," Mason told them.

"Were you expecting it?" my husband Kevin asked Ana.

"No, just chubby," she replied.

We had five solid seconds of just ocean sounds until we realized what she had heard.

We were still invited to the wedding.

— Amber Lynn Dykstra —

68

Ms. Glam No More

Mistakes are a fact of life. It is the response
to error that counts.
~Nikki Giovanni

It was a hot July day in Dallas, Texas. We were going to a high-school baseball game with my husband Larry's new boss whose teenage son was the pitcher. Needless to say, the Boss Man was extremely proud of his boy.

A group of Larry's new employees was also attending the game. I had never met any of them before.

Larry and I had dressed appropriately — he in a T-shirt and shorts, and I in cool capri pants with a simple but elegant, white cotton blouse.

I had always taken good care with my appearance. In those days, my friends used to call me Ms. Glam.

At that time in my youth, I didn't go anywhere without lipstick, foundation, mascara, eye liner and, yes, some very subtle false eyelashes. And a soft pink blush on my cheeks. Not that I needed any pink that day. The heat was enough to keep my cheeks bright red.

Of course, my hair had been styled to perfection... or so I thought. A bit of hair spray would keep the humidity in check.

As the day progressed, the humidity and the temperature were rising. We took plenty of drinking water to keep us hydrated.

Men! They don't care how hot they get, especially when observing players on a field hitting a ball and running around like crazy! Larry and most of the men had perspiration running down their faces before the first inning even started. It didn't seem to bother them a bit.

Outside sports were not my thing, but I took it all in stride. After all, a woman is supposed to suffer for the man she loves, right? That's what my mom had taught me.

I'm only joking. Not *my* mom.

But making the best of the situation, I took a paper napkin, poured some cold water from my cup on it, squeezed out the moisture, and placed it on the back of my neck. It felt good, but only for a few moments.

I didn't want to put the napkin directly on my face. It might ruin my meticulously applied makeup. I was also careful not to get it on my hair, which I had colored the night before. I used a well-known product that produced a lovely result, darker than my natural shade. Almost black. Dramatic. Even my husband declared: "Eva, your hair is stunning!"

I had given it a color lift, hiding the few gray strands that were beginning to appear. Miss Glam couldn't be seen with gray, right?

With the heat getting more intense, I continued to dab at my face using Kleenex whenever I'd feel the perspiration starting to drip down. No sooner had I wiped it when more sweat started dripping until it felt like hot, pouring rain.

The new boss's wife handed me her two-year-old boy, who seemed to take a liking to me. I sat him on my lap, and he giggled and wiggled all over me as we watched the game together. Just what I needed in that heat… not!

Our team scored, and everyone cheered. The toddler echoed the cheers with his "Yay!" Larry, also excited, turned to me to give me a high-five and exclaimed, "Wow!"

I proudly assumed he was going to compliment me on my beautiful hair and makeup again. But this time, his baffled expression made me wonder if he was feeling ill.

"Honey, are you okay?" I asked.

He exclaimed, in a loud enough voice to attract the crowd around us, "I'm fine. But what's wrong with you? What's that black stuff on your face? And is that a bug?"

"Eva," he continued with alarm, "you have a black bug crawling down your cheek!"

The toddler in my lap turned to look at the monster he was sitting on and let out a piercing scream, "Arrrrrrgghhh! Mommy!" followed by pathetic tears of panic and fright. Then, he proceeded to wet himself. And me.

Appalled, I took out my mirror to see what the youngster and my husband — and by now half the spectators at the game — were witnessing. Black drops were dripping down my face. One of my false eyelashes had become loose and was crawling slowly down my cheek, hence the bug.

The semi-permanent hair dye I had used to tint my hair the previous night had turned to black liquid trickling down and onto my crisp, white blouse. I knew it hadn't been permanent dye, but it was supposed to last a couple of weeks at least. Maybe nothing could withstand the smoldering July afternoon in the Texas sun, but Miss L'Oréal Semi-Perm, could you not hang in there with me for even one day?

—Eva Carter—

69

Terrible Timing

*Sometimes we're a three-ring circus, but I
wouldn't trade my family for the world.*
~Author Unknown

That Sunday, like most Sundays, my husband, high-school son, and I sat in our usual pew in church listening to our pastor. I sat between them. The sun shone through the window next to our pew, and I could see a bird making a nest outside the window.

The church my family attends has a small congregation and meets in an old building on the outskirts of the downtown area of a medium-sized city. The old building is in need of repairs. Slowly, as finances allowed, the church had been working on it bit by bit.

That morning, about two-thirds of the way through our pastor's sermon, my son Ty leaned into me and whispered, "I need to go to the bathroom." I nodded my head and motioned my okay for him to go. He slid out of the pew on his side and made his way quietly out of the sanctuary to the bathrooms on the floor below us. The church only had three small, old bathrooms, each with only one toilet in it, and all on the first floor.

Ty was gone for a very long time.

Finally, Ty returned to our pew just as the service was about to end. He slid in next to me, leaned into me again and whispered, "Does our church have a plunger?"

I turned my head to look at him, and he lowered his head and nodded it in a mock shamed look that acknowledged what I assumed by his question. I didn't know the answer, but I thought his father might since he was one of the lay elders in the church. So, as the pastor was offering a departing blessing to everyone, I leaned into my husband sitting on the other side of me and whispered, "Ty wants to know if our church has a plunger. Do you know?"

My husband leaned forward and looked past me at Ty. By this time, Ty was a bit amused, obviously suppressing a smile while again nodding to his dad in acknowledgment of what we all now knew was the condition of the toilet he had just used. It had gotten stopped up when he tried to flush it and was in danger of overflowing. My husband stretched toward Ty, moving his body past me and whispered, "I don't know, but I'll ask Pastor Mark when church is over."

At that very moment, Pastor Mark finished his parting blessing, and the people started standing up from their seats to head home. Then, the pastor remembered something and exclaimed, "Wait! I have one announcement I forgot to mention earlier." Everyone stopped where they were and turned their attention back to the pastor.

He walked back to the podium from the steps where he had been and said loudly and clearly into the microphone, "I meant to publicly thank the Johnsons in our congregation for the work they did this past week on our bathrooms. They spent many hours during their vacation time sprucing up our bathrooms. They scrubbed them thoroughly, applied fresh paint on the walls, and switched out some of the old fixtures for new ones. Let's all give them a hand of applause to show our gratitude."

The congregation all clapped for the Johnsons. When the clapping subsided, Pastor Mark added one more parting word when he said, "And be sure to stick your heads in the bathrooms downstairs before you go and see how nice they are!"

I have been attending church for as long as I can remember, and I have never laughed out loud in church in my life. I didn't that time either, but it took all the self-control I had in me to keep from doing it. I looked over at my husband and then at Ty, and I could tell they were about to burst out laughing, too. Thank goodness church was then officially over because we all did end up laughing uncontrollably.

My husband told Ty to go ask the pastor about a plunger as quickly as he could. Ty did so, only to find out that the church did not have a plunger. Pastor Mark said he would purchase one and make sure he had the problem fixed by the next Sunday. The three of us slipped out the back door of the church to escape to our car.

— Harriet E. Michael —

70

The Girdle

Style is something each of us already has,
all we need to do is find it.
~Diane von Furstenberg

The wedding invitation that my husband Jeff and I had been anticipating arrived, so we arranged our travel plans. I was already overwhelmed by the beauty and size of the event. Then, Jeff began naming a few of the Major League Baseball players who made up the wedding party. As he rattled off their stats, my intimidation grew.

The fact that the wedding guests would be young, vibrant, and beautiful sent me to my closet to confirm what I already knew. I lacked an appropriate dress for an occasion of this magnitude, so I turned to the power of the mouse for rescue. I found a beautiful liquid knit dress in my chosen color, mid-calf length, and a pair of shoes that coordinated perfectly. With a few clicks, I had my ensemble on its way.

When the packages arrived, I tried everything on, including the jewelry that Jeff gave me to complete my look. My reflection in the mirror was just what I hoped for... until I turned around.

The rear view looked as though I'd laid the dress across a riverbed of small pebbles. I faced my new reality with bravery and embraced the idea of a girdle. Back at my computer, I remembered the day my mother handed me my first training bra. I chuckled at my maturity, and "click," my first girdle was on its way.

When it arrived, I slithered into the fabric as it enveloped each curve, giving me the smooth appearance it was meant to. I layered the liquid knit dress over it and promenaded back to the mirror. My confidence grew when I examined the rear view from all possible angles. I called my husband for confirmation and spun a few times for him.

"How do I look?"

"Nice!"

We were set. Shopping for the trip was finished. Soon, we packed and traveled to our hometown, excited to see the entire family under one roof.

I dressed with a little spunk on the day of the wedding, knowing my worst side would be smooth as spandex. When my husband and I completed our finishing touches, I took a few steps toward the door and felt the girdle shift. I adjusted accordingly, and we left the hotel room. Seated in the car, I tugged the girdle in place. When we arrived at the extravagant venue, I exited the car and found privacy between parked vehicles, reached under my dress, and yanked the girdle in place again. The short walk to the entrance looked like a mile as I feared every step would unleash the squirmy beast. It constricted the length of my steps to four for every one of Jeff's strides.

He took my hand and said, "You'll get used to it, and everything will be fine."

Inside the grand event center, my girdle shuffle was camouflaged in the crowd of hundreds. I settled into my chair and did my best impression of a mannequin throughout the lavish wedding. As we moved to the reception area, my girdle and I learned to work together. For the first time that evening, I began to relax, and the girdle seemed to be under my control — just like Jeff promised it would.

He suggested we dance.

I hesitated but then told him, "Sure, I'll just go in the ladies' room afterward and make adjustments."

With the first move on the dance floor, though, that girdle snapped like a slingshot and rolled into a horizontal rubber band. Under the beautiful liquid knit dress that revealed every rough patch now sat a jelly roll around my waist, inches thick. And everything I was trying to hide by wearing the darn thing was exposed. My panicked expression stopped Jeff in mid-motion. I declared, "I must go to the ladies' room. Now!" And then I ran for sanctuary.

What do you find at the entrance to every ladies' room? A line. That is where I stood sideways, with my back against the wall and my arms awkwardly around my waist. I had plenty of time to wonder if my husband's laughter on the dance floor was being mistaken for a new dance craze.

Once I made it through the line and inside a stall, my dress came off, and then the girdle. With my dress back on, I stood with the girdle in my hands. I wasn't free yet. I folded it. I wadded it. I turned circles looking for a place to put it. I considered handing it to the towel attendant outside. Then, I pondered the idea of tossing it over the top of the door like a bouquet toward the single ladies waiting in line. After all, it was a wedding. Finally, I decided I had only one choice. I stuffed it and departed the sophisticated stall, leaving the mini trashcan overflowing with girdle.

I headed back to the dance floor a free woman. We never mentioned it again while we danced the night away.

— Tracie Lobstein —

71

Chicken Soup for the Soul

Southern Exposure

I'm sorry you find communicating so difficult.
Next time I'll read your mind.
~Author Unknown

After my new husband and I arrived in Florida for a summer vacation we were anxious to take advantage of the refreshing outdoor pool. Before leaving our hotel room, we donned our bathing suits and cover-ups, readying ourselves for a little swimming after a quick meal.

Dinner was perfect, we felt rejuvenated, and headed outside. Poolside, we found two lounge chairs next to each other. As it was the dinner hour, the pool wasn't crowded.

Before the trip, I had purchased a beautiful, flower-patterned, stretchy bikini stitched in such a way that the material looked puckered. That was the style of many blouses, and I was elated to find it in a bathing suit.

Having never worn the suit before, I had no idea how well it would hold up once it was wet, but it was sold as a bathing suit, so why should I think twice about it?

The one blouse I had made of that material became heavy when wet and needed to be wrung out. It made sense the bathing suit would do the same, but it never occurred to me at that time.

I jumped into the pool and began swimming back and forth. My husband was more of a dunker than a swimmer and decided to sit at the edge of the pool with his feet in the water.

I glanced over at him a few times, still sitting there with a drink in his hand, watching me swim past. Collecting the little umbrellas out of the drinks made him happier than jumping into the water.

At some point, I got tired of swimming, turned around, and started floating with little backstrokes here and there. The water was a perfect temperature, the air was warm and humid, and the sun was going down. It was a lovely first night.

As I was keeping myself afloat, I noticed my husband standing up, probably preparing to walk over to the stand to buy us more drinks, or maybe he was even hot enough to jump in.

Instead of heading for the refreshment stand, he stood at the edge of the pool and started waving at me. *How cute he is!* I thought to myself, waving back.

Then, he waved again, so I waved back, too.

Isn't that sweet? He can't keep his eyes off me. What a perfect gentleman I married! He is so generous, always planning these amazing trips for us and concerned for my wellbeing.

Now, he's just being silly. He's waving both arms at me frantically as if there's a shark in the water or something.

Still floating on my back, I gave him a "What the heck?" sign with my hands. He started pointing at his chest, then pointing at me.

Is he using some kind of sign language? What is he trying to tell me? Maybe we haven't been married long enough for me to know his hand signals because, whatever he's trying to tell me, I have no clue. What an odd thing to do. Why doesn't he just yell over to me instead of looking like he's landing an airplane?

Still floating on my back, I gave him the Italian "Hey, what's up?" sign with my right hand. You know the one: palm up, tips of your fingers touching, and a firm shake of the arm.

What's wrong with him? Now, he's very demonstrably pointing at his chest, then at me, then at his chest, then back at me. Why is he pointing at his chest, or is he pointing to my chest? And why is some guy standing at the edge of the pool staring at me with a grin on his face?

It finally dawned on me to look down, and there it was: my right breast, out of my bathing suit, floating above my chest for all to see.

And this guy was enjoying every minute of it!

Yep, my husband was pointing to my chest alright. How embarrassing!

The bathing suit I bought — my beautiful, new, pucker-style bikini — became so heavy that it had slipped right off me.

As I pulled it back on, I realized the material had become water-logged and was not very practical for its intended purpose. Who knew? Well, I should have remembered what happened to the blouse when I washed it, but I didn't.

I did wonder how many other women bought that bikini and what their story was.

My new bathing suit was thrown out that night. I was lucky to have brought my old one with me on the trip.

The embarrassment stayed with me for the rest of that trip and far beyond.

The picture of my husband standing at the side of the pool, waving at me, is an image I'll never forget, any more than the image he probably has of my floating breast — baring itself to an unintended but seemingly pleased audience!

— Vera-Marie Landi —

I Kid You Not

72

One Funny-Looking Chip

How do people make it through life without a sister?
~Sara Corpening Whiteford

As a homeschooling, stay-at-home mother of six, my mom had to come up with creative ways to earn money to make ends meet. She was the one who had to make birthdays and Christmas happen.

My mom came up with the creative idea of entering sweepstakes. She would start her day at 4:00 a.m. because that was her lucky time to enter instant-win sweepstakes. She sent in thousands of sweepstake entries every month.

It worked. She won things we needed: a grocery-store shopping spree, a kitchen-supplies gift card for hundreds of dollars where we traded in our Goodwill cookware for Le Creuset Dutch ovens and pots, as well as getting a KitchenAid mixer and food processor, all of which I still use in my own kitchen fifteen years later. We got bikes for Christmas, mini fridges and TVs for our bedrooms, new iPods and handheld gaming platforms. What prizes we couldn't use, we sold, and then used that money for groceries or little extras that we couldn't afford otherwise.

We went from no money for anything outside of bills to having enough money and merchandise for wonderful holidays.

There was no better sound than the jingle of our driveway alarm system announcing that UPS or FedEx had arrived with a new surprise. My siblings and I affectionately called our DHL man, who just so happened to have a long, white beard, Santa Claus. The UPS guy knew our dog by name and always brought her an extra treat. He later mourned with us when she passed away.

I knew at the age of fourteen how to fill out an affidavit. My younger siblings would spend art class decorating envelopes with crayons. They'd do self-portraits, sun and flowers, and all kinds of eye-catching designs for my mother's written essays and sweepstakes cards to go in. I listened to the radio all day, just to tell my mom exactly when to call in to win their daily contests. The radio hosts knew her well and sometimes even gave her extra tries. Although she could call in right on time, she was awful at the games they put her through. Still, I went to many concerts as a teen, and all of them were free.

It meant my mom worked for hours, though, searching for sweepstakes to enter and keeping track of everything in her notebooks. She had blocks of time where we all knew that Mom was busy and couldn't be interrupted, like it was an actual job.

One day, though, my four younger siblings helped themselves to an approved snack during my mom's sweepstakes time. My five-year-old sister walked into my mom's office, waving a chip in her hand.

"Mom, my chip looks funny. Should I still eat it?"

My siblings were always very fussy eaters. If anything was slightly discolored or differently shaped, they wouldn't eat it. My mom, in the middle of writing an essay for a contest, waved her off without a glance.

"This is my busy time. I'm sure it's fine. Just eat the chip," she answered, continuing to type.

"But it looks funny. Look!"

My mom was good at essay ideas, but if she stopped the flow of writing, the idea tended to evaporate from her mind forever. She waved off my sister with an assurance that it was okay to eat.

My sister ate the chip.

At dinner that night, my sister pointed to the chip container. It showed a photo of the sweepstakes they were running. To be the lucky grand-prize winner of thousands of dollars' worth of amazing prizes, you had to find the one barbeque-grill-stamped chip they released. Even though my mom loved sweepstakes, the chances of this were so rare that it wasn't even on her radar.

With my sister's finger on the image of that winning chip, she said, "Look, Mommy, that's what the funny chip looked like that I ate today!"

My mom was never so dismissive about a funny-looking piece of food again.

My sister is now in her twenties, and she has yet to live down the day she ate thousands of dollars' worth of summer prizes and cash. Gathered around family, my mom will still laugh about the time she was so busy entering sweepstakes that she lost an even bigger prize right next to her! It's now one of the favorite laugh-until-we-cry stories we share at family functions.

— Jill Keller —

73

The Flying Tomato

Laughter is the shortest distance between two people.
~Victor Borge

The first time my husband and I lived on Canada's west coast, one of our favorite destinations for weekend skiing was the Mount Baker ski resort in Washington State, just south of the Canada/USA Peace Arch Border Crossing. After skiing on Mount Baker, we would stop for dinner at the Black Angus Steakhouse in Bellingham before crossing back over the border to head home to Vancouver. When my husband took a new job that required moving to another city we had one final romantic dinner there, and it was a memory that I treasured.

Eight years later we returned to Vancouver for a holiday with our three-year-old son and seven-year-old daughter. After spending a day visiting Pike Place Market in Seattle, we stopped for dinner at the Black Angus Steakhouse in Bellingham on our way back to Vancouver. The restaurant was as special as we remembered, still a great place for a romantic dinner. As it turned out, it was fine for children too, and we ordered a veggie appetizer plate from the children's menu.

At one point, I looked over at another table and noticed a younger-looking couple deep in conversation. The young man reached over for his girlfriend's left hand. I smiled to myself when he kissed the top of her hand, charmed by his intimate gesture.

The veggie plate arrived just then, and our three-year-old tried to stab a cherry tomato with his fork. The tomato flew up into the air in a perfect arc, headed to the young man's plate. By then, he had a ring in his hand and was proposing to his girlfriend. I locked eyes with the young man and mouthed, "Sorry," while his girlfriend dissolved into laughter after the tomato plopped onto his plate. Thankfully, it didn't take long for her boyfriend to erupt into laughter, too.

It's often said that restaurant memories feel so nostalgic not only because of the context of when, where and who you were eating with, but because of the occasion being celebrated. The memory of our previous romantic dinner at the Black Angus Steakhouse after a ski day at Mount Baker years ago had just been superseded by an evening with our children and a flying tomato. And I'm sure the flying tomato became an important part of that young couple's "proposal story" as well.

— Kathy Dickie —

74

Hotels Where You Can't Do Anything

I brought children into this dark world because it needed the light that only a child can bring.
~Liz Armbruster

With a six-year-old son on the autism spectrum who struggled to adapt to new situations, my wife and I spent a long time discussing how we could make a family vacation work. Perhaps it would work if we started small. Maybe the zoo. Maybe Myrtle Beach. Both were a bit over three hours away. If we needed to cut our time short, those destinations were close enough to home to be manageable.

Tonia and I presented some options, and Brandon chose Myrtle Beach without hesitation. Auntie Kim had recently visited there, and his favorite YouTube character, Handyman Hal, filmed in that area. It would be new but also familiar.

When we talked about the area, Brandon asked what we could do there. I told him about the activities I thought he would like: the beach, Ripley's Aquarium, mini-golf, and the huge SkyWheel that Handyman Hal rode on. Brandon was excited about all the options.

Brandon asked if Mom would go on the SkyWheel with us. She hesitated before agreeing very reluctantly. I explained that Mom is afraid of heights, so he would have to hold her hand and be brave for her.

"I'm not afraid of heights very much," he informed us.

"Oh, good!" Tonia replied.

"But," he added, "I don't know if I like them. So, how about no SkyWheel?"

"I thought you wanted to do the SkyWheel, just like Handyman Hal," I replied. "You don't want to do it anymore?"

"No. I just don't want to very much," he confirmed. "Do I have to do things there?"

"If you want to do things, you can," I told him. "If you don't want to, you don't have to."

"Okay, good," he replied. "I don't want to. Can you look up hotels where you can't do anything?"

We tried explaining that there were all sorts of activities in the area. Some of them could be at the hotel while others would be outside the hotel. Regardless of where the activities were, we could pick what we wanted to do and skip the things we didn't want to do.

"I just, I don't want to do anything. So, that's what I picked. I'm just not gonna do anything," he informed us.

"Okay, that's fine," Tonia reassured him. "What are we going to do at the hotel if we don't do any activities?"

"We'll eat breakfast and dinner, for sure. So, that's what we'll do. We're going to need pajamas. You should probably bring my toothbrush."

Tonia started looking up hotels with him. They found a really nice one that was probably outside of our budget, but that wasn't going to be an issue because there was way too much to do there. We needed to find someplace else.

"Hmm," Brandon pondered. "Can you look up other hotels? Like hotels where you can't do anything? Because that's what I picked."

I had stepped out for part of the evening to go to the movies. When I got home, Tonia told me she spent hours planning our vacation with Brandon.

"It shouldn't have taken that long," I joked. "It's not like you had to plan any activities."

Apparently, it took a great deal of time to find a hotel where there is nothing to do. They settled on the DoubleTree, even though there was a pool and a restaurant. The following day, Brandon and I were leaving the local grocery store when he spotted a large building across the street.

"Is that a hotel, Dad?" he asked.

"Yeah, bud," I replied. "That's a hotel."

"What kind of things can you do there?" he inquired.

Being jaded with the area, I gave a sarcastic answer. "Bud, there's probably nothing to do there at all. There's nothing to do anywhere around here."

"Hmm," Brandon thought aloud. "Maybe we should just go to that one then."

— Elton A. Dean —

75

Teen Talk

Once you sign on to be a mother,
24/7 is the only shift they offer.
~Jodi Picoult

"The power washer is on fire," my daughter yelled as soon as I picked up the phone.

"Actual fire?" I asked, not missing a beat and continuing to shuffle through the stack of papers on my desk. I get a lot of these calls, so I usually like to assess the seriousness before fully committing to the conversation.

"Flames are shooting out," she said.

I put down my papers to focus on the fire conversation. "Maybe 911 would have been a better option," I said.

"Not helpful!" she wailed.

This was just the most recent in a series of calls from my older daughter. They always go like this. No greeting. No "How are you?" Just a blunt, matter-of-fact statement that requires some type of immediate action (and usually obscure specialized knowledge) on my part.

Things were supposed to get easier as she got older. I knew this because I saw my life flash before my eyes during her inaugural drive on the highway when she was working toward her license. The part I saw about her adulthood looked deceivingly calm.

These days, my brain needs to retain an exorbitant amount of information. At any given moment, I'm expected to know the capital of Tanzania, her Social Security number, her dad's Social Security number, what carry-on luggage is allowed to weigh for an international flight, the secret ingredient in Great-Grandma's spaghetti sauce, the latest tax code, how to launder a cashmere sweater (you don't), and what happens when there is no oil in your car (something really bad).

Since I clearly had failed with her, I pinned my hopes on her younger sister. She seemed to be successfully balancing an internship and her summer job. Well, at first, anyway.

"You don't understand," she said, flopping down on the couch about two weeks into summer. "I work ten-hour days. It is exhausting." The word "exhausting" was drawn out like it was taking every last ounce of energy for her to utter the word.

I had to clap my hand over my mouth to stifle the laugh that wanted to burst out. "You're right," I said. "I have no idea what it's like working full-time and then carpooling kids to soccer, basketball and cross-country practice or to cello and violin lessons, making lunches, washing uniforms, volunteering for class parties, grocery shopping, cleaning the house, cooking dinner and making Halloween costumes."

She stared back at me, thoroughly unimpressed. "Work was the only time I actually sat down," I continued. I didn't add this part, but I'm pretty sure I slept for a total of sixteen hours during a six-year period.

At this point, she was fast asleep on the couch.

My phone pinged with an incoming text from her sister. If I did not respond within 3.4 seconds of hearing the ding, I would be bombarded with follow-up texts until I answered.

If I texted, though, it would go something like this.

Me: How many hours are you working on Saturday, and how many vacation days do you get?

Four days later, this would be the response: "Yes."

The thing is, we all know that I am absolutely not the best person to handle most of these situations. I realize that both girls are on the cusp of greatness, teetering on the edge between childhood and adulthood. And that is exactly why I continue to answer my phone. I'm not ready to let them go, and I like to think that they're not ready to let me go either.

My phone rings. It's my older daughter. I am equal parts thrilled and terrified. Taking a deep breath to prepare myself, I answer, "What's wrong?"

"What? Nothing. I just wanted to say hi and tell you about my day."

There's hope.

— SJ Fellenstein —

76

Animal Kingdom

Laughter is poison to fear.
~George R.R. Martin

My friend Kim called to tell me she'd secured One Direction tickets for her daughter Claire and for Claire's friend, Emily. The concert venue was close to me, and there were lots of late-night cafes where Kim and I could hang out and catch up, so she was wondering if they could spend the night with me. The only fly in the ointment was that I'd already promised my friend Pam (who lived even closer to the venue) that I'd pet-sit for her. Pam was fine with it, so we made our plans. The four of us would stay at Pam's house with her two cats.

Pam lived in a suburb that seemed more like a rural area. I always felt like the huntsman from *Snow White* when I drove up her very long and steep gravel driveway. It's edged on both sides by trees that slope toward the center of the pathway. When driving through this forested tunnel at nighttime, I swear I can see pairs of eyes watching me.

Kim wasn't a nature girl; she thought glamping in luxurious yurts where room service was provided was "roughing it," so I didn't tell her about the time I had to gently coax a rattlesnake off the driveway. It had been sunning itself and didn't appreciate the interruption. Nor did I mention the giant rat that had chewed through a window screen so that she could realize her birthing plan of a warm closet stuffed with blankets, where her six tiny pups would begin their life.

When it was time to pick up the girls after the concert, I joked about all the creatures that had probably already snuck in through the pet door. It wasn't like Pam had a dog that would scare off any invaders.

We pulled up to the house, and the girls jumped out of the minivan with their backpacks dangling off their shoulders. Kim and I got out a little more carefully. Our eyes weren't as quick to adjust to the dark. As we walked up to the door, Kim glanced back to remotely lock her car and noticed that the girls had left their door open.

"Mom, I'll go back and close it after I go to the bathroom. My bladder is about to burst."

I unlocked the front door and pointed Claire to the bathroom.

Then Kim, Emily, and I walked into the family room, where we were greeted by a huge raccoon dipping cat kibble into an adjacent water bowl and tasting it before devouring it. Right next to her was a juvenile raccoon copying his mama.

Kim froze, while Emily grabbed my arm. When poor Claire walked into the family room, she screamed. Kim ran out of the house, darkness be damned, and jumped through the minivan's open door, locking it before the girls could climb in with her.

This was a surreal experience because Kim was one of those perfect mothers. So, naturally, I was torn between hysterical laughter and needing to be the responsible one. The girls started crying. I tried to distract them with really cool facts about raccoons like, "Hey, did you guys know that raccoons often score nearly as high as monkeys on intelligence tests? They have more neurons and higher IQs than dogs!"

This was not helpful. Nor was the fact that the raccoons were not leaving. I pointed the girls toward their bedroom while I gently shooed the raccoons out through a sliding door. The coast was clear. Just as we were about to tell Kim that it was safe to come back inside, we heard a scream and an earsplitting car alarm.

We soon learned that when Kim had jumped into the minivan she discovered that an opossum had already climbed in through that open door. It was nestled into one of the newly purchased One Direction T-shirts. With all the screaming, the opossum decided to play dead and not budge from its new nest. In her panic to try and get back out of the minivan, Kim had set off the car alarm.

I turned off the alarm and walked Kim and the girls back into the house. I offered Kim a glass of wine. Then, I grabbed a beach towel and headed toward the car. The little guy was still there. I saw one eyelid flutter open, then quickly shut tight. I gently wrapped a towel around him and lifted him out. I placed him underneath a bush and let him keep the towel. Then, I snatched the One Direction shirts, locked the car, and walked back to the house, hoping I was done playing wildlife safari guide.

Claire hugged me and said, "Oh, you saved our shirts! Thank you! The opossum didn't touch them, did it?"

Kim and I exchanged glances. "I don't think so, but let's wash them just in case."

Kim said, "Are we done with the Wild Animal Planet show tonight? Or should we expect a skunk to stop by?"

"I sincerely hope not," I said. Just then, we spotted movement underneath the couch. All three looked at me like I was about to unleash Cujo on them. I, too, was tense until I saw a familiar set of little, orange paws. Out from under the couch and behind the bookcase came the two resident cats.

The girls sat down on the carpeted floor, and the cats began rubbing against them. They asked if the cats could sleep in their room, and I said, "Yes."

"They'll protect us," Emily said, and Claire nodded in agreement.

I refrained from telling them the fun fact that raccoons are really good at problem-solving. The long fingers on their front paws are perfect for picking locks and opening latches.

— Victoria Lorrekovich-Miller —

Patches and Patience

You can learn many things from children.
How much patience you have, for instance.
~Franklin P. Adams

The woman at the counter held out her hand knowingly and nodded toward a small desk. "You can take Josh over there and have a seat. I'll be right with you, Melissa." I handed over the mangled pair of tiny prescription eyeglasses and steered my three-year-old son to a nearby fitting station. Our visits to the eyeglass store had become so frequent that they knew our entire family by name. Each visit went much the same, with the fitting specialist marveling over how the angelic-looking little boy in front of them could make such a big, twisted mess of his glasses.

Joshua had recently been diagnosed with what is commonly referred to as a "lazy eye." He was given a prescription for glasses designed to strengthen the affected eye. As a rough-and-tumble country boy, Joshua was not happy about having to wear glasses. Trying to keep them on my little guy had become a constant fight, but nothing compared to the battle waged over the adhesive eye patch he was required to simultaneously wear over his "good eye."

"Joshua, what did you do with your patch?" I would ask daily as I adjusted his crooked glasses on the bridge of his nose. Josh always seemed to conveniently forget, but I found them everywhere: stuck inside my car's center console, attached to the back side of his bedframe, and even glued to the windshield of our farm's tractor. But the place

I most dreaded finding them was in the pockets of his jeans after removing them from the dryer. The melted adhesive caused quite the sticky mess!

One Sunday morning, as we prepared for church, I placed Joshua's patch securely over his eye as I gave him the obligatory "be good at church and don't mess with your glasses" speech. It was a pep talk of sorts, one which I made sure to reiterate on the car drive there, and again just before we walked into the building.

Things seemed to be going well as the church service progressed. Joshua kept himself busy by drawing on the back of my bulletin and did not bother with his glasses one single time. I must have delivered that pep talk with a little added fervor for it to have worked so well, I reasoned. I was feeling quite proud of myself as Josh left his seat to go forward for the children's sermon.

Joshua half-walked, half-ran up the aisle before plopping himself down next to the pastor. The large altar, adorned with seasonal linens, loomed directly behind the seated children. Above it, an even larger cross hung on the wall. It was always a sweet sight to see the children gathered for their very own sermon.

I took the opportunity to browse the bulletin, and before I knew it, Josh had returned to our pew. I looked up at him and let out a deep sigh. Joshua held his glasses in his hand as he climbed into his seat, sans eye patch.

"Where's your patch?" I whispered to my son. My three-year-old shrugged his shoulders, feigning ignorance.

"Put on your glasses right now and don't take them off again," I said in the best "mad-mom voice" I could muster without being heard by the people sitting in front of us. I made a mental note to check his pants pockets before throwing them in the wash when we got home. I was in no mood to clean adhesive from my freshly laundered clothing that afternoon.

I turned my attention to the cross at the front of the church. I said a quick prayer, asking for patience and grace to handle the situation with Joshua. Just as I uttered "Amen," something just below the cross caught my attention. I immediately sat up straighter, leaning forward to get a better view.

"No, no, no," I said to myself as my face flushed. There would be no need to check my son's pockets that day because Joshua's eye patch was plastered to the front of the altar, plain as day for all to see.

I sat in my pew waiting for what seemed to be the longest church service I had ever attended to end. This turned out to be a good thing because it gave me time to devise a plan on how to remove the eye patch undetected.

When the service ended, I waited until the church had largely cleared out. I could see the pastor standing at the door of the foyer as he visited with the last of his parishioners. My mom was one of them, and I knew she liked to talk, so I figured I had plenty of time to make my move. I exited the pew, warning Joshua not to leave his seat, and moved hurriedly toward the large cross.

My plan was simple: take the steps up to the front of the church two or three at a time, rip the adhesive patch from the side of the altar, and retreat as fast as possible to avoid detection. But, of course, that is not how things went.

Once I made it to the altar, I bent down to remove the patch, but it wouldn't budge. I scraped it with my thumb nail and it finally came off, but a gooey, adhesive outline of the patch remained in its place. I decided to cut my losses and retreat.

I stood and turned to make my getaway, only to be stopped in my tracks. Standing there, blocking my only escape route through the open prayer railing, was my pastor with Joshua right at his side.

"I... I... He lost his eye patch, but I found it!" I blurted out as I thrust my hand in the pastor's direction as proof of my claim.

He looked down at Joshua and then up to the altar before his gaze settled back on me. A wide grin spread across his face, and he began to chuckle. "It would appear that someone has been paying attention in church," he said as he placed his hand on Joshua's shoulder. "I may have given a sermon or two about leaving one's burdens at the foot of the cross."

It was now my turn to laugh. As Joshua and I gathered our things to leave, I said one last silent prayer: "Lord, please let next week's children's sermon focus on obeying your parents."

Amen.

— Melissa H.B. Bender —

Best Reason Ever

I am your Mom. Your argument is invalid.
~Author Unknown

It seemed like every summer or holiday break, our son came home with a new one — a new tattoo, that is!

It began with a penguin. Then, a huge skateboard logo that looked like a devil with flames for hair. Then, some Chinese characters that, according to our boy, meant "integrity" and "equality" but probably really meant "5 Crab Rangoon for $6." Then, "Dying 2 Live."

We got worried. Ian seemed determined to get every inch of his skin tatted up.

So, we begged. We told Ian, "A perfect Christmas present would be to just wait a while for the next tattoo," and "Don't get any more tattoos until your frontal lobe is fully developed." We explained that the frontal lobe of the brain helps make rational decisions, and it doesn't finish developing until people are in their mid-twenties. We pleaded, but we wondered, *Would our son's frontal lobe ever mature? Did he even have a frontal lobe?*

The tattoos kept on coming.

One evening after graduating from college, Ian made my husband and me sit down on the couch. We got nervous. What now?

He said, "I want to do something for you because you've done so much for me over the years. You paid for college. When my bank account would get low, you'd put in some money. You sent me care packages full of cookies. I want to show you how grateful I am."

We both breathed out a huge sigh of relief. Maybe he had a homemade card for us or a gift.

He continued, "I want to honor you. I want to get your portrait inked right here, on my chest."

Oh, no! This was too awful to even consider. But what could we say? So far, nothing had slowed down his trips to the tattoo salon.

My husband and I sat there, speechless, until a brilliant idea came to me. I looked directly at him and hissed, "Ian, no girl is gonna wanna have sex with you if your parents are staring at her the whole time."

I'm happy to report that our faces are not on his flesh, and there were no more tattoos after that.

— Sioux Roslawski —

The Concerned Citizen

Laughter gives us distance. It allows us to step back
from an event, deal with it and then move on.
~Bob Newhart

Back in the day, my husband and I, along with our two little girls, would drop into the video store to browse for something new. We would hit the new-release section while our girls, four and five years old at the time, happily scanned the kids' section. With wide eyes, they'd sift through all their favorite doll and puppy DVDs.

We kept an eye on the girls and were cognizant of the different folks perusing the store. All was peaceful and calm as I read the back of a DVD. Suddenly, a small child's voice rang out.

"Your tummy is so big!" she cried.

I imagine I must have looked like a deer caught in the headlights as my eyes shot to my husband's face. He stood just feet from me, his face configured in the same panicked manner. Our younger daughter was the culprit.

"Oh, dear!" I uttered under my breath as I rushed to her.

This four-year-old child held nothing back. If it was in her brain, it came out of her mouth. And she saw everything.

There she stood, in her blue jeans and little red jacket, with tiny blond pigtails and inquisitive blue eyes. Her pointer finger aimed right at the very pregnant belly of a young woman.

I have to say, I was relieved. It would have been even more

awkward if the poor woman had just been a bit on the heavier side. I tried to coax my child away from this mother-to-be quietly, but she stubbornly pointed at the protruding belly and announced again, for the whole world to hear, "Momma, her tummy is so big!"

The woman appeared to be quite young. This was more than likely her first pregnancy. She stood there, seemingly stunned, gazing down at this small person pointing at her tummy. She didn't crack a smile or anything. The same can't be said for the man accompanying her. Bent over at the waist with his hand covering his mouth, he tried controlling his laughter.

It was time for a teaching moment, then a quick exit.

"Well, honey, see here?" I made a small gesture. "She has a baby in her tummy," I explained hoping to show I was educating my manner-less little one. At the same time, I was trying to grab her hand and bid the probably traumatized mother-to-be farewell. But, alas, as I noted before, nothing gets past this little, blond bundle of mine.

"Wait... WAIT!" she squawked resoundingly, pulling her hand away from mine. The room went quiet.

With heavy breaths, she questioned, "There's a baby in there?" Her eyes opened wide in utter shock and disbelief as she stared toward the belly right at her eye level.

"Yes, there's a baby in there," I reassured. I noted the man with her turning and walking down the aisle, trying to stifle his laughter. My own husband stood by with a look on his face that said, "I don't know what to do. I got nothing." So, the guys were of no help, and I felt trapped in the middle.

My daughter asked again with extreme urgency, "There's a baby in there?"

"Yes, there is a baby in there," I affirmed while I tried to gently move her along.

She still resisted my lead. With a furrowed brow, she thought quietly for a moment.

Finally, and with pure conviction, she rendered her decision. "You gotta get that baby outta there!"

And, on that note, the man spewed belly laughter while the expectant mother still stood dazed. It was time to head in the opposite direction with my child, who was still exclaiming, "Momma, we gotta get that baby outta there!"

— Carrie Linde —

80

Body of Christ?

The innocence of children is what makes them stand
out as a shining example to the rest of Mankind.
~Kurt Chambers

W e called it Saturday school. All public-school kids (called "publics") who were members of the Catholic religion were required to attend Saturday school to help combat the heathen ways propagated by the state-sanctioned public-school system. If you did not attend Saturday school, there would be consequences.

I never found out the true extent of those consequences, but not being able to partake in the sacraments was a biggie. At age seven, I knew the sacrament of holy communion was right around the corner, so Saturday school took on even greater significance. I dutifully attended, thereby missing the cartoons that were another major educational influence in my early life.

Several nuns from the local Catholic school were in charge of ensuring that we had "sufficient knowledge and careful preparation in order to understand the mystery of Christ according to their capacity, and are able to receive the body of Christ with faith and devotion." This was according to the 1917 *Code of Canon Law*.

Please focus on a key phrase in the above quote: "the body of Christ." This is a phrase that is used repeatedly in the church liturgy and teachings and tossed around with little fanfare. But when studying to receive your First Communion, the concept of partaking in "the

I Kid You Not | 239

body of Christ" is hammered home. (Wine being the "blood of Christ" is for another story.)

At no time did the nuns of Nativity, or my parents, or any other adults or kids for that matter, describe the wafer used in the communion service as a symbol or a metaphor. We were taught in Saturday school that, at the appointed time, a magical, mystical transformation took place in which a wafer of wheat flour and water became the body of Christ. Literally. Christ's body. No one suggested that there was anything figurative about it. No one ever explained that it was supplied by the nuns or the Cavanagh Altar Bread company. It was Christ's body.

So, on the second time taking communion — after the major ceremony and invocation of First Communion — I unceremoniously vomited Christ's body into my mother's handkerchief.

I'm not sure why this didn't happen at the First Communion event, but I guess there was so much pomp and circumstance that I didn't have time to think about what was dissolving in my mouth. Now, I knelt in the pew and felt an almost gelatinous blob forming on my tongue. I assumed this was what flesh tasted like. I had a sliver of Christ's body on my tongue, and I was supposed to chew it or swallow it or something. Obviously, the appropriate course of action for me was to throw up.

For the next week, I badgered my mother about the handkerchief. She couldn't wash it or throw it away. It contained a consecrated "piece" of Christ's body. She assured me that she would take it to the rectory where the priest would know what to do. I wasn't so sure that she would follow through, but what could I do? She then proceeded to explain the true nature of the communion wafer as a symbol.

"But it felt and tasted like flesh," I yelled. Since we were in the local grocery store at the time, the other customers watched with a strange interest and intensity. My mother hustled me out, forgetting to order the salami and braunschweiger we were to have for lunch.

I was gradually able to take communion like everyone else as I undermined all the diligent work the nuns took in convincing me of the mystical wafer transformation. I gained the ability to keep the wafer down, but I lost something innocent and profound in that knowledge:

A purity of belief was shattered. This process of juggling fact with faith continues to this day and is always bittersweet.

— Brad Korbesmeyer —

81

Little Pitchers

Children have never been very good at listening to
their elders, but they have never failed to imitate them.
~James Baldwin

had always wanted to be a wife and mom, so I was thrilled when we had our first child a year after we were married: a beautiful, red-headed baby boy. Several months after our son's arrival, we were reassigned to Davis-Monthan AFB in Tucson, Arizona. There, we were blessed with miracle number two: another beautiful baby boy. He had shocking red hair! It was so red that it was really closer to orange. He was so tiny and so cute!

My two sons! They were adorable. It seemed like every time we went out, someone would comment on their red hair. We were happy with the size of our family and decided not to have more children. A couple of weeks before we made that decision permanent, we found out that our family of four was going to be a family of five. Tell me that God doesn't have a sense of humor! We were not the least bit upset. In fact, we were grateful that God had chosen to bless us with another child.

The first two boys must have gotten all of the red gene. Our new little man was blond. Two redheads and a blond! That was what everybody always said. It actually got irritating after a while, and we started making the comeback of "Yeah, different mailman." I know, I know... bad joke! Looking back now, I wish we had handled things differently.

We ended up moving onto the base, and a couple of doors down was another young mother and her three boys. We became fast friends. Between our daily tasks, we would sit outside and watch the boys play. We were always looking for ways to save money, as an airman's budget is really tight. We came across a grocery store in town that would triple coupons up to a dollar and allow you to use them in conjunction with their in-store coupons. The savings were amazing!

One day, I stopped in the supermarket with my three sons. They were approximately four, two, and six months old at that time. I was the only adult on this excursion but was quite confident in my mothering skills. After all, my boys were usually complimented on their good behavior. What could possibly go wrong?

I don't remember much of anything about the shopping trip, so it must have gone fairly smoothly. That is, until we got up to the checkout. While I was paying, the cashier was admiring my little darlings. I heard her say, "Oh, look! Two redheads and a blond!" My sweet, little four-year-old didn't miss a beat. He put his little hand on his hip, dipped his head while shaking it, and pitifully replied, "Yeah, different mailman."

I was mortified! I couldn't get mad at my son. After all, he was only innocently repeating what he had heard us say over and over again. The cashier was laughing so hard. She told me it was the funniest thing she had ever heard. I thanked her, grabbed my kids and groceries, and hightailed it out the door.

"Little pitchers have big ears" came to life for me that day in a very big but funny way. That cute, little redhead is now a grown man raising two daughters. You can bet he has had his own embarrassments from his "little pitchers." Like me, he has no one to blame but himself!

— Angela L. Stuck —

Chapter 10

Not What I Meant

Seriously Embarrassing

The embarrassment of a situation can, once you are
over it, be the funniest time in your life.
~Miranda Hart

The first time I gave birth was an awful experience. The hospital was overwhelmed with women in labor and not enough rooms to house them. I ended up on a gurney in a storage closet with my doctor missing in action. As my pains grew stronger, I urged my husband to find her so she could give me an epidural. He found a nurse, but then she went MIA, too. Finally, a casually dressed man came in and administered an epidural.

After he left, I asked my husband, "Who was that?"

He said, "I think it was the janitor."

Things went downhill from there.

Since there may be young people out there contemplating becoming parents, and my Social Security checks could hinge on such a decision, I won't go into further details. Let's just say that after my first birthing experience, I decided to switch doctors and hospitals.

I could only find male doctors available, but one clinic offered a choice between two. I asked the receptionist, "Which one would you recommend?"

She said, "It depends on what you want. John is funny and likes to joke, but Mark is serious."

Considering what I had just been through, I said, "I'll go with Mark. I don't want anyone heeing and hawing around when I'm getting examined or giving birth."

Mark turned out to be young like me, but he always carried the air of a more seasoned doctor.

After a couple of years as his patient, I needed to go for my routine exam, but the woman who normally babysat my son, Josiah, backed out at the last minute. I took Josiah with me to the exam, reassuring myself that he was only two years old. Surely, I could distract him during the exam so that he wouldn't see what Mark was doing behind the sheet!

At my appointment time, Mark was running late. He rushed into the exam room, not seeming to even notice Josiah. He asked me some quick questions, and I lay down with Josiah standing near my head.

Mark set up the white sheet over my knees and disappeared behind it.

Immediately, Josiah headed toward him. I caught my young son by one hand and held him back. He tugged me toward Mark, straining to see what was going on behind the sheet.

I needed a diversion for my two-year-old son. I held my free hand over my eyes and called invitingly to him, "Peek-a-boo!"

Even though this game was one of his all-time favorites, Josiah ignored me as I lowered my hand and peeked at him.

I tried a little louder. "Peek-a-boo!"

Still, no response other than another tug toward Mark. Who said two-year-olds are easily distracted? I was struggling to stay in place.

More insistently, I sang out, "Peek-a-boo!"

One of Mark's hands appeared at the top of the sheet, and he slowly lowered the sheet to where he could peek over the top. His voice, tentative and dubious, responded, "I see you?"

My face probably grew as white as the sheet as I realized the quiet doctor thought I was trying to entice him into a game of peek-a-boo. "I'm p-p-playing with my son," I stammered.

He looked down at Josiah, disappeared behind the sheet, and quickly finished his work. He was all business when he reappeared, and no more was said about the game of peek-a-boo, but I think I became a favorite patient of his after that.

He helped me deliver my second son and told me that delivery was one of the easiest he had ever had. He even started joking lightly with me and teasing, "So, when are we having our next child?"

I'm not sure whether he told anyone else in the office about our game of peek-a-boo, but I was glad I had not chosen the funny doctor, John. I'm sure his laughter would have been heard throughout the clinic.

— Ronica Stromberg —

It Means What?

*Everybody laughs the same in every language because
laughter is a universal connection.*
~Jakob Smirnoff

learned to speak Spanish in the Dominican Republic as a Peace Corps volunteer. They give you three months of intense language training, immersion-style. I became fully fluent, never realizing that the Spanish spoken in my village in the DR was different from the Spanish spoken everywhere else. I married a Dominican, and when our family returned to my pre-service home in Southern California, it was surprising to learn our Mexican neighbors often struggled to understand us.

Most of the time, intent was obvious. If the neighbor asked to borrow a tool that happened to be on my husband's truck, I would tell them it was on the *guagua* (the Dominican word for truck, which doesn't exist in Mexican Spanish), and they'd get the gist. The problems happened when the same Spanish word meant two different things in Dominican and Mexican Spanish.

The most ridiculous of these incidents occurred for me with the word *chichi*. In Dominican Spanish, a *chichi* is a small child, a baby usually up to about three years old. It is common practice for Dominican parents to show babies other babies when out and about. You walk down the street, you see another mother holding a baby, and you point to them and say to the baby you are carrying, "Look at that pretty baby!" *[Mira chichi lindo!]* Everyone smiles, and you go on about your day.

In the US, when we'd go out with our baby to the store, see other mothers with babies and point them out, I'd say, "Look at that pretty baby" in English, and everyone would smile. But when my husband did it in Spanish, "*Mira chichi lindo*," people would look at us strangely. I thought this was because he was a man, and that perhaps Mexican men didn't interact with their children in the same way. I later found out it was because *chichi* in Mexican Spanish means breast.

I learned this in the most ridiculous way possible, too. We had gone out of town to visit friends for a few days. When we came home, I realized we were out of milk for the baby. We unloaded the car, and I was going to run to the store to get it before he woke up.

My Mexican neighbor saw me and asked about our trip. I told him, in Spanish, that I couldn't talk right then because my baby [chichi] was out of milk. He looked at me very strangely, and I left. When I got back, his wife was waiting for me. She told me I had made her husband very uncomfortable, and that I shouldn't be talking about my breasts with him!

I had no idea what she was talking about. I told her, in Spanish, that all I had said was that my baby [chichi] was out of milk. I showed her the Enfamil I had purchased and told her I needed to prepare it before my baby [chichi] woke up. She figured out what was happening, clarified that I was talking about my *bebé* — the word that Mexican Spanish speakers use for baby — and explained what *chichi* means in Mexican Spanish. I nearly died of embarrassment.

— Mei Emerald Gaffey-Hernandez —

Higher Education

An exchange student is like a human cultural decoder
ring, except sometimes you're not sure if they're
translating your slang correctly
or just making stuff up.
~Author Unknown

"Jojo, do you have fortune telling in America?"

"Oh, I'm sure we do. Do you mean like palm reading? Tarot cards? That sort of thing?"

"Oh, no, I mean Japanese-style fortune telling."

"I don't think so. What kind of fortune telling do you mean?"

"Did you know in Japan that your bra type is used for fortune telling?"

I look a bit shocked but then quickly regained my composure. I mean, after all, different cultures have different norms. But seriously, I had never heard about a girl's bra being used in that way.

I was a naive eighteen-year-old heading into my freshman year of university in a small, southern Oregon town. My parents thought it would be a good idea to acclimate to college life by taking part in the "One Week Early" program.

This program allowed incoming freshmen to settle into dorm life, unpack, and maybe make a friend or two before classes actually started. It was a godsend for socially awkward and extremely shy me. My high school graduating class had a total of twelve students. So, you can imagine that anything over double digits in a crowd or class was utterly foreign and intimidating.

I had always enjoyed other cultures, and even in high school had an affinity toward Asian styles, colors, and art. I loved Japanese fabrics, historical art, and culture, and I had learned a little bit about the food and drink.

In my junior year, I had even applied for and won a scholarship to spend a year abroad with a family in Tokyo due to an essay I had written. However, I didn't get a full scholarship to go, so I wasn't able to afford the trip.

The next best thing was to offer to be a roommate to an international student at university. Of course, I made a request for someone from an Asian country and was thrilled to know I'd been paired with a Japanese roommate.

Megumi, or Meg as I called her, was as cute as a button and full of energy and humor. She was trying her best to make friends with this shy country girl by asking me questions, offering me some questionable Japanese snacks, and generally being sweet. As I was finally getting settled, she started that conversation with me in her heavily accented English about my bra type. What?

It didn't surprise me, though. Boobs have been judged for millennia, so who's to say they can't predict your future, too? I shrugged. Maybe they were a bit magical. Just ask any heterosexual male, and I'm sure he'd say boobs were definitely on some sort of mystical spectrum.

"No, I've never heard of that before."

"Oh, good! Can I give you your fortune?"

"Suuuuuuurrrre?" I looked at her a little fearfully. This girl was nice, but should we start trading cup sizes already?

She bounced on her bed a bit and grinned at me. "Okay! I'll start. I'm an A-type, and A-types are usually sweet, innocent, and shy. We have a hard time with boys but can always find a boyfriend." She giggled.

I looked at her chest and nodded in agreement. She was most definitely an A-type. So, her explanation made sense.

She continued, "I don't know about the accuracy of this kind of fortune telling, but mine is sometimes true." She giggled again. She looked at me and asked, "What about you? What's your type?"

I looked down at myself and then back at her. I blushed a bit and slowly said, "Beeee?"

"Oh, that's my sister! Do you like to party? B-types are always the party girls. They are good at business and will get married early."

"No, that's not me at all." I laughed, imagining myself at a party, and turned red.

"Well, what about the rest of the sizes?" I asked.

"You mean O?"

"No, I mean C, D, E, and F."

"In Japan, we don't have anything else other than A, B, and O."

"You don't?" In some ways, I could definitely see that there were no other cup sizes than A and B, but then she threw in O, and I was baffled. What cup size is an O?

I couldn't even imagine the torpedoes that must be worthy of an O designation.

My eyes widened, and I looked at her in confusion.

"What's an O-type? I mean, how big is the cup? That must be huge! And what does it mean that you don't have Cs and Ds?" I must have looked shocked because she looked at me quizzically.

"Bra types in America must be very different. I didn't know that it would be so different. Here, look at this article in my magazine about fortune telling."

I looked at her Japanese magazine with the text in Japanese, but it also had illustrations and a few photos. Immediately, the lightbulb turned on, and I busted out in the biggest uncontainable giggle.

"Meg!" I laughed out loud. "You mean blood type, not bra type!"

I pulled an undergarment out of my dresser drawer and dangled it suggestively in front of me.

She gasped audibly, and her mouth fell open in a perfect circle. We both started laughing so hard that we ended up crying and hugging it out. It was our inside joke for the rest of the year. She was a great girl and is now an accomplished publisher and photographer in Tokyo.

Meg was definitely more of a B-type than I ever was. She was a party girl and hung out with a larger group of international students who would have wild benders every weekend. But she was a wonderful roommate, sweet and always inclusive if I was alone. It was definitely one of the best lessons in cultural communication I ever had.

— Jojo Teckina —

The Advertisement

*Back of every mistaken venture and defeat is the
laughter of wisdom, if you listen.*
~Carl Sandburg

"My fellow writers, good morning! What better way to start a brisk Saturday morning than to share a warm conversation while sipping a hot cup of coffee. So, welcome. Please grab a bagel, a muffin, or a croissant and settle in. In just a few moments, we will begin our journey."

There I was, addressing a group of recovering heart surgery patients, ranging in age from their late sixties to one remarkable gentleman in his mid-nineties. We were gathered in the community room of a local hospital.

I was presenting a program that would encourage the participants to use creative writing as a therapeutic tool for emotional healing and coping with anxiety, illness, grief, and fear of the unknown. Everyone seemed engaged as I discussed the art of writing and encouraged them to find the time to write daily and even consider starting a gratitude journal. At the end, I said, "Okay, folks, are we ready for our writing journey? All aboard!"

I had brought a pile of brand-new, colorful notebooks and two unopened boxes of pens. I handed out the notebooks and explained the workshop format. Part would be devoted to actually writing, the remainder to sharing and discussing written pieces.

I then directed their attention to some random objects I had brought to use as writing prompts. I held up each one and asked the participants to look at the item. I assured them that some sort of memory or thought from last week, last year, even from childhood, was certain to be triggered. The room began to fill with a bit of mumbling, followed by audible "oohs and aahs" and lots of chuckling. I had intentionally brought a collection of generation-specific objects certain to resonate with the participants: a Slinky, Gumby, an old metal lunch box, a rotary phone, a Nancy Drew book, an old key, a roller skate, and a vinyl record.

Next, I reached for the boxes of pens to hand out, but I happened to notice a basket of pens on the shelf above the wooden table I was using. I reached for the basket instead and said, "Okay, folks, I am going to circulate this basket. Please take a pen and let's focus once more on these objects. No stress. No worries. See where the pen takes you. It is truly amazing how the pen always takes you where you need to go."

I then explained we would write in silence for fifteen minutes or so, then re-group. Anyone who felt comfortable and wanted to read their piece was most certainly welcome to share. Once more, I reminded the group to look at the objects or, alternatively, to look out the window, to take a deep breath, slowly exhale, relax, and enjoy the writing journey. I encouraged the participants to write whatever came to mind: a few sentences, a paragraph, or a poem. I then repeated, "Folks, see where the pen takes you. It's amazing. It always takes you where you need to go."

After fifteen minutes, I asked those who were willing to share what they had written. The participants were receptive and enthusiastic, and it certainly seemed like the workshop had provided a therapeutic oasis, a creative distraction from the group's medical issues and concerns. I thanked the group for their participation, wished them good health, and encouraged each of them to keep writing.

Then I heard a woman's voice say, "Wait, can I add something?"

I had already told everyone the notebooks were theirs to keep, but I thought perhaps she was going to ask if the pens were parting gifts as well.

She cleared her throat and said, "You have mentioned the pen a few times. It takes you where you need to go."

I nodded and added, "Yes, it sure does. Correct. Thank you for reminding all of us."

With an impish grin, the woman continued, "Well, the pens you handed out… There's an advertisement printed on them."

I immediately answered, "Oh, that's okay."

She responded, "Well, the advertisement is for a local cemetery!"

Everyone started laughing. You could have heard them down the hallway. It was truly a testament to the old adage, "Laughter is the best medicine."

— Patricia Rossi —

Birthday Suit

Language is the source of misunderstandings.
~Antoine de Saint-Exupéry

Let me take you back to the time when I was in my early twenties, naively navigating the treacherous waters of online dating. Picture this: I was a young French woman, happily chatting with a guy named Phil on a dating app for about a week. He was a pleasant fellow, and his birthday was fast approaching. Now, when you're in your early twenties and you're gearing up to celebrate a special occasion, there's a certain level of excitement and preparation that goes into it, right? You and your friends have those go-to ensembles for such events, and you're all set to paint the town red.

So, it was Phil's birthday, and he was getting ready to head out with his buddies to commemorate the big day. We were texting back and forth as he got dressed, sharing our excitement and plans for the evening. And then, in the midst of this innocent banter, I casually asked Phil, "Do you have your birthday suit on?" Innocent enough, right?

Well, remember, I'm French, and in the French language, we don't have any equivalent to the English phrase "birthday suit." It's just not a thing. So, I was genuinely asking if he had donned a special outfit for his birthday celebration, like any sensible person would do.

To my surprise, Phil confirmed that he was indeed wearing his birthday suit. His birthday was still a few days away, but I thought he might have tried on the outfit to see if it worked. I was excited to see what he had chosen for his special evening.

I can't emphasize enough just how clueless I was about this linguistic quirk. So, when I received a photo from Phil with him wearing nothing but a smile, I was absolutely horrified. I mean, there I was, innocently asking to see his special birthday outfit, and I got a much more revealing picture than I had ever anticipated.

In my shock and confusion, I quickly responded to him, telling him how inappropriate and offensive I found it to send such an explicit picture without even knowing me well.

Little did I know that Phil, in his own innocent way, thought I was playing along with his little birthday game. To him, I was in on the joke, asking him if he was in his "birthday suit" and then receiving his playful response.

That night, our conversation took an awkward turn, and I went to bed utterly bewildered and slightly perturbed by what had transpired. I had thought Phil was a nice, genuine guy, but now he seemed like a completely different person.

The next day, still somewhat in the dark about what had happened, I decided to confide in a close friend about this bizarre turn of events. I recounted the entire story, from my innocent question to the unsolicited photo that followed. As I described the situation to my friend, her eyes widened.

She burst into laughter, explaining that, in English, "birthday suit" is a cheeky way of saying someone is naked — stark, raving naked. I couldn't believe it!

Feeling utterly mortified, I realized that I needed to set things right. It was time to reach out to Phil and explain my side of the story. With my cheeks still flushed from embarrassment, I sent him a message, apologizing for my misunderstanding and clarifying that I had no idea what I was asking when I inquired about his "birthday suit." I was prepared to laugh it off, hoping that he'd see the humor in our language-barrier mishap.

And then I waited. And waited. But alas, no response came from Phil. It seemed that the damage was done, and he had likely moved on to less linguistically confusing pastures.

— Faynixe White —

The Worst Line

"I think you need a hearing test."
He responded, "Why the heck do
I need a hairy chest?"
~Author Unknown

The driver's mouth moves again, but I can't hear what he's saying over the traffic. "I'm sorry, what?" I ask. "Say again, please?"

He leans farther out his window. He's obviously speaking, but I can't discern a thing from my spot on the sidewalk. "Sorry, still didn't catch that."

His smile is turning into a frown. And behind me on the sidewalk, my dorm-mates are in fits of giggles. We've gone past the point of social niceties now and me continuing to ask just feels embarrassing. The poor man probably only caught my attention to ask for directions. Part of what he said may have been "Do you know the way to…," so I take a shot in the dark and point ahead.

"If you keep going, take a left. There's a roundabout with a lot of road signs. I'm sure it will show you the way to go."

I smile. He looks sullen and confused as he drives on. And now my dorm-mates have collapsed into absolute hysterics. One is laughing so hard that she leans over to clutch her knees.

"Did you hear what he actually said?" I ask.

Apparently, their ears are better than mine.

Only one of them sobers enough to reply, "He said, 'Do you

know the way to Heaven, or am I already there?' And you gave him directions!"

—Nemma Wollenfang—

88

Richly Breast

Scientists now believe that the primary biological
function of breasts is to make males stupid.
~Dave Barry

The most magical day of my life. The most elegant day of my life. The most captivating day of my life.

My beautiful bride stood across from me. Our closest family members and friends stared in awe at her and the green, rolling hills in the background.

The preacher asked us to repeat after him — a simple task to officially start our life of wedded bliss. I was up first.

"You are the woman..."

"You are the woman," I repeated.

"God richly blessed me with," the preacher uttered.

I attempted to repeat the next line.

"God richly breast me with."

My bride — once stoic and listening to my every word — was now bent over, laughing uncontrollably with her hand on my chest for extra support to keep from literally falling over in laughter. She couldn't stop. She giggled. She gasped for air. She even snorted. She couldn't stop the laughter. But the preacher knew the show must go on.

"Let this ring be a constant reminder," he continued.

My bride was laughing uncontrollably between each word.

I repeated. My bride was still laughing uncontrollably.

She finally composed herself enough to correctly repeat the same words I had. The wedding concluded, and down the aisle we went.

I honestly had no idea what I had actually stammered out of my mouth. I was greeted at the end of the aisle by my grinning groomsmen.

"What was on your mind?" my best man asked.

"Getting married? I was nervous? I don't understand."

"You said 'breast,'" he informed me.

No, I didn't. Absolutely not.

I turned my head to see all six groomsmen and my wife surrounding me, all smirking, nodding their heads, confirming that I had just said "breast" during my wedding vows.

— Dekota Gregory —

89

My Daddy Put It There

Yet the best determining factor of how comfortable we
are with ourselves, is our ability to laugh at ourselves.
~Wes Adamson

When my daughter Vivian was almost four we shared the news that she was soon to have a sister or brother. "Where is the baby now, Mommy?" she asked.

"The baby is growing in Mommy's tummy where it is safe, and when it's big enough it will join our family," I answered.

My husband and I had discussed how to explain human reproduction to a three-year-old. We decided to do as all the books on the subject suggested and keep our answers honest but simple, not volunteering more information than needed to satisfy her curiosity.

Then came her next question. "How did the baby get into your tummy, Mommy?" she asked innocently.

All kinds of possible answers paraded through my mind, but I wanted to keep it honest but simple. "Daddy put it there," I blurted. Oh no! Did I really just say that? Silently, I prayed she wouldn't ask me how or why?

"Oh!" She shrugged then hugged my legs and ran off to play with her friends.

Glancing at my husband, who sat innocently reading his newspaper in his comfy chair, I commented, "Whew! That was quick thinking, don't you agree?" I was feeling a little smug, maybe a little proud of the way I'd handled the situation.

"Yeah, you were lucky this time around." He grinned and left me thinking about what I should say if she asked for more information.

Later that day my in-laws dropped by for a visit and were sitting on the sofa when my daughter rushed in from playing next door. Not noticing her grandparents, she ran directly to me, all out of breath. She was always happy to see her grandparents, but she had exciting news to share that day.

"Mommy," she proudly announced, "Wendy has a baby in her tummy too!"

Wendy was my friend and next-door neighbor who had a son the same age as Vivian. They were playmates. She was so excited about her news she hadn't noticed her grandparents in the room until now. She ran and gave them hugs then continued her tale, barely stopping for air.

"Hi, Grandma, Hi, Grandpa. Wendy has a baby in her tummy just like Mommy and I know how it got there too cause Mommy told me so!" She rattled this off so quickly that I barely had time to process it all before she did a quick turn toward me as if for assurance, then back to her grandparents.

Both grandparents were grinning as they gave me an inquisitive glance, probably curious how I had shared this information with my daughter. Giving her their full attention, they awaited little "Miss-know-it-all" to reveal her newfound knowledge. Before I could think of a way to intercede, my mother-in-law inquired, "And how did Mommy tell you the baby got into Wendy's tummy?"

I groaned. Oh nooooo. I knew exactly what was coming next but was helpless to stop her!

"My daddy put it there!" Vivian announced proudly.

The looks on my in-laws' faces were priceless.

— Christine M. Smith —

90

The Lesson

To all of the grandmothers who make the world more gentle, more tolerant and more safe for our children. Never doubt your importance.
~Mary-Lou Rosengren

M y four-year-old grandson was sick enough to miss two weeks of school. Feverish with pneumonia, his small body ached from coughing. He also could not attend one of his favorite activities — an after-school sports program his pre-K teacher coached on Wednesday afternoons. He loved kicking a soccer ball into a goal and running relay races in the yard. Carrying the baton made him feel "special."

When he was well again, his teacher suggested he come for some extra lessons, hoping he'd see that even though pneumonia had made him feel exhausted and sad, he still could have a little of his usual fun.

"Guess what!" I said. "Put on your soccer jacket. I know how disappointed you were to miss sports, but now that you're all better, you can have a makeup lesson. We're heading back to school!"

Dropping the Lego pieces he was holding on the kitchen floor, he looked at me with disbelief. "No!" he cried. "I'm not going! I don't wanna go!" He rushed to his room, his face as red as when he had the fever.

"What's wrong?" I pleaded, totally astounded. "You've always had so much fun on Wednesday afternoons. Did something happen before you got sick that makes you want to stay home? Do you think you're not good enough at the sports? Did somebody say something mean to you? Please tell me what's wrong."

My grandson caught his breath and tried to stop sniveling. With a quavering voice, he stammered, "I don't — wanna go — please don't — make me. No children in my class ever wear makeup."

— Lynn Hess —

Chapter
11

Sometimes, You Just Have to Laugh

91

The First Date

I went out with a guy once who told me I didn't need to
drink to make myself more fun to be around.
I told him, "I'm drinking so that you're
more fun to be around."
~Chelsea Handler

was a nurse in the cardiac intensive care unit at a Level 1 trauma center in Tampa, Florida. Our department would frequently receive acute heart patients by helicopter. During one shift, a patient was brought in by our flight team, which included a nurse I'd never seen before. While he helped me hook up the patient to a monitor, I couldn't stop staring at him. Aside from being tall and filling out his flight suit quite nicely, he was drop-dead gorgeous! I was so flustered that I could barely speak when the flight nurse introduced himself as David and proceeded to give me a bedside report.

For the next several weeks, whenever David and his team brought patients to our unit, he would strike up a conversation with me. He often made me laugh with his quick wit. I was so excited when he asked me out for dinner that it took every ounce of self-control not to jump around.

I took great care with my appearance when date night finally rolled around, and David, looking devastatingly handsome, drove us to a casual restaurant on the coast. We had a great time talking and laughing at each other's stories, and after the sun had set and dinner wrapped up, he asked if I'd like to go for a walk on the beach.

I felt like I was in a dream! With the warm, gentle waves rolling over our feet, our conversation took a more serious turn as I asked David about his family and heritage. He answered all my questions and then asked me about mine. I told him my dad came from a long line of Scottish blood, hailing from Cape Breton Island in Canada. Trying to be funny, I slapped my butt with great emphasis as I said, "My mother is half-Italian with the background to prove it. She doesn't have a mustache, though."

I thought he was going to kiss me when he bent down and looked at me intently. Without missing a beat, he replied, "Well, then, I guess that means you got yours from your dad."

— Katherine Bradbury —

92

A Wedding Debacle

Make sure to marry someone who laughs
at the same things you do.
~J.D. Salinger

My wedding was a comedy of errors. But a comedy was not what I had in mind!

We were getting married at my parents' home a week before Christmas, and I wanted a festive Christmas gathering. In my mind, I saw a sumptuous table piled high with hors d'oeuvres and garnished with twinkling white lights and evergreen boughs. But that's where the vision stayed. In my mind.

Every time I talked about the wedding, I felt my panic increasing. Decisions were hard for me, and the Big One was more than I could handle. I had called off the engagement once, so in order to make it to the wedding this time, I had to quit talking about it.

I lived a few states away from my parents and, when I arrived the day before my wedding, I learned that the photographer's equipment had been stolen; he wouldn't be able to photograph the wedding. That sent my mother into a frenzied search until she found a friend who had a friend who could "take pictures."

But no frenzied search turned up our singer. She was supposed to arrive that day to practice with the musicians for the ceremony the next day. But she was nowhere to be found.

This should have been a foreshadowing of things to come. On the day of the wedding, the ladies from church, whom my mother had hired to "do" the wedding, arrived with flower arrangements that looked like they belonged on top of caskets. There wasn't a pine bough or a twinkly light in sight. At that moment I knew we were in trouble. No one had understood my directions.

But wait! Had I given them any directions? Probably not. The ideas were all swirling in my mind, but I just hadn't been able to talk about them. And now I realized they weren't transmitted through mental telepathy.

A friend arrived to see if she could help with anything, and we jumped in her car to search out Christmas tree lots, hoping to collect boughs so she could make wreaths and swags. I wanted a Christmas wedding, not a funeral! We ran into a store and grabbed spools of festive ribbon and glossy berries. With clippers, ribbons, and a few flowers hijacked from the casket arrangements, we tried to create Christmas ambiance. We only partially succeeded.

With just a couple of hours to go before the wedding, I threw off the garden gloves, jumped in the shower, and did my hair. The guests gathered, the groom was late, and the musicians had to proceed without the missing singer. I had to figure out when to march into the room without the cue from her song. Luckily, I heard my mother, as did everyone else, saying, "Now, now!" in a very loud whisper. That's when I saw my soon-to-be husband looking sickly pale. For once in his life, he was not tan. My handsome groom, who had always been the positive cheerleader in our relationship, was experiencing last-minute panic. I almost laughed.

Right on cue, my best friend's father, who was a member of the clergy, began the ceremony. Just as he was getting close to some rather important parts that required a response, my sister's baby started crying. Immediately, my sister-in-law's baby, across the room, burst into tears as well. Soon we had stereophonic wailing.

My sister-in-law stood up to comfort her little one, and her husband thought she was leaving the room, so he pulled out her chair. But baby settled down, so she sat back down. The trouble was, the chair was no longer there. She tumbled to the floor with a re-charged baby and a chair collapsing behind her. This sent one of the uncles into uncontrollable giggles, and the babies, not wanting to be outdone, screamed louder.

With the clattering chair, the screaming babies, and a great uncle who couldn't contain his laughter, the whole scene was rather comical — if you weren't the one getting married. With all the chaos, I was straining to hear the ceremony. Somehow, I managed to hear the part when I was supposed to say, "I do." And I actually said it, which I'm sure was somewhat of a surprise to my brand-new husband.

So, I was officially married in spite of funeral decor, a missing photographer, an absent singer, two crying babies, a sister-in-law on the floor, and an uncle who found it all hilarious. But then it was time for pictures.

The guy who could "take pictures" stood there like a dumb rock and asked what we wanted. "Well, pictures, I guess," was my brilliant reply. He clearly had no idea what he was doing, and the resulting photos were of odd groups of people with lamps coming out of their heads and teenagers flashing peace signs between them, not to mention a little nephew picking his nose. The photos never made it into a wedding album.

After that ordeal, we began receiving guests for our reception. In about an hour, we were getting hungry. We wandered out to the patio in the hopes of filling our plates from a table of holiday delights. What we found were a few plates of cookies. Cookies? Where were the bacon wrapped chestnuts and the cherry tomato bruschetta? Still rolling around in my brain somewhere, I suppose. I went back to the kitchen and found stacks and stack of cookies, but apparently my mother's dear friends from church were preparing for legions of late arriving guests, or they were hoarding cookies for some impending apocalypse. Didn't they know we were in the middle of one? Each of our guests was carefully nibbling on a single cookie out on the patio.

At that point, I realized the whole thing was a complete disaster. But I didn't cry. In fact, I might have even laughed. I was married, and much to my surprise I actually felt good. So, grabbing a cookie, we got out of there as fast as we could and headed out on our honeymoon which, much to my delight, was as good as the wedding was bad.

Forty-six years of marriage later, I am able to laugh about my disastrous wedding day. I quickly learned that it's the marriage that counts, not the wedding. And that's the advice I always give to young brides who are stressed about their weddings. Mine couldn't have been worse, but the marriage couldn't have been better.

—Jan Cameron—

93

Now Boarding Everyone but You

Seems like half my anxiety dreams are about airports.
~Lois McMaster Bujold

Whenever I book a flight, I always end up in Group 7. Even when I check in twenty-four hours ahead of time, the first minute you're allowed to.

Group 7 is the equivalent of being picked last in PE.

Except the ticket agents are the captains, and not only do they not want me on their team, but they don't think I deserve any overhead bin space.

But I'm not always in Group 7. Sometimes, I'm Group E.

"E" as in EVERYONE gets to board but you!

This is why I decided it was time to try a new airline. Delta.

When my boarding pass popped up, I almost fell out of my chair. MAIN CABIN #2!

It was like I was a silver medalist. *Delta likes me! They really like me!*

I stood at my gate, beaming, boarding pass in hand, facing upward, in perfect scanning position.

"In just a few minutes, we will begin boarding," the agent announced in a cheery voice.

I extended my arm back and positioned my carry-on so it was ready to roll. My right leg was forward, knee slightly bent. Obviously,

I had already stretched.

"We will start with our Delta One passengers," the agent gushed, blowing them kisses.

That must be their fancy name for First Class. That's okay. Main Cabin #1 will be next and then moi!

After all the fancy-pants people boarded, the agent announced, "Active Military, you may now board." She saluted them.

Not going to argue that one. Also, thank you for your service.

I edged forward. *Any moment, she'll be calling the good folks of Main Cabin #2.*

"First Class and Delta Premium, you may now board." The agent gave them a round of applause.

I thought Delta One was First Class! And what's this Delta Premium you speak of?

More fancy, smug people boarded. But I didn't lose faith. I was so close.

"We now invite our Diamond Medallion members to board," the agent declared with a big smile.

I sighed. *As if I could compete with a club based on diamonds and medallions.*

However, most of the Diamond Medallion members were wearing neither diamonds nor medallions, so obviously it was a club based on lies.

"Families with small children, you may now board," the agent said, giving a thumbs-up to a couple of frazzled parents and their screaming toddler, who kept neither his hands nor his bronchial cough to himself.

But I had bigger problems. The herd had thinned, and overhead bin space was disappearing fast. I knew I had to get the ball rolling.

I raised my fist in the air. "Main Cabin! Main Cabin! Main Cabin!" I chanted, trying to engage my fellow Main Cabin passengers. But they were a listless bunch, completely devoid of team spirit.

I slumped against a pillar as the agent welcomed Delta Comfort.

Still smiling, but with her enthusiasm waning, she announced, "Sky Priority, you may board."

A bunch of average Joes shuffled past me.

I'm losing to these guys?

"We will now board Main Cabin #1," she said, forcing a smile.

The below-average Joes boarded.

When there were only us riffraff left, the agent yawned, "Main Cabin #2? I guess."

I dragged myself over to the agent. After scanning my boarding pass, she said, "We're out of overhead bin space, so you'll need to…"

"Yeah, yeah, yeah," I sighed, surrendering my carry-on.

That's what happens when you're in Main Cabin #2.

Which is the equivalent of Group 9.

Also known as Group I.

And we all know what "I" stands for…

I can't believe I was excited about Main Cabin #2!

— January Gordon Ornellas —

94

The Procedure

*My colonoscopy wasn't the best experience
of my life, but it was up there.*
~Author Unknown

B e forewarned. Not all personal accounts of life are pretty. There is a good chance that the following will be too frightening to read for even most grown men. This is especially true of grown men who just recently turned fifty; men such as me.

Since that eventful birthday, I now fear only two things: my own mortality and my colon. I apologize for my bluntness, but the fact is that an unhappy colon can kill you. Thus, doctors invented the colonoscopy, a procedure that is safe and allegedly painless, although it does involve a device known as a colonoscope, the medical equivalent of a garden hose with a camera mounted on the business end. I suspect that it is considered painless because the victim is rendered nearly unconscious before it all transpires. It's preparing for it that will do you in.

By 10 a.m. of my prep day, I was in what felt like day four of a twenty-four-hour fasting period. During this time, I was allowed a boiled egg for good behavior, plus the threat of beef bouillon if I misbehaved. Unlike legitimate fasting for religious or financial purposes, this suffering is done to make the colon tester's job easier. As I was about to be medically violated for the first time by people I barely knew, I'd rather they had to work for the privilege.

But since these same professional colon-teers could cause me intense discomfort if I disobeyed their wishes for a clean colon, I continued the fast knowing that if I woke up from the procedure I would get to eat the nearest edible thing, even if it required me chasing it down and killing it.

It is reported by some people that fasting leads to profound thoughts. As I pondered the accompanying hunger hallucinations, I too asked myself the profound: "If it seems like I've been hungry forever, then why is it called fasting?" Unlike most experienced fasters, I didn't wait for an answer, preferring instead to try to capture the imaginary dancing pizza floating before me. Besides, the answer came soon enough as I entered step two of the preparations for my initiation into colon-hood: The Cleansing.

At the risk of harming sensitive folks and children who might be reading this, I'll spare the details. I will say that I was required to drink six ounces of magical colon-cleansing medicine that immediately expanded to a gallon once it took up its very temporary residence inside me. I was also given orange juice and Jell-O, but in a cruel trick wasn't allowed to keep either in my stomach for more than a few minutes. It is no coincidence that this medicine is called Fleet, although Swift, Quick, Sudden, or Too Late would also be suitable names. Unlike the orange juice and Jell-O, it's the gift that keeps on giving.

When I was first informed as to what I would receive for my fiftieth birthday, the doctor took great pains to explain the procedure. Although he was quite enthusiastic about my colon, I just needed to know two things: Would I be heavily sedated during the procedure, and would I ever walk again?

"Don't be silly," he said. "I've had the procedure, and I don't remember a thing!" He then limped out of the room to mistakenly answer another doctor's page.

After being assured that it was painless by several young, female nurses—none who had ever suffered at the hands of a professional colonoscopier—I agreed to the procedure. I did not agree to the foodless fog that I was now in as I prepped.

What I wanted at that moment was to visit an exotic place with no regard as to bathroom locations and eat a six-course meal when I arrived. I wanted to cough without fear and bask in the confidence that it isn't necessary to always carry a change of clothes. I wanted to be a normal person with a contented colon. After tomorrow's procedure, I would be.

I don't wish to berate those who specialize in the nether region of colons. It takes lots of money, years of school, and experience with plumbing tools before one can become a colon specialist. My hat's off to these people, as are my pants. But what other business makes the customer suffer for the ease of the employees? Okay, plenty, but those businesses don't require me to pay money to, well, be violated. With a camera, no less. I cried myself to sleep feeling cheap and uncared for.

The next morning's drive to the hospital went quickly, thanks to light traffic and another bottle of colon cleanser. It should be noted that the check-in personnel who complete the paperwork for colonoscopies are the fastest seen inside the medical profession, a haste they undoubtedly learned the hard way. Once the papers were signed, including what I suspect was a release for all film rights, I was wheeled into a cubicle, told to disrobe, and given a standard-issue, relaxed-gap hospital gown. Nothing more, not even a kiss or a glass of wine. Meanwhile, my attendants spoke of food and giggled menacingly.

Soon, I was ready, or rather *they* were ready, not giving me much of a say in the matter. I relaxed only momentarily when I saw there was a TV screen nearby, but that turned to horror as I realized the colon channel was on, and I would be the star. I readied myself to scream with the start of the procedure and mentally noted the best route if I attempted escape. Then, I waited, and waited.

"You ready to go home?" the nurse asked.

I blinked my eyes in disbelief. They hadn't done anything yet.

"When are you going to start?" I replied groggily.

"We're finished. You slept through it all."

I've slept through storms, loud music, and even nagging ex-bosses, but not through something as traumatic as this. No matter how great the anesthesia was, surely I'd remember something.

Soon, I did remember something: the colon-cleansing juice. Or rather, it remembered me. I rushed stat into the restroom, but nothing happened.

Sometimes, You Just Have to Laugh |

It was all over. I was allowed to dress, pay my fee, and briefly talk to the doctor before leaving. I noticed he was wearing a full three-piece suit and tie, with nary a hint of the blood and gore that must accompany any lower GI (Gastronomical Incorrectness) work. As I can get twice as dirty taking out the kitchen trash, I developed a theory. Just like crop circles and recent Elvis sightings, colonoscopies are staged. The whole idea of a camera being used inside of the colon is a story concocted to give these people a job, bless their hearts. Quite frankly, the thought of it having never happened leaves me relieved — and yes, that was a deliberate pun.

So, after this, I'll swear to the world that, yes, I'm certain the procedure really was done, and it will be our little secret. I for sure won't complain to the management because if the preparation for this staged procedure was any indication...

The amount of colon cleansing needed for a real procedure would've killed me.

— Butch Holcombe —

Out of Control

I often laugh at extremely inappropriate times... Not
because I'm nervous or anything. Mainly because I
think inappropriate things are funny.
~Author Unknown

"Why is your face all red? Were you laughing?"

"No. I was just waiting for you."

I lied. How could I explain to my six-year-old son, J.W., that I was about to die of embarrassment?

This "embarrassment" actually started about a month earlier when J.W.'s teacher told me the school district was screening students for a program that offered enriching activities beyond the regular classroom. They're looking, she said, for students "who process things a little differently, who link ideas in creative ways, and who think out of the box." At first, I had no idea what she was talking about, but in the ensuing weeks, as J.W.'s teacher explained how students in the program built robots and did experiments, I began to think my son might really enjoy such instruction. The more J.W. heard, the more he also wanted to attend the program.

J.W.'s teacher, however, cautioned both of us that it was very difficult to qualify for this program, and J.W. would have to pass a one-on-one test with a specially trained examiner to be accepted. It was a long exam, she said, and could be stressful.

Initially, I wasn't concerned, but as the date for the test came closer, I began to worry. I knew if J.W. didn't qualify, he would be disappointed.

When the day finally arrived, I had to take him to a different school building where we met the test examiner and the proctor who would supervise the exam. The examiner took J.W. to a brightly lit room filled with toys, puzzles, and computers. The room looked very inviting, and the proctor told me it was designed to make the student feel at ease.

I was told I could watch the test through a two-way mirror in an adjacent, darkened room. I could see the examiner and J.W., but they could not see me. I was cautioned by the proctor not to make noise in the room because the room was not soundproof, and any noise might distract the student. She told me not to touch the glass or to interfere in any way with the test, and then she left.

I found myself alone in a small, quiet, dark room... and that's when it began. I suddenly felt strange because it seemed so surreal to watch my child interacting with another person through the window. I felt like I was watching a television sitcom but I was personally acquainted with the star.

The examiner started the test by showing J.W. a picture of a dog. The dog was lying on a rug, curled up, and sleeping by a fire.

Examiner: "What is the dog doing, J.W.?"

J.W.: "He's making a circle."

Examiner: "Why do you say that?"

J.W.: "Because he's curled up in a circle."

I sighed loudly, dismayed that J.W. had not simply said, "The dog is sleeping," which I felt certain was the correct answer.

I began to feel claustrophobic. Restrained by the instructions not to speak or act, it didn't take long for me to want to do both. I had a strong desire to knock on the glass. I wanted to tell J.W. to stop being funny and to simply answer the questions.

Examiner: "J.W., do you know what H_2O is?"

J.W.: "It's a TV station my mother won't let me watch."

"No, J.W.," I said out loud from my chair behind the glass. "She said H_2O, not HBO, and I know you know the difference!"

With each new question and J.W.'s tangential answer, I got more anxious.

About fifteen minutes into the examination, it suddenly started. I started with a little giggling but was soon full-blown laughing. I couldn't stop.

Suddenly, the door opened. I froze. With a very disapproving look, the proctor admonished me to remain quiet during the testing so the student's evaluation would not be disrupted. As she closed the door, I did my best to smother a laugh. I put my hand over my mouth to muffle the sound, but I realized it was beyond my control.

I could hear the proctor discussing my poor behavior with someone beyond the door, but I couldn't stop laughing. Her tone was one of condemnation, but I couldn't help it. I kept laughing.

Examiner: "J.W., can you tell me how a yard and a pound are related?"

J.W. will get this one, I told myself. We had talked about units of measurement, and he knew how many feet are in a yard and how many ounces are in a pound.

Examiner: "Can you tell me how they are similar?"

J.W.: "Well, if you have a dog, you can put him in a yard or in the pound—but it's better to put him in the yard because he might get euthanized in the pound."

With this answer, a particularly loud paroxysm of laughter exploded from me. I remember holding my ribcage because the force of my laughter was actually hurting my left side.

It seemed to me that J.W. was trying to entertain the examiner, but the irony of the situation was that he was entertaining me... and that realization only made me laugh more.

J.W. kept glancing at the mirror during the entire test. Perhaps, he simply heard my guffaws, but I think he knew from the beginning he was being watched... and that, I believe, encouraged him to be creative... and to perform.

When the test ended, the examiner and J.W. left the room. The door opened in my little room, the lights came on, and I bolted. I was too embarrassed to hang around and try to explain my behavior.

I grabbed J.W., and we exited the building as the proctor called after us that we would be contacted with the results of the test.

Despite my inappropriate conduct, J.W. did get accepted into the program. I think they may have felt sorry for him for having such a strange mother, but they said it was because he did indeed think "out of the box." J.W. truly enjoyed participating in the program, and he learned a great deal.

All I learned, however, is that sometimes your mind and body work against you, and you laugh despite your best intentions.

— Billie Holladay Skelley —

It's the Shoes

*Give a girl the right shoes and
she can conquer the world.*
~Marilyn Monroe

When I started college at Emporia State University, it was with equal parts excitement and fear. Like all college students, I was there for the academics and to get training for my future career. But since I was hundreds of miles away from home and everything familiar, I hoped to make good friends during this chapter of my life as well. I didn't expect it to happen so quickly.

I met Dale after a church service during my second week on campus. He was friends with one of the girls who lived on my floor in a dorm, and after he said hello to her, she introduced him to me.

"Hello, Lorraine," he said brightly. The enthusiasm in his eyes spilled over into his voice. "It's really nice to meet you!"

The first thing I noticed was his big smile. The second thing I noticed was that he didn't seem to be at all uncomfortable around my wheelchair. That was something I couldn't say about many people whom I was meeting.

Since Dale was a resident assistant at the dorm I lived in, we ran into each other often over the next few weeks. He got to know about my love of the New York Giants, and he witnessed the way other people tended to dismiss me. I learned of his love of basketball and video games as well as his affection for Ernie and Bert from *Sesame Street*. He had dolls of them displayed on a shelf in his room, and he was just as playful and lovable as they were.

One night, he knocked on my door at 2:00 a.m. When I answered, he stood there dressed in a gorilla suit. He gave me a hug, handed me a banana, and left. Another time, when we were invited to have dinner with some friends, some kids in their apartment complex saw us and asked why I was in a wheelchair. Before I could say a word, Dale turned to them and said, "She ate too much sugary cereal when she was young." I giggled for the rest of the evening.

We got into the habit of having late-night conversations and shared meals in the cafeteria almost every day. After a while, Dale even had a nickname for me. He teasingly told me he had a theory that I was named after food: Quiche Lorraine. As the years passed, Dale became one of my closest friends. To this day, he is the only person who calls me "Quiche."

One of the things Dale and I had in common was that we were both members of the Baptist Student Union. BSU was comprised of a large group of students who did their best to live by faith and did lots of social things together. One Friday night during my junior year, the group decided to go bowling. My plan was to stay behind and curl up with a good book in my room. I never had a good time when a group of people around me were doing something physical and all I could do was sit and watch. But Dale didn't want me to stay home. When I told him I didn't want to go, he did his best to convince me to join the group.

"Lorraine, if you go bowling with us, I promise you will have fun. Come with us. Please?"

I just couldn't refuse a request that was so sincere from a guy whom so many young girls had a crush on.

At the bowling alley, almost everyone in the group tried to help me hit some pins. They held my wheelchair in various ways and suggested I sit in various positions. One guy even took me out of my wheelchair and helped me to sit on the floor. He thought if I could push the ball from between my knees, it might go straight down the lane.

None of it worked. Even though I had the lightest bowling ball that we could find, and I thought all my efforts were incredibly entertaining, the end result was nothing but gutter. I put my foot down when an employee at the bowling alley offered to put those air-filled tubes in the gutters for me. I appreciated that he was trying to help, but I wanted to leave with at least some of my dignity intact.

Dale had been watching everything from the corner where he was sitting. When there were only a few frames left in the game, he came over to me with an amused look on his face.

"I think I know the problem, Lorraine. It's the shoes. You don't have any bowling shoes."

With that, he took the tennis shoes I was wearing off my feet and replaced them with the bowling shoes that he had worn all night. Then, he pushed my wheelchair up to a bowling lane and adjusted it so it was straight.

"Concentrate, Quiche. Focus. You can do this."

I took a deep breath, threw the ball toward the pins, and hoped for the best.

What happened next defied all logic and reason. Not only did I hit some pins, but I got a strike!

People in the entire bowling alley, who had watched me struggle all evening, reacted like I had just scored the game-winning touchdown in the last seconds of the Super Bowl. The whooping, cheering, and dancing around lasted a full five minutes.

When the fanfare died down, Dale leaned in and whispered, "I knew it was the shoes."

Many years have passed since college, and Dale and I have kept in touch. He still makes me laugh and looks out for me in every way that he can.

I still try to make new friends with every new chapter in my life. But compared to Dale, everyone else has some pretty big shoes to fill.

Even if they aren't bowling shoes.

— Lorraine Cannistra —

How Not to Open a Gin Gin During Takeoff

*I was irrevocably betrothed to laughter, the sound of
which has always seemed to me to be the most
civilized music in the world.*
~Peter Ustinov

O f all the flights I had taken during my forty-five years on Earth, the one I took from Detroit to Philadelphia during the summer of 2022 was undoubtedly the worst. And, as luck would have it, that flight was also my children's first.

I, on the other hand, was no stranger to the friendly skies. Between the miles I had racked up traveling for business and the countless times I had flown to the east coast and back while my husband (then boyfriend) and I maintained a long-distance relationship, I was steadfast in my belief that I had seen, heard, and smelled it all.

I was wrong.

As the plane ascended into the clouds, I took my eight-year-old daughter's hand in mine and simultaneously peered through the gap between our seats to offer a reassuring glance to my son, who was sitting behind us. He failed to notice me because both of his eyes were pressed shut as he clung to his father's elbow for dear life.

I then turned back around, took in a deep breath, and surrendered to the sensation of the rising plane.

It's going to be fine, I thought. *Like always.*

The next thing I knew, I was overcome with a pain I can only describe as ghastly and all-encompassing. It was as if someone had crammed the Goodyear blimp between my ears and decided to inflate it at warp speed.

The only thing worse than enduring this intense pressure was the sudden realization that my son and daughter were likely feeling it, too.

I turned my head toward my daughter, and the look of sheer panic and desperation on her face told me everything I needed to know.

My son wasn't faring any better. He was biting his lip and grimacing in such a way that, if I hadn't known any better, I would have thought he was receiving a flu shot.

"Mom, this hurts!" my daughter said through shallow breaths. "You said takeoff would be easy."

I had no counterargument. And the inherent discomfort of it all introduced me to a new first: Having to eat crow alongside your young, trusting daughter in a soaring airplane is no fun.

Fast-forward twelve months. Same airport. Same month. Same time.

Our family was again headed east. Thankfully, the nightmare we had endured the previous year had long since been forgotten.

Or so I assumed.

But then, after the pilot instructed the crew to prepare the cabin for takeoff, my daughter began to shift nervously in her window seat. She leaned in. "Mom," she began, "what if that thing that happened last year happens again? You know, our ears?"

Remaining stoic, I feigned obliviousness. "Oh, that? It was a fluke. It probably won't happen again. Honey, we've got this."

But I would have been lying if I didn't admit to saying a silent prayer.

As we taxied, I decided it was time to reveal my ace in the hole, which no one knew I had: I reached inside the right pocket of my jacket and produced a Ziploc snack baggie containing a handful of Gin Gins.

I had picked up a small box of them on clearance months ago because the price was too good to pass up. I like to have Gin Gins on hand because I've discovered that these tiny, chewy, individually wrapped ginger candies are the perfect cross between a confection and a lozenge.

And that makes them a prime accessory for a flight.

You see, I had read somewhere that sucking on candy — or chewing gum — encourages swallowing, which can help open our Eustachian tube. That, in turn, can alleviate the pressure in our ears when there's a change in cabin pressure.

I passed one Gin Gin to my daughter and one to my son, who was again seated directly behind me. "Just in case," I motioned toward my head. "For our ears."

They tore open their respective candies and popped them in their mouths as if on cue.

At this point, the plane was breaking through the fog as a whooshing noise dominated the aircraft.

My daughter confidently made a thumbs-up sign, which indicated that she was good to go; my son was, too.

Me? Not so much.

It was as if I suddenly possessed the motor skills of an uncoordinated toddler: I couldn't open my Gin Gin wrapper.

My daughter stared at me incredulously. She initially thought I was pulling her leg. I wasn't. For the life of me, I simply couldn't pierce the wrapper.

When my daughter realized that the difficulty I was having was, in fact, real, her quiet giggle morphed into a ginormous snort, which opened the floodgates to uncontrollable cackling.

And I couldn't help but join her.

The grumpy businessman in front of us turned around to see what the hubbub was about. I shrugged at him, pointed at my Gin Gin wrapper, and tried in vain to put a halt to my laughter. He shook his head and turned back around.

His reaction made us laugh even harder. My fumbling ensued.

Have you ever tried harnessing all your might to open something in the face of irresistible hilarity?

Well, believe me when I say that it's an impossibility.

Now we had finished taking off and were at cruising altitude.

And my Gin Gin was still unopened.

My daughter had all but collapsed in her seat. Apparently, she laughed so hard that she developed a cramp in her side.

Unfortunately, Gin Gins wouldn't serve as an effective remedy for that particular ailment. But those little suckers (pun totally intended) sure did have a way of saving us during that flight. Just not in the way I had imagined.

— Courtney Conover —

Your Garden Is Boring

The best way to garden is to put on a wide-brimmed
straw hat and some old clothes. And with a hoe
in one hand and a cold drink in the other,
tell somebody else where to dig.
~Texas Bix Bender

Gardening season is going full throttle, which means that many of my friends are outside, knees in the soil, tending their gardens.

If you're one of them, this also means that when I stop by, you'll want to show me your garden, lead me through it, and tell me the story of every last green, growing thing.

Here's the problem: Your garden is boring. Don't take it personally. I think all gardens are boring.

I'm just not into plants, and I pay Angela to do my landscaping. When you come over, I'm not going to take you through the garden and tell you the name of every last plant and how it came to be there. I don't know the names of any of them, and the only thing I know about how they came to be there is that I paid Angela, and she put them there.

You already know these things about me. My indifference to green, growing things is no secret. And yet, here we are, traipsing out into the sunshine together so you can show me how well your tomato plants are doing.

And because we're friends, I will follow you around your garden pretending to care as you show off each plant and tell me about when you planted it and how you take care of it.

But what I'm really doing is counting the minutes until I'm back on the porch with a cool drink.

As far as I'm concerned? Gardens should be seen and not heard about.

I don't care about your garden's backstory. How you decided to put the rhododendrons over there. Your epic battle with the broccoli-devouring bugs. How wonderful mucking around in the soil makes you feel.

Don't get me wrong. I'm really glad your garden makes you happy. But hearing about your garden doesn't make me happy.

It makes me want to howl with boredom.

Let me put it to you this way:

I'd rather do my taxes than tour your garden.

I'd rather have my teeth cleaned than tour your garden.

I'd rather vacuum the basement steps than tour your garden.

I understand. You either just can't believe that I really feel this way, or you don't care. You need to talk about your garden. It's not enough to just garden. Gardening is an adventure that must be shared!

I get it. I feel that way, too. Not about my garden, but about my grandchildren. I absolutely adore them. I think they're remarkable. And I love to share stories about every last thing they say and do.

I particularly love to share photos of them.

I know that you don't care about my grandchildren with quite the same intensity. And that, amazingly, you think that looking at photo after photo of my three perfect grandsons can get a little boring.

I understand that you think your begonias are every bit as beguiling as my two-year-old grandson. You're wrong, of course, but I'm willing to cut you a deal.

Every time you show me a plant, I get to show you a photo of a grandchild.

As my six-year-old grandson Benji often says, "Sharing is caring."

I can share my adorable grandkids with you, and you can share your beautiful garden with me.

Then, we'll both be happy! And bored.

— Roz Warren —

Killer Food

A puritan is a person who pours righteous indignation
into the wrong things.
~Gilbert K. Chesterton

When my friend Ingrid left after a five-day visit, I nearly danced a jig. Benjamin Franklin had been spot-on when he had observed, "Guests, like fish, begin to smell after three days." They smell even worse — in a manner of speaking — if they had failed to disclose that they had become health-food zealots since you had seen them last.

The Ingrid I had known for years had been reasonably normal. Health-conscious but still fun, chill enough to enjoy a dish of ice cream or even the occasional tuna melt on a supersized bagel.

The new Ingrid who arrived on my doorstep had become a Holy Roller of the gluten-free, BPA-free, sugar-free, organic kale variety. Think about having someone like this in your house for five days, tut-tutting over your white rice and cookies-and-cream ice cream and see how quick you'd run to the nearest Dunkin' for an apple fritter and a large coffee doused with some half-and-half the minute she left.

Ingrid's marriage had gone bust and she was traveling to see friends as part of her recovery tour. She was smart, funny, and blunt, and we had shared many views about life. But before she had even unpacked, she flung open the doors of my kitchen pantry and frowned. Next thing I knew, she had borrowed my car for a trip to Whole Foods, returning with chicken-less chicken, eggless eggs, and loaves of brown bread

Sometimes, You Just Have to Laugh | 295

that could have doubled as hand weights.

As she unloaded the groceries, I saw that Ingrid's arms had become depressingly toned, and her skin positively glowed. Was that the divorce or the organic kale? I know it isn't nice to hate a girlfriend for getting in better shape than you and having glowing skin like you haven't had in fifteen years, but who says life is fair?

That first evening, I ate less during dinner than usual, feeling competitive with Ingrid and resenting every minute of it. Still hungry, I planned to sneak into my own kitchen later that night for a cheese sandwich when she had gone to bed. What happened to the Ingrid who used to rail that pressure on women to be fit and lean was a patriarchal construct? Who could tuck into a steaming-hot pizza without obsessing about its carb content? I began to wonder if this friendship could be saved.

The next morning, as my kids ate normal breakfast cereals like Apple Jacks and Cheerios, and I sipped my non-organic coffee and enjoyed my own healthy-choice cereal, which claimed to have quinoa and was bursting with twiggy-looking things in it, Ingrid breezed in after her morning run. "Just burned 436 calories according to my Pacer app!" she announced, as I slid my cereal bowl behind my newspaper so she wouldn't see the chocolate chips I had sprinkled on top.

I don't think Ingrid meant to gloat, but it was only Day 2, and I didn't think I could survive three more days of this.

I tried to look at the bright side: I might lose five pounds from aggravation and by only eating what she ate, mostly marinated tofu and arugula salad dressed with lemon juice and a speck of olive oil. Then, I anticipated the worst: I might gain eight pounds from aggravation that led to binge eating when she wasn't looking.

Fortunately, I was distracted by living my life, working from home, and taking care of my family. But while Ingrid wasn't always hanging around doing push-ups or yoga, a little bit of her went a long way. She couldn't help but talk about food and exercise and calories at every opportunity.

On the evening of Day 3, when Ingrid insisted that I was pronouncing "salmon" wrong — she said it was "SOL-mon" not "SAM-un" — a thought occurred to me: I get why she's been divorced twice. Who could tolerate such a know-it-all? Who cares how I pronounce "salmon"? Waitstaff at restaurants understand me when I place my order.

The next day, Ingrid had plans to burn calories outside the house all day long. I was so happy that I played "Sherry Darling" on Spotify and sang along. It's one of my favorite Bruce Springsteen songs about a guy stuck driving his girlfriend's annoying mother around town each week. He finally tells Sherry to tell her mother, "Tell her she wins if she'll just shut up, but it's the last time that she's gonna be ridin' with me." I sang it loud and proud!

I also resolved that this was the last time Ingrid would ever stay with me. Her militancy about exercise, food, and calories made me not even want to keep in touch with her. She was welcome to her magnesium supplements, but I'd get my magnesium from SAM-un and dark chocolate.

That evening, I made shepherd's pie for dinner with real meat, and Ingrid asked why I wasn't making my kids' sandwiches for the next day with the Dave's Killer Bread that she had bought for me. "Ingrid, my kids won't eat bread with seeds sticking out from it."

On Day 5, she left, taking the leftover Dave's Killer Bread and açai powder with her. I went a little crazy eating comfort foods for two days, none of which included arugula salad or organic chicken-less chicken. Our friendship was finished, but Ingrid had left something behind. I hated to admit it but Ingrid was right — to a degree — about diet and exercise. I grudgingly recommitted to exercising four times a week and limiting my chocolate intake to once a day instead of with every meal. My magnesium levels may dip, but I can probably up them with enough SAM-un.

— Judy Gruen —

The Hotel Balcony

*New York City is one of the greatest places on the
planet. You have the best in food, art, theatre,
and definitely people-watching.*
~Matt Bomer

I t was our annual theater trip to New York, my favorite city in the world. The taxi pulled up in front of our hotel on 54th Street. We checked in at the front desk, got the keys to our room, and headed to the elevator. It was midnight and we were exhausted from a day of traveling and flight delays.

We entered our room and I immediately started to unpack. About an hour later we were ready to go to sleep. My husband walked to his usual side of the king bed and I walked to mine. We climbed into bed and suddenly we were thrown into the middle of the bed, crashing into one another. For a moment we could not speak and just looked at one another.

"What happened?" my husband finally blurted out.

"I don't know," I answered.

We tried to roll toward the edges of the bed to go to sleep but we kept rolling back to the middle. After several minutes of frustration, we got out of the bed and stood looking at it.

"This bed is broken," my husband finally concluded. "Look at the frame. It has totally come apart."

I got on the phone and called the front desk. It was by now almost two in the morning. The night manager officiously informed me that the hotel was full and that we would have to wait until the morning to change rooms. That news was not what we wanted to hear. I argued with him but got nowhere. "Would you like us to sit up all night?" I asked in my most sarcastic tone. He let me know that whether we used the broken bed or not was certainly our choice. We were livid.

I let my tired husband have the middle of the broken bed to himself and I took one of the overstuffed chairs. I did not need an alarm clock that morning. I was on the phone to the morning manager before she could have her first cup of coffee. She asked to come up and see the bed. That meant waking and moving my husband. I told her yes. He was not pleased.

"This bed is definitely broken," she declared.

"So is my back," my husband retorted.

I was too tired to comment.

"We will move you to another suite as soon as it is cleaned," she offered. We nodded our acceptance. Because we were unpacked, I wanted to supervise the change of rooms. This was not the way I had hoped to spend my first day in New York.

Finally settled in our second room, I walked into the bathroom. At first it looked fine, but then I realized that the sink had literally pulled away from the wall and was ready to fall.

"Oh honey," I calmly called to my husband. "Would you please come in here?"

"What is that?" he asked incredulously.

"Let me call our friend the morning manager," I responded.

She came up and agreed. "Oh, this is very dangerous." She called for the yellow tape they use to block off crime scenes and proceeded to place it over the bathroom entrance.

Completely sleep deprived, at that moment I had had enough. "What are you going to do for us next?" I asked in my most determined voice.

"Mr. and Mrs. Aleskow, we would like to offer you the hotel apartment for the remainder of your stay," she answered apologetically. I could see that my husband was beyond caring where his bed would be at this point. One of his least favorite things was having to change rooms. I, on the other hand, was intrigued by this new proposition.

The hotel apartment had a bedroom, a living room, a dining room, and a balcony. It was lovely. The manager had us test the bed and handed us the keys.

We woke up Sunday morning and walked out on our balcony. We could see Central Park on our right and midtown Manhattan on our left. My husband put his arm around my shoulders. I sensed a romantic moment about to happen when I felt his body suddenly freeze.

"Don't look, don't look," he whispered.

"Look at what?" I asked, barely finishing my question before I saw the answer. From our rooftop balcony we were staring straight into an office-building window where a man and a woman were having a great Sunday morning visit on a swivel chair.

Not only was my husband whispering for some strange reason, but he was watching this X-rated scene but pretending not to. His face was pointing forward, but his eyes were as far to the left as possible. He didn't want them to notice he was looking.

"I don't think they are aware of anything at this moment but their own pleasure," I assured him. Yet, he still would not turn his head toward them for fear of being discovered.

That afternoon we went to a matinee. But nothing on Broadway could match the scene we had watched from our hotel balcony that morning.

— Elynne Chaplik-Aleskow —

Let's See That Smile

We don't laugh because we're happy—
we're happy because we laugh.
~William James

t had been a couple of years since my wife Ellie and I had moved to what we hoped we would be our last home: Pearl Oaks Retirement Center. We had recently celebrated our sixty-fifth wedding anniversary and were ready to relax and enjoy our golden years.

Our years of marriage had presented us with many challenges. They started on our wedding night in 1959 when I forgot Ellie's luggage. As I checked into The Drake hotel in Chicago without her garment bag and suitcase, the male night clerk gave me a smile and a wink.

On the other hand, Ellie wasn't smiling as she walked through the lobby all weekend wearing the same plain, cotton dress. Only purchasing her several new outfits when the stores opened on Monday saved the day for me.

The months flew by, and in September of 1960, Ellie spent over twenty hours in labor giving birth to our son. Needless to say, that brought a big smile to my face. However, Ellie wasn't laughing when she found herself soon pregnant again. Thirteen and a half months after the birth of our son, we barely had time to get to the hospital before our daughter arrived.

We had the usual ups and downs for the next few years. Finally, in 1984, when both of our children were in college, Ellie and I moved to Florida. We soon found new jobs and were settled into our home.

I was very surprised when, at the age of seventy-two, I was informed that my PSA reading was very high. A biopsy determined that I had prostate cancer. We found ourselves praying, "Dear Lord, help us get through this." After radical surgery, I was declared cancer-free.

The next few years passed quickly, and in 2020 we sold our large home in Clearwater and moved to a five-star, independent-living community. We quickly settled in our two-bedroom apartment and tried to adjust to living with two hundred close neighbors.

Once again, we were faced with a major problem. It was Covid time, and we were greatly limited in our activities. For three years, we adjusted to dealing with Covid and the limitations it presented to our community.

Slowly, the dangers of Covid receded, and we made many new friends. We even helped the newer residents of our facility get adjusted by serving as their ambassadors.

One evening, as we headed to the dining room for our dinner, we encountered a new resident exiting her apartment. She said, "Excuse me. I'm new, and I'm looking for the mailbox."

We introduced ourselves and replied, "Follow us. We're heading that way."

We directed her to the mail room, and I added, "We're heading in to supper. Would you like to join us at our table?"

"No, thanks. I always eat in my room."

For the next several days, we never saw her again. Finally, we asked about her. The concierge at the front desk said, "Oh, that's Jane. She only comes out to pick up her dinner and get her mail. She even has all her medicines delivered."

As time passed, my wife made several inquiries about Jane. Her nearby neighbors said that they never saw any family visit her room. And her next-door neighbor said she thought she saw Jane crying when she encountered her in the hall. She never smiled and had an almost angry look on her face.

Finally, one Friday afternoon, when we were on our way to Comedy Hour in the upstairs theater, Ellie decided to take action. "I'm going to stop at Jane's room and invite her to go to Comedy Hour with us."

Our new activity director had introduced many new programs on our monthly calendar. One that had proved to be very successful was Comedy Hour where the residents told jokes and presented different skits.

I nodded. "Good idea. Maybe she's ready for a few laughs. I'll get us some good seats up front."

To my surprise, Jane agreed to come upstairs to the Comedy Hour in the theater. Once we were seated, the Master of Ceremonies announced, "Okay, folks, sit back and get ready for a few laughs."

The first couple of residents who told jokes were quite funny, and I noticed that Jane was laughing.

"Like the show?" I whispered to her.

"Not bad. When I was younger, I did a few stand-up routines in college and in the comedy clubs in Manhattan."

"Oh, maybe you could do some jokes now," Ellie suggested.

Jane thought for a few minutes before she slowly nodded.

Ellie put up her hand and said, "Mr. Master of Ceremonies, my friend Jane would like to do some comedy."

Jane got to her feet and pushed her walker to the front of the room. She started out slowly and then rapidly progressed as she saw how much everyone enjoyed her material.

To my amazement, she spent the next ten minutes telling joke after joke. Finally, she announced, "That's all, folks."

Everyone in the room stood up and applauded her.

When the program ended, many of the residents approached Jane and congratulated her on her great presentation. One man said, "Hey, Jane, great routine. You should work the clubs in New York."

She smiled. "As a matter of fact, I did work the clubs for a while before I got married."

I took Jane by the arm and said, "How about eating dinner with us now? We are ready to go to the dining room, and I heard they have a great salmon with dill sauce tonight."

"Sounds good to me," she replied.

While we ate our dinner, we had a chance to really get acquainted. Jane told us about living and working in New York for several years before she met her husband. After retiring, they had moved to Florida to be near her sister. She told us that her sister had died a couple of years ago, and her husband had passed a year ago. Since then, she had been sitting alone in her condo. She grieved over the fact that she and her husband had never had children. All she did now was think about him and cry.

Now, it seemed like she had finally broken through her shell of grief and was ready to relate to those around her.

When we finished eating, one of the residents came up to us. "Say, Jane, there's a new fellow in apartment C 309 next to me. He seems very despondent and doesn't want to come out of his room. Maybe you could stop by and cheer him up."

Jane turned to us and said, "You'll have to excuse me, Ray and Ellie. It seems like there is someone who could use my humor. You know laughter is always the best medicine."

I tried to hide my surprise at this statement. "Well, maybe we'll see you at exercise tomorrow morning, Jane. It's at 10:00 in the activity room."

She grinned. "Save me a place."

— Ray Weaver —

Meet Our Contributors

DeVonna R. Allison's stories have been featured both in print and online. She is a Marine Corps veteran, wife, mother and grandma who lives in Central Florida. She writes every day and enjoys reading and "playing" in her flower beds. Learn more at devonnarallisonauthor. wordpress.com.

Katie Avagliano is a lecturer in the English department at Rollins College in Orlando, FL. When not teaching she can be found reading in the sunshine, playing cooperative board games, or exploring National Parks with her friends and her German Shepherd. She is a four-time bridesmaid.

Dave Bachmann is a retired teacher who worked with special needs children in Arizona for thirty-nine years. He now lives in California with his wife Jay, a retired kindergarten teacher, writing stories and poems for children and grown-ups.

Eric J. Barr is a retired forensic accountant. During his career he had more credential letters after his name than in his name. He now spends his time sharing (hopefully) funny and occasionally inspiring family stories with his disbelieving wife Linda, two adult children, and a granddaughter.

Steve Barry is an international geographer, currently living in Florida. A natural storyteller with a diverse and interesting background, he finds humor in unusual situations, which are making their way into a comical and entertaining book series. He and his wife live with two Galgos and are active with sighthound rescue.

Diane Ganzer Baum has been writing and publishing since 1990. Her many stories about animals include *Patrick the Wayward*

Setter, the book that propelled her professional writing career. She went on to write nonfiction books relating to alcoholism, domestic and child abuse and others.

Following a career in nuclear medicine, **Melissa Bender** is joyfully exploring her creative side. She recently moved to the Texas coast where she and her husband are renovating a thirty-five-year-old former Parade of Homes fixer-upper. She shares her home renovation and her stories at www.facebook.com/chicvintique.

Katherine Bradbury is a Registered Nurse and published author of *Triple Exposure: You Are What You Hide*. She loves traveling, writing, entertaining, music, belly laughing and is a collector of oil paintings. Her two sweetest spots are hanging with family and friends, and getting lost for hours in her writing. She is blessed!

Cathy Bryant worked as a shoe shop assistant, civil servant and childminder before writing professionally. She has had hundreds of poems and stories published, and four books. Cathy has won thirty-four literary awards. One poem has been used in a literacy programme and in a schoolbook. E-mail her at Cathy@cathybryant.co.uk.

Jan Cameron was a kid who liked to write stories. Although real life often got in the way, she never stopped writing and has collected an untidy heap of manuscripts. When she is not writing she enjoys traveling, the great outdoors, and crafting custom bedtime stories for one of her adorable grandchildren.

Lorraine Cannistra has proudly been published in the *Chicken Soup for the Soul* series fourteen times. She is the author of *More the Same than Different: What I Wish I Knew about Respecting and Including People with Disabilities*. She is passionate about advocacy, empowerment, writing, cooking, exercise, and her dog, Levi.

Eva Carter is a frequent contributor to the *Chicken Soup for the Soul* series, having had forty-four of her stories published so far. She lives in Dallas, TX with her Canadian husband and two cats. Eva loves dancing, traveling and writing.

Elynne Chaplik-Aleskow is a published memoirist including her book *My Gift of Now*, Distinguished Emeritus college professor, and founding general manager of WYCC-TV/PBS Chicago. Her husband

Richard and her dog RG are her muses. Elynne loves to perform her memoirs and to hear from her readers. E-mail her at elynne4@gmail.com.

Rachel Chustz lives in Louisiana with her husband and three children. She loves traveling, reading, writing, and playing Mahjong. This is Rachel's third contribution to the *Chicken Soup for the Soul* series. She is also the author and illustrator of the children's book, *The Bubble's Day at LSU*. E-mail her at rachelchustz@gmail.com.

After a forty-plus-year stint as a graphic designer and creative director, **Patty Cimlov-Zahares** is now retired, but not fully. In her free time she still creates humorous greeting cards (zazzle.com/store/cimzahdesigns), writes and illustrates children's books (on Amazon), and still loves to travel, wine and dine and have fun.

After military service, **Richard Cintorino** had a forty-year career as a bank officer, retiring in 1998. In 2004, he joined the Department of Defense as a flight attendant and helped transport military personnel worldwide. A native of Connecticut, he and his wife now reside in South Carolina. E-mail him at rick1029@aol.com.

Christine Clarke-Johnsen is a retired English as a Second Language teacher. She is a storyteller and event coordinator from Nanaimo, BC, Canada who loves writing short stories, exploring new places, hiking, creating beauty in her garden, developing new recipes and playing her guitar.

Courtney Conover has an insatiable sweet tooth, so it's apropos that a candy wrapper malfunction inspired her story. She and her husband Scott, a former NFL player, just co-authored their first book, *AI Turf: Playing Against All Algorithms*, and have two children. This is Courtney's eighteenth contribution to the *Chicken Soup for the Soul* series.

Elton A. Dean is a higher education leader, author, and retired soldier. He owns Big Paw Publishing and recently published two children's books titled *A Yeti Like Freddie: Talking to Kids About Autism* and *Brandon Sets Sail: A Story About Sharing Success*. The second was co-authored by his then seven-year-old son.

Kathy Dickie lives in Calgary, a western Canadian city nestled in the foothills of the majestic Rocky Mountains. She enjoys adventures with her remarkable granddaughters, traveling with her husband, family events, quilting, ancestry research and writing. Kathy is a recurrent contributor to *Chicken Soup for the Soul* series.

Barbara D'Antoni Diggs loves international travel and trying ethnic foods. She was an ESL teacher for twenty years in the states and also overseas. She and her husband, James, live in East Tennessee. Barbara enjoys writing nonfiction stories, attending writers' conferences and encouraging other authors in their work.

Amber Lynn Dykstra studied English, Creative Writing and World Literature at Florida Gulf Coast University. She lives in South Florida where she teaches middle school students with disabilities. She enjoys spending time with her husband and two sons. E-mail her at AmberLynnDykstra@gmail.com.

Michelle Eames lives on a hobby farm near Spokane, WA. She is the author of a humorous memoir, *Riding Lessons: Things I Learned While Horsing Around*, and has had a poetry chapbook, "Fire Triangle (Heat Fuel Oxygen)" included in *Triple No. 23*, published by Ravenna Press. Read her blog at MichelleEames.com.

Ivy Eisenberg is an award-winning humor writer, storyteller and comedian. Her essays have appeared in *New York* magazine, *Tablet*, *Narratively*, *Next Avenue*, *Business Insider*, and essay collections. Ivy is working on a memoir about growing up in the groovy and turbulent 1960s in Queens, NY.

SJ Fellenstein spent most of her career as a newspaper reporter and editor. Today she works in programming at a retirement community where she finds inspiration daily. While she loves traveling and meeting new people, her favorite place is home.

Glenda Ferguson received her education degrees from College of the Ozarks (Missouri) and Indiana University. She writes devotionals for *All God's Creatures* and performed stand-up comedy at the 2024 Erma Bombeck Writers Workshop. Glenda's mom discovered something to laugh about every day.

Marilyn Frey's re-ignited passion for writing has led to her stories being published in anthologies and placed in several contests. When she isn't reading or writing, she loves talking with a friend over a steaming cup of coffee, dreaming about possibilities.

Mei Emerald Gaffey-Hernandez received her Bachelor of Arts in Economics from the University of Redlands in 2002. She was a Community Economic Development volunteer for the Peace Corps stationed in the Dominican Republic from 2006-2007. She currently lives in San Luis Obispo, CA, and enjoys spending time with her family.

TG Gilliam, to her astonishment, enjoys writing nonfiction and is amazed people read her stories. She has two other stories published in the *Chicken Soup for the Soul* series, a Tips for Self-Care book and a book about ghosts and angels she self-published on Amazon. She is currently working on a book detailing a quest to dance in all the old dancehalls in Texas.

Robbie Gorr is a retired elementary school teacher from the Ottawa Valley in Ontario, Canada who now spends his days enjoying his hobbies of gardening, family history research, reading, writing and photography. He has learned that a little humor goes a long way in any endeavor.

Holly Green is a lifelong storyteller. Her childhood in France and her life as a wife, mother, grandmother and RN have provided her endless material. Under her pen name, Anne Ashberg, she has written six novels: *What Julia Wrote*, *Linger*, *Exactly Enough*, *Swan in Winter*, *The Target* and *Gemma's Woods* available on Amazon.

Dekota Gregory is from Locust Grove, OK and graduated from Oklahoma State University. He has a wife and son. Dekota and his family enjoy traveling and sports.

Judy Gruen is the author of five books, including *Bylines and Blessings* and *The Skeptic and the Rabbi*. An award-winning columnist for the *Jewish Journal*, she is also a book editor and writing coach. Based in Los Angeles, CA she loves mysteries, dark chocolate, yoga, and divine coffee.

Karl Haffner is V.P. at Loma Linda University. He has two B.A. degrees, two master's degrees and a Ph.D. He's crazy about his wife and their two daughters. Karl loves stories, Costco, and ice cream (he orders broccoli à la mode). He's the award-winning author of thirteen books and 1,000+ articles published in a variety of journals.

Bonnie Compton Hanson, author and speaker, has had sixty-three books published besides many articles—including forty-seven in the *Chicken Soup for the Soul* series. She has spoken at many writers' conferences, plus taught at several colleges and universities.

Susan M. Heim is a longstanding editor and co-author for Chicken Soup for the Soul and a Communications Coordinator for a major university. A graduate of Michigan State University, Susan loves her adopted home in Florida where she raised her four boys. Contact her via her website at www.susanheim.com.

A retired teacher, **Lynn Hess** also conducted weekly poetry workshops for students in grades K through 8. Her writing has appeared in literary journals, and a book of her poems for children was published by Lime Rock Press. A mother of two, grandmother of three, and teacher of thousands, Lynn loves writing about "her kids."

Butch Holcombe of Georgia has the dream job of publishing *American Digger*, a high-quality periodical concerning his lifelong passion of metal detecting. He also publishes hardcover books on contract as founder of Greybird Publishers. In his spare time, he enjoys writing and has been published several times in the *Chicken Soup for the Soul* series.

Charlotte Hopkins was a social worker for five years and a preschool teacher for ten. She wrote a children's book series with two lovable characters, Pixie Trist (a fox) and Bo (a monkey), that teach fun facts to children in a rhyming pattern. In 2024, she wrote two YA books titled *Secrets of Flower Mound* and *Charm*.

Teresa B. Hovatter is a real estate broker, a devoted single mother to three children and a proud "TeTe" to six loving grandsons. She is thrilled to be part of the Chicken Soup for the Soul family, and recently published her memoir, *Grace Beyond the Gate*. Teresa is a North Carolina native who faces life's highs and lows with faith and courage.

A.J. Hughes got her break as a humor columnist with a small monthly newspaper; an opportunity that continued for nine years. Now, she is a busy freelance writer/editor and loves to write humor whenever her clients request it. She lives in Arizona, and loves hiking, edgy art, concerts, and sunshine.

Jeffree Wyn Itrich was inspired by her 7th-grade English teacher who saw her potential and encouraged her to pursue writing as a career. Twenty-one years later, her book, *The Art of Accompaniment*, was published. Four more books have been published since, including her latest novel, *The Wedding Dress Quilt*.

Story Keatley writes material drawn from her knack for landing herself in complicated situations ranging from funny to tragic. Her goal is to bring joy and inspiration to the human race. Story, also a guitarist and yodeler, lives in Texas with her husband and their two Dachshunds. Above all, her favorite role is "Grana."

Krista Kell went to Bible College, and is now a stay-at-home mom who homeschooled her teens. She's a proud Canadian who loves good family values and laughter. She enjoys board game nights with her family, history and blessing others.

Jill Keller lives in a small town in Southern Indiana with her husband and two children. She enjoys writing novels, making desserts for her home bakery, being a reborn artist for therapy dolls, running a business helping those going through baby loss, and reading to her children. Learn more at kellerjf.wixsite.com/author.

As E. E. Kennedy, **Ellen Edwards Kennedy** is the author of the *Miss Prentice Cozy Mysteries*. Her most recent publication, a picture book, *Walk with a Stranger*, won the 2024 Eric Hoffer Book Award first prize in its category. Her alma mater Huntingdon College named her one of their Outstanding Alumni in the Arts in 2024.

Chip Kirkpatrick and his wife Grace are lifelong residents of NE Florida. He has published several books and writes for metal detecting magazines in the U.S., U.K. and Scotland. He is a popular storyteller, and his hobbies include historical metal detecting, gardening, fishing and poker.

Brad Korbesmeyer is an award-winning playwright, screenwriter, editor, and educator. His favorite "job" is as "Pop" to three wonderful granddaughters. He currently resides in Minneapolis, MN. Learn more at brateragency.com.

T. Jensen Lacey specializes in history and travel writing and is author of a series of "tour-able history" books. Lacey has twenty-three published books and has appeared in nineteen anthologies, including the *Chicken Soup for the Soul* series. Her latest, a cookbook, *Around Our Southern Table*, has recipes from six generations of family cooks. Learn more at www.TJensenLacey.com.

Vera-Marie Landi retired early from a major pharmaceutical company as a senior systems analyst, during which time she completed her MBA. She then pursued another passion by working in the food industry before retiring again. She enjoys time with family, dancing, walking, baking, and writing. Her dream is to one day publish a book.

Before living in Europe for several years, **Lynne Latella** taught English, Russian and Creative Writing. In her spare time, she has been an opera singer, personal chef, public speaker and newspaper columnist. She writes to amuse, educate and inspire. She lives lakefront in Upstate New York with oodles of Standard Poodles.

Mary Elizabeth Laufer has a degree in English education from SUNY Albany. Her stories and poems have appeared in magazines, newspapers, and several anthologies. She received a Kirkus star and a Moonbeam Children's Book Award for her middle-grade novel, *Katelyn's Crow*, and is now working on a sequel, *Katelyn's Cat*.

Jody Lebel, a voice actor who narrates audiobooks, writes romantic suspense novels and funny short stories on the side. She was raised in charming New England, was an only child who had an only child (claiming she didn't breed well in captivity) and now lives with her two cats in sunny Florida.

Karen M. Leet enjoys life in Kentucky with her family, friends and assorted dogs. She's been writing since she was ten years old and also enjoys reading, feeding wildlife, and spending time with family and friends. Her previous publications include *Sarah's Courage*, a middle-grade historical novel from The History Press.

Carrie Linde and her husband Tim traded city life for a farm, where their family now includes chickens and bees. Carrie's passions include cooking, baking, and collecting books by the armload. After years of dedicated writing, she's nearing the finish line on her first novel, *Water Like Glass*—stay tuned!

Annie Lisenby writes teen fiction and romance. Her debut novel *A Three-Letter Name* was chosen as the best book by an indie author from the state of Missouri for the 2022 Indie Author Project. Annie teaches theatre at a local college and leads workshops at writing conferences. Learn more at www.annielisenby.com.

Tracie Lobstein is an author and podcast host who is passionate about encouraging single Christian women who want to flourish. She resides in Arizona. When she is not writing or podcasting, she photographs wildlife and landscapes and spends time visiting her grandchildren. Learn more at tracielobstein.com.

Barbara LoMonaco graduated from USC and has a teaching credential. She is the Senior Editor for the *Chicken Soup for the Soul* series and has had stories published in many titles. She lives and works from her home in Southern California.

Victoria Lorrekovich-Miller is a writer, editor, and MFA Candidate at St. Mary's College of California. Her stories and creative nonfiction have been published in *Pithead Chapel Literary Journal, Kveller, Piker Press, Reader's Digest, The Bark,* the *Chicken Soup for the Soul* series, *Dog and Kennel, Animal Wellness Magazine,* wow-womenonwriting.com, YourTeen.com, *Cricket* magazine, and more.

Born in Africa as the daughter of missionaries, **Harriet E. Michael** discovered her passion for writing about fifteen years ago. Today she has authored twelve books and hundreds of articles, short stories, and devotionals. Married for over forty-five years, she and her husband have four children and five grandchildren.

Ronald Milburn received his B.A. from Eastern Illinois University. He has four children and fourteen grandchildren. Ron enjoys posting TikTok videos and writing children's books about his pet, Robert "Bobby" Squirrel. He's published short stories, novels, and screenplays. His movie *Beyond Detention* is now streaming.

Courtney Lynn Mroch is the Editor-in-Chief for Haunt Jaunts, a travel and lifestyle site for restless spirits. When she's not traveling or writing, it's a safe bet you'll find her on a pickleball court somewhere in Nashville, TN, where she currently resides.

Jill Nogales writes stories for a variety of children's magazines, including *Highlights for Children*, and she is the author of *Zebra on the Go* (a picture book). She and her husband recently moved to a coastal town in the Pacific Northwest where they live in a tiny beach house in the woods.

January Gordon Ornellas is a humor writer whose work has appeared in the *Los Angeles Times*, the *Chicken Soup for the Soul* series, *The Belladonna*, and the Erma Bombeck Writers' website. Her debut novel, *My Above Average Colon and Other Midlife Adventures*, was published in December 2023. Learn more at midlifebloomer.com.

When **Sharon Pearson** and her husband moved to Arizona because they loved the rugged scenery of the Southwest, Sharon's parents (featured in the story) followed.

Chrissie Anderson Peters lives in Bristol, TN. She holds degrees from Emory & Henry College and the University of Tennessee. She has been published in *Still: The Journal*, *Women of Appalachia Project*, *Red Branch Review*, *Untelling*, and *Salvation South*, among others. Learn more at www.CAPWrites.com.

Mary C. M. Phillips is a caffeinated writer and musician. Her essays have been widely published in numerous bestselling anthologies. Her poetry can be found in various literary journals and was featured in Lancaster Pennsylvania's public transportation as part of Poetry-in-Transit's 2024 campaign.

Amy Leah Potter has traveled to over eighty countries and remains eager to discover more. Though her work now focuses mostly on writing e-mails and policies, she began documenting the missteps and mishaps from her travels as a way to dispel any envy toward her seemingly exotic — yet far from glamorous — lifestyle.

This is **Becky Lewellen Povich's** seventh publication in the *Chicken Soup for the Soul* series. She has stories included in other anthologies, small-town newspapers and magazines. She published her memoir, *From Pigtails to Chin Hairs*, in 2013. Find her on Facebook under her name or e-mail her at Writergal53@gmail.com.

Evan Purcell is an author and teacher who has worked with kids in Kazakhstan, Bhutan, Zanzibar, China, and Ukraine. He's helped over 200 young people from developing countries write, edit, and publish their first stories and poems. He also writes scripts for podcasts, cartoons, and other media.

Mark Rickerby is a screenwriter and co-owner of Temple Gate Films. This is his thirty-first story published in the *Chicken Soup for the Soul* series. The creations he is most proud of are his daughters, Emma and Marli. Visit his YouTube channel "Mark Rickerby's Stories of Mystery and Adventure" where his stories are narrated (by him) with beautiful visuals.

Nancy Roenfeldt lived in Peru where she acquired Henry the Macaw. He lived with the family for fifty years giving joy, fun and some aggravation.

Sioux Roslawski is a middle-school teacher, and one of the producers of the "Mama Said, Mama Said" show, based in St. Louis. In her free time she loves to read and rescues dogs for Love a Golden Rescue. Her greatest writing accomplishment was getting her historical novel *Greenwood Gone: Henry's Story* published.

Patricia Rossi is a published writer and avid reader. Her written works have been featured in literary journals, magazines, newspapers and academic textbooks. For years she has facilitated writing to heal workshops for cancer as well as heart patients and the bereaved. She is an active member in her community, currently serving on various nonprofit boards, as well as her college alumni board.

Nancy Saint John is a retired Public Information Officer. Her M.S. degree is from California State University. She volunteers with refugees and is learning Spanish. Nancy and her husband enjoy spending time in Mexico.

Chris Maday Schmidt is a Publishers Weekly bestselling author and self-professed princess who believes it's always the "write" time for hope, humor and heart. She relocated to the Southwest with her real-life hero and daughter and writes clean and wholesome stories about family, friendship and faith. Learn more at chrismadayschmidt.com.

Susan Schuerr is a retired English/drama teacher, and a current blogger at www.lifewithlarry.org. She has a Master of Arts degree from Concordia University and enjoys time with her husband Larry, her three adult children and five grandchildren. She volunteers playing piano and working at a care center.

Scott Scovel is a writer and businessman who was raised in

Minneapolis, worked in Manhattan, and retired in Miami. His boundless curiosity has led to adventures both close to home and in over 100 countries. Learn more at sites.google.com/view/scottscovel/home.

Mandy Shunnarah is a writer, skater, and cat lover in Columbus, OH, who authored *Midwest Shreds: Skating Through America's Heartland*. Their poetry collection, *We Had Mansions*, will be published in 2025. Read their work and get to know their six cats at mandyshunnarah. com/ and on Instagram @offthebeatenshelf.

Billie Holladay Skelley received her bachelor's and master's degrees from the University of Wisconsin. A retired clinical nurse specialist, she is the mother of four and grandmother of three. Billie enjoys writing, and her work crosses several genres. She spends her non-writing time reading, gardening, and traveling.

Doug Sletten is a retired attorney who worked as a weekly columnist for a local newspaper. He is a graduate of Concordia College in Moorhead, MN and grew up in rural North Dakota, but now lives in Mesa, AZ. Doug is an avid sports fan who takes great pleasure in writing humorous articles for a number of magazines.

Christine Smith is simply a person who loves storytelling. Most of her stories originate from her own experiences with her children, grandchildren, friends and extended family. Personal comments or appreciation can be shared anytime at chrissmith680@outlook.com.

By day, **Laurie O'Connor Stephans** works at a law firm. By night (when not fighting crime), she happily exercises her writing muscles instead of the other ones. Laurie shares an empty nest in Plano, IL with husband Mike, cat Opie, and dog Ernest T. Bass. Learn more at laurieoconnorstephans.com.

Ronica Stromberg has twenty-six stories in compilations including the *Chicken Soup for the Soul* series and is the author of four traditionally published children's novels. She specializes in wholesome, humorous writing.

Angela L. Stuck resides in Nebraska. She raised three wonderful sons and is now a proud grandma of five. She enjoys serving in her local church. She hopes this is the beginning of more published stories.

Tsgoyna Tanzman is a Certified Life Coach and the author of three books, including *Just Decide: Fail-Proof Strategies to Up-Level Your Life, Career, and Relationships*. She's an expert at helping women rediscover their vitality, visibility, and verve and for now she's reimagining her third act of life while vagabonding through Europe.

Jojo Teckina is a wife, mom, artist and amateur writer. She received her Bachelor of Science in Commercial Art in 1996 from Southern Oregon University. Currently a graphic designer, she enjoys baking in her free time and being a full-time mom to a busy nine-year-old boy and a very needy guinea pig.

Karen Bodai Waldman, Ph.D., has been happily married to her best friend Ken for thirty-eight-plus years. Both psychologists, they are co-writing a book, *Self-Help for Couples: A Simple and Effective Guide*. They love spending time with their eight awesome kids, twelve amazing grandkids, and a sweet Doodle. Karen also enjoys acting and nature walks. E-mail her at dr.karenwaldman@gmail.com.

Roz Warren writes for everyone from *The Funny Times* to *The New York Times*, has appeared on both *The Today Show* and *Morning Edition* and is happy to have been included eighteen times in the *Chicken Soup for the Soul* series. Roz is also a writing coach and editor who helps writers improve and publish their prose. E-mail her at roSwarren@gmail.com.

Ray Weaver has been living in Florida for over forty years. He has been writing novels and short stories for fifteen years. He and his wife Ellie have been married for sixty-five years and have two children, six grandchildren and one great-grandchild.

Faynixe White, a French Canadian from Quebec, now lives on Vancouver Island. Growing up surrounded by animals on hobby farms led her to become a pet loss grief counselor. She enjoys cooking, hiking, painting, and writing, and dreams of creating a small animal sanctuary one day.

Leslie Wibberley lives in Canada and is represented by Naomi Davis of Bookends Literary. Her work is published in literary journals and award-winning anthologies and has placed 1st in Writers Digest's Annual Competition and Popular Fiction Awards, The Chanticleer International Book Awards, and the PNW Association Literary Contest.

Jeannie S. Williams is a prolific author/lecturer and a master storyteller. She is a frequent contributor to the *Chicken Soup for the Soul* series and has been entertaining audiences for years with her creativity. Jeannie lives in Sikeston, MO. E-mail her at jeanw483@gmail.com.

Carole Williams-Morrison holds a master's degree in education, and is a retired public school teacher, a mother and grandmother, and resides in Northern California. She is the author of *Nellie Estelle*, a memoir of growing up in Georgia with her grandparents, available on Amazon.

Nemma Wollenfang is a prize-winning, short story writer who lives in North England. Her stories have appeared in several venues, including *Northern Gravy*, the *Chicken Soup for the Soul* series and Flame Tree Publishing. She loves her cats, has worked at several animal rescues and can be found on Facebook and Amazon.

Christy Wopat is the author of three books: the award-winning memoir, *Almost a Mother*, a picture book titled *Always Ours*, and *After All: Pregnancy After Loss*. Her personal essays have been featured in the *Chicken Soup for the Soul* series and *The Educator's Room*, among others. She now spends most of her writing time working on books for kids.

Vic Zarley lives with his wife in a log cabin in southern Indiana. He and his wife enjoy writing Christian songs together. He loves to write poetry and a recent hobby is taking old hymns and giving them new life by reading the lyrics to beautiful instrumentals which can be found on Amazon (digital music). E-mail him at vic@zarley.net.

Meet Amy Newmark

Amy Newmark is the bestselling author, editor-in-chief, and publisher of the *Chicken Soup for the Soul* book series. Since 2008, she has published more than 200 new books, most of them national bestsellers in the U.S. and Canada, more than doubling the number of Chicken Soup for the Soul titles in print today. She is also the author of *Simply Happy,* a crash course in Chicken Soup for the Soul advice and wisdom that is filled with easy-to-implement, practical tips for enjoying a better life.

Amy is credited with revitalizing the Chicken Soup for the Soul brand, which has been a publishing industry phenomenon since the first book came out in 1993. By compiling inspirational and aspirational true stories curated from ordinary people who have had extraordinary experiences, Amy has kept the thirty-two-year-old Chicken Soup for the Soul brand fresh and relevant.

Amy graduated *magna cum laude* from Harvard University where she majored in Portuguese and minored in French. She then embarked on a three-decade career as a Wall Street analyst, a hedge fund manager, and a corporate executive in the technology field.

Her return to literary pursuits was inevitable, as her honors thesis in college involved traveling throughout Brazil's impoverished northeast region, collecting stories from regular people. She is delighted to have come full circle in her writing career — from collecting stories "from the people" in Brazil as a twenty-year-old to, three decades later, collecting stories "from the people" for Chicken Soup for the Soul.

When Amy and her husband Bill, the CEO of Chicken Soup for the Soul, are not working, they are visiting their four grown children and their spouses, and their six grandchildren.

Follow Amy on X and Instagram @amynewmark. Listen to her free podcast — Chicken Soup for the Soul with Amy Newmark — on Apple, Google, or by using your favorite podcast app on your phone. You can also find a selection of her stories on Medium.

Thank You

We owe huge thanks to all our contributors and fans. We received thousands of submissions for this popular topic, and we spent months reading all of them. Barbara LoMonaco, Crescent LoMonaco and Laura Dean read all of them and narrowed down the selection for Publisher and Editor-in-Chief, Amy Newmark. Susan Heim did the first round of editing, and then D'ette chose the perfect quotations to put at the beginning of each story and Amy edited the stories and shaped the final manuscript.

As we finished our work, D'ette continued to be Amy's right-hand woman in working with all our wonderful writers. Barbara LoMonaco, Kristiana Pastir, and Elaine Kimbler jumped in to proof, proof, proof. And, yes, there will always be typos anyway, so please feel free to let us know about them at webmaster@chickensoupforthesoul.com, and we will correct them in future printings.

The whole publishing team deserves a hand, including our Vice President of Production & COO, Victor Cataldo, and our graphic designer, Daniel Zaccari, who turned our manuscript into this entertaining book.

Sharing Happiness, Inspiration, and Hope

Real people sharing real stories, every day, all over the world. In 2007, *USA Today* named *Chicken Soup for the Soul* one of the five most memorable books in the last quarter-century. With over 110 million books sold to date in the U.S. and Canada alone, more than 300 titles in print, and translations into nearly fifty languages, "chicken soup for the soul®" is one of the world's best-known phrases.

Today, thirty-two years after we first began sharing happiness, inspiration and hope through our books, we continue to delight our readers with ten to twelve new titles each year but have also evolved beyond the bookshelves with super premium pet food, a podcast, adult coloring books, and licensed products that include word-search puzzle books and books for babies and preschoolers. We are busy "changing your life one story at a time®." Thanks for reading!

Share with Us

We have all had Chicken Soup for the Soul moments in our lives. If you would like to share your story, please go to chickensoup.com and click on Books at the top of the page and then Submit Your Story. You will find our writing guidelines there, along with a list of topics we're working on.

You may be able to help another reader and become a published author at the same time! Some of our past contributors have even launched writing and speaking careers from the publication of their stories in our books.

We only accept story submissions via our website. They are no longer accepted via postal mail or fax. And they are not accepted via e-mail.

To contact us regarding other matters, please send an e-mail to webmaster@chickensoupforthesoul.com, or write us at:

Chicken Soup for the Soul
P.O. Box 700
Cos Cob, CT 06807-0700

One more note from your friends at Chicken Soup for the Soul: Occasionally, we receive an unsolicited book manuscript from one of our readers, and we would like to respectfully inform you that we do not accept unsolicited manuscripts, and we must discard the ones that are sent to us.

Changing lives one story at a time®
www.chickensoup.com